PELICAN BOOKS

A293

ETHICS

P. H. NOWELL-SMITH

P. H. NOWELL-SMITH

ETHICS

PENGUIN BOOKS

Penguin Books Ltd, Harmondsworth, Middlesex

U.S.A.: Penguin Books Inc., 3300 Clipper Mill Road, Baltimore 11, Md

AUSTRALIA: Penguin Books Pty Ltd, 762 Whitehorse Road
Mitcham, Victoria

—

First published 1954
Reprinted 1956, 1959

Made and printed in Great Britain by
Unwin Brothers Ltd, Woking and London

Contents

Editorial Foreword

MR P. H. NOWELL-SMITH's book on ethics is one of a series of philosophical works which are appearing in a similar form. The series consists mainly in original studies of the work of certain outstanding philosophers, but it covers also a number of more general topics, including, besides ethics, political philosophy, logic, the theory of knowledge, and the philosophy of science.

The series is not designed to reflect the standpoint or to advance the views of any one philosophical school. Since it is addressed to an audience of non-specialists, as well as professional philosophers, the contributors to it have been asked to write in as untechnical a manner as their subjects allow, but they have not been expected to achieve simplicity at the cost of accuracy or completeness.

There is a distinction, which is not always sufficiently marked, between the activity of a moralist, who sets out to elaborate a moral code, or to encourage its observance, and that of a moral philosopher, whose concern is not primarily to make moral judgements but to analyse their nature. Mr Nowell-Smith writes as a moral philosopher. He shows how ethical statements are related to, and how they differ from, statements of other types, and what are the criteria which are appropriate to them. His book deals with the most important problems in the field of moral philosophy, from the objectivity of values to the freedom of the will.

A. J. AYER

PART I

Theory and Practice

CHAPTER 1

The Task of Ethics

[1]

A BROAD distinction may be drawn between theoretical and practical sciences. The purpose of the former is to enable us to understand the nature of things, whether the things be stars, chemical substances, earthquakes, revolutions, or human behaviour. These sciences consist in answers to such questions as 'What is an acid?', 'What are the laws of planetary motion?', 'How do bees find their way about?', 'Why does wood float and iron sink?', 'What are the marriage laws of the Arapesh?'. The answers take the form of statements, descriptions, generalizations, explanations, and laws. I shall call such discourse 'theoretical', 'fact-stating' or 'descriptive' discourse; but it must not be supposed that every sentence in such discourse is a theory or states a fact or describes something. Newton's laws belong to descriptive discourse, but they do not *describe* anything.

Practical discourse, on the other hand, consists of answers to practical questions, of which the most important are 'What shall I do?' and 'What ought I to do?'. If I put these questions to myself the answers are decisions, resolutions, expressions of intention, or moral principles. If I put them to someone else his answer will be an order, injunction, or piece of advice, a sentence in the form 'Do such and such'. The central activities for which moral language is used are choosing and advising others to choose.

Traditionally, moral philosophy has always been regarded as a practical science, a 'science' because it was a systematic inquiry the goal of which was knowledge, and 'practical' because the goal was practical knowledge, knowledge of what to do rather than knowledge of what is the case.

The words 'morals' and 'ethics' are derived from words meaning 'custom' or 'behaviour'; but the role of the moral philosopher was never conceived to be that of describing or explaining the customs or behaviour of men. That is the task of the psychologist, sociologist, anthropologist, historian, dramatist, and novelist. Moral philosophers set out to perform different tasks. The first was to answer practical questions, the second to criticize, evaluate, or appraise customs and behaviour. They claimed, not to tell you what men do, but to tell you which of the things that men do are good and which are bad. This second type of judgement, which is expressed in verdicts or appraisals, seems closer to theoretical than to practical discourse. To say that Jones is a good man is not – on the face of it – to tell anyone what to do, but rather to tell you what sort of man Jones is. It states a fact and from its grammatical form alone we should conclude that it is more like 'Jones is a tall man' than like 'Do what Jones does'.

But the great philosophers of the past always treated questions of appraisal as subordinate to practical questions. They assumed – and who would not ? – that the point of telling you that Jones is a good or a bad man is that you should imitate or not imitate Jones, that you should or should not give Jones the job or do whatever else might be in question. When they depicted the Good Life they would have thought it very odd if someone had said: "You have told me what the Good Life is and I agree with everything you say. Now tell me what I ought to do". Such a man has obviously misunderstood the philosopher's talk about the Good Life. For this talk was never intended to be a description of anything; it was from the start assumed to be an injunction to do something, to adopt this or that course, to subscribe to this or that moral code.

Moral philosophers did not, of course, undertake to give detailed practical advice as to how you should behave on this or that occasion. A philosopher is not a parish priest or Universal Aunt or Citizens' Advice Bureau. As we shall shortly see, different philosophers held very different views as to the way in which moral philosophy can help you to answer practical questions. But they all agreed that the goal of moral philosophy is practical knowledge, not that we should know what goodness is but that we should become good. From Plato, Aristotle, and Epicurus, from Hobbes, Spinoza, and Butler you can learn how, in their opinion, you ought to live.

And these philosophers were agreed also on another important point. They take for granted the fact that men have certain aims, purposes, and desires which they wish to achieve, fulfil, and satisfy. The achievement of these aims is variously called 'The Good Life', 'The Good for Man', 'Happiness', and 'Felicity'; and the task of the moral philosopher was to depict this state in broad outline and to tell you how you can achieve it. Although Plato starts his most elaborate treatise on moral philosophy with the question 'What is Justice?', the principal question with which he is concerned is 'Which of the two (justice or injustice) will bring happiness to its possessor?'.[1] The notion of duty does not play the central role in traditional that it plays in modern ethics and the notion of doing one's duty for duty's sake hardly appears before Kant. Earlier philosophers thought it quite sensible to ask 'Why should I do my duty?'; the obligation to do one's duty needs justifying and can only be justified by showing that doing his duty is, in the short or long run, advantageous to the agent; indeed the classic treatises on the subject might be said to be mainly concerned with this justification. This point of view is called 'teleological' and is opposed to that called 'deontological', according to which duty rather than purpose is the fundamental concept of ethics.[2]

If we turn to the great religious systems of the world we find the same emphasis on the practical nature of moral questions, the same assumption that life has a goal, be it the Christian or the Moslem Paradise or the Buddhist Nirvana, and the same assumption that the rules we are enjoined to live by are rules for achieving this state. This assumption is of the

1. *Republic*, 427 d.
2. From the Greek 'telos' meaning 'purpose' and 'deon' meaning – roughly – 'duty'.

greatest antiquity. The Egyptians had a word 'Ma'at' which is translated in three different ways. It means (a) 'being straight, level, or even', (b) 'order, conformity, regularity', and (c) 'truth, justice, righteousness'. It has obvious affinities to our word 'right'. Now the earliest moral document we possess is a manual of instruction on good behaviour to budding civil servants. In this the aspiring official is enjoined to follow the rules of Ma'at, but only because, by so doing, he will get on in the world. In later times the fruits of Ma'at were thought to lie in the next world rather than in this, but the basic conception is the same. We are to practise virtue because, in the short or long run, it pays.[1]

In Christian ethics we find the same basic assumptions. "What shall I do", asks the lawyer, "to inherit eternal life ?".[2] The difference between this question and Plato's is simply that felicity is now thought to lie in the next world, not in this. No question is raised as to whether the lawyer wants to inherit eternal life; this is treated as a datum of the problem. Still less is there any question as to whether he ought to want this or ought not rather to have some other aim. In Christian, as in Greek ethics, there is no suggestion that moral rules ought to be obeyed irrespective of any purpose which will be served by obeying them. The answer does indeed take the form: "What is written in the law ? How readest thou ?". But this would not be an answer at all if it were not assumed that the rules contained in the law are to be obeyed because obedience is conducive to what the lawyer wants to achieve. Without this assumption the answer is simply irrelevant to the lawyer's problem.[3]

But to say that moral rules are rules for achieving happiness or the Good Life does not tell us much. In what does happiness consist ? How can we tell a good life from a bad one ? How do

1. H. Frankfort and others: *Before Philosophy*, Ch. IV.
2. Luke x. 25.
3. It might be thought that to look at Christian Ethics in this way is to give it an unplausible and shocking egoistic twist. On this see below, chapter 10.

14

we know whether obedience to the proffered rules is really going to lead to happiness? It was to these very general questions that the great philosophers mainly devoted themselves. In order to answer them they had to range over a wide field. Since man is a social animal, the Good Life must be life in society and politics must be discussed; indeed ethics and politics were, for these philosophers, one subject. Since it is idle to tell men what they ought to do unless we know what men are, psychology also comes into the picture, and philosophers spent much time analysing the human soul. It is also, for reasons to be given later, necessary to study logic; though this was more apparent to some philosophers than to others.

[2]

Students of ethics are apt to be disappointed to find that, although the subject has been studied for over two thousand years, it does not seem to have produced any established system of truths comparable to those of mathematics and the natural sciences. Why is Aristotle's *Ethics* still worth reading, while his *Physics* is of interest only to scholars and historians? If moral rules are rules for achieving happiness it ought to be fairly easy to discover which rules are good and which are bad, which to adopt and which to reject.

Part of the answer to this criticism of moral philosophy lies in the fact that as soon as any progress is made in solving any general type of problem that problem ceases to be a philosophical one and becomes a problem for someone who is called, not a 'philosopher', but a 'scientist'. Suppose, for example, that a man wants to bring up his children as well as possible. He is faced by two quite different types of problem, which we may call 'problems about ends' and 'problems about means'. (*a*) What sort of person do I want my child to become? and (*b*) What method of up-bringing is most likely to turn him into this sort of person?

In answer to the first question it is no use saying that he

wants his child to lead a good and happy life. Of course he does. But in what do goodness and happiness consist? What, in more detail, is the ideal life for him – or for anyone? These are philosophical questions because the ability to answer them is not a matter of special expertise. But if we turn to the second type of question the position is different.

Suppose that he has decided that he does not want his child to be grasping and aggressive. The question 'What sort of up-bringing prevents people from becoming grasping and aggressive?' is a question of fact, the ability to answer which could be a matter of expertise. If it is true that early weaning makes people grasping and aggressive, which is something that psychologists might be able to establish empirically, that settles the matter. Psychology is a young science; but enough is now known to make many questions about the best method of achieving an end 'scientific' questions. That they continue to be treated as philosophical or moral questions is a matter for regret.

But is the man's problem really solved when he has learnt the facts about weaning? It might not be. Suppose that his wife is so ill that it would be dangerous for her to go on suckling the child. He is now faced with a problem of the first kind again. For he now has to decide, not between two methods of achieving a given end, but between two different ends consisting in the effects on both his wife and his child of either weaning or not weaning. And no 'science' can help him solve this problem; he has to discover which of these two complex states he really wants.

The second part of the answer is of greater philosophical interest. Why cannot we discover a body of general moral truths that would help us to solve particular moral problems in the way that geometrical truths help the surveyor and mechanical truths help the engineer to solve their practical problems? Some philosophers have thought it possible to discover such truths. Plato, for example, seemed to think that, although it would be very difficult and no one had yet done it, it might be possible for a man to come to know The Form of the

Good; and this would give him an insight into moral rules not unlike the insight of the geometer into geometrical axioms. Like Plato, Hobbes was much impressed by the method of geometry and he thought that moral rules were Rules found out by Reason for avoiding social calamity; and Spinoza frankly casts his ethics into a deductive, geometrical form.

But the analogy with mathematics or with any of the natural sciences will not do. I shall try later to explain in detail why it will not do; here it must suffice to notice that the conditions which make the deductive method so fruitful in the sciences do not all obtain in the field of conduct. The success of the sciences is in part due to the possibility of discovering functional relations between measurable quantities and in part due to the possibility of giving precise meanings to the words employed. The classical Utilitarian theory was an attempt to produce a sort of mechanics of behaviour; and it failed just because these necessary conditions do not obtain. Even if we neglect the fact that ethics raises questions about ends and take the duty to produce the maximum pleasure all round us as a datum, it is impossible to measure amounts of pleasure in the way that we can measure amounts of heat or energy; and the duty to produce the maximum of pleasure all round can certainly not be accepted as a datum unless 'pleasure' is construed so vaguely as to be useless.

Moreover the view that no progress has been made in solving the fundamental problems of ethics is an illusion based on the fact that some of these problems were solved very early in the history of mankind. Both the practical difficulties of deciding what to do and the difficulties encountered in theoretical ethics are unlike those encountered in mathematics and science. In practice difficulties arise mainly from the conflict of moral rules and in the application of well-known rules to particular cases; in theoretical ethics they are, as we shall see, mainly difficulties of understanding the logical behaviour of and relations between the concepts used in practical discourse.

Problems of conduct arise on particular occasions, and difficult problems arise only when the circumstances are unfamiliar. Indeed they can only so arise, since we all know what to do when the case is covered adequately by some familiar rule. Sceptical doubts about the validity of our moral code or its application to familiar circumstances reflect no genuine uncertainty about what we ought to do.

There are a few fundamental rules of conduct that have never changed and probably never will; indeed it is difficult to imagine what life in society would be like if we abandoned them. The more we study moral codes the more we find that they do not differ on major points of principle and that the divergencies that exist are due partly to different opinions about empirical facts, for example about the effects of certain types of conduct, and partly to differences in social and economic organization that make it appropriate to apply the fundamental rules now in one way, now in another. Thus all codes agree that we have a duty to requite good with good; but obedience to this rule will involve behaving in ways that will differ according to the view that a society takes of what it is to do good to someone. In some societies it is rude for a guest to eat everything on his plate, in others it is rude for him not to do so; but both agree in enjoining that we should not be rude to our hosts.

It is not enough to know the general, unchanging rules; we must also know how to apply them. And it is for this reason that moral rules, like the law, cannot be codified for all time. One of the main tasks of the lawyer is to apply well-tried and stable general principles to cases that could not have arisen in an earlier age simply because the facts involved could not have arisen. New social and economic relations between man and man give rise to new rights and duties that could not have been contemplated by the authors of a particular moral or legal code.

The idea of a 'scientific morality' – if it means anything more than the laudable recommendation to make use of discoveries in psychology when we are thinking about means – is as chimerical as the ideal which inspired the *Code Napoléon*. A detailed moral code, a sort of handbook to which we might turn for the answer to every moral problem, cannot help us, because difficulties will always arise about the application of the rules to new cases and because the cases in which the need for practical thinking is particularly acute are just those which are new and those in which we suspect that there is some good reason for breaking the accepted code. The need to think afresh about moral problems is ever present and particularly great in a period of rapid economic and social change and rapid advance in knowledge of human nature. Most of our detailed rules were evolved in societies very different from our own and by people who knew far less about human nature than we now do. This is particularly true in matters of sexual morality, where the rules are, or were, considered to be hypothetical and justified by reference to the consequences of obeying them to the individual and to society. If we know, as we now do, that obedience to some of these rules does not promote the desired end, we must either abandon them or make them out to be absolute, categorical rules of morality, which in many cases is very unplausible.

[3]

The impossibility of a 'scientific morality' and the reasons why it is impossible were more clearly understood by Aristotle than by any other philosopher. Like other philosophers he believed that the aim of moral philosophy was to make men good, but he did not think that he could make them good by lecturing on ethics or by writing a handbook. He thought that the help that moral philosophy can give was of a more indirect and subtle kind; and since the scope and method of this book are of a more Aristotelian than Platonic kind, it is necessary to explain what this is.

Suppose someone were to ask me to give him a moral code to live by, I should reply – as Aristotle in effect did – "I can't give you a code; go and watch the best and wisest men you can find and imitate them". I should not have given him what he asked for; but I should have given him the sort of help that a moral philosopher can give. If I went on to give the reasons for this advice, I should help him by explaining that he has put his question in the wrong way. What he really wanted was practical knowledge; he wanted to know how to live. But he had jumped to the conclusion that this sort of knowledge could be contained in a moral code. It is as if someone who wanted to learn how to play the piano were to ask for a manual of instructions and to suppose that when he had mastered the manual he would be able to play. Now whether morality can be learned from books or only by practice is a typical philosopher's question. I am not claiming to give the answer – which is in this case obvious – but only to use this as an illustration of the sort of help that a philosopher can give.

Some of our practical difficulties arise because we are not sure about the facts of the case. But we have other difficulties which are of a kind that is not so easily detected. These are due to our inexpertness in handling the concepts or words that we use for solving practical problems. We have a specific vocabulary for dealing with moral questions. It contains such words as desire, appetite, will, voluntary, choice, approval, conscience, remorse, guilt, deserve, pleasure, pain, duty, obligation, good, and evil. These, unlike the technical terms of a science, are not the property of specialists; in a way, everyone understands what they mean; and people who do not know what they mean, who do not know, for example, what pleasure or remorse is, will never learn anything from ethics.

But there is another way in which people who are unversed in philosophy do not understand these words. They do not always know the connexions between these words or between the ideas which they express. Under what precise conditions do we hold a man responsible? Why do we punish thieves and not kleptomaniacs? What is the connexion between responsibility and deserving punishment? How is choosing related to wanting? How does duty come into the picture? Is it necessary to justify obedience to a rule of duty? Does it even make sense to try to do so? All these are typical questions of moral philosophy.

And there is another range of questions that are even more obviously questions about the meanings of words. How are these different concepts related to each other? Can 'good', for example, be defined in terms of 'pleasure' or 'desire'? Can it be defined at all or is it an irreducible moral term?

There is a similar range of questions also about sentences. Do all the sentences that appear to do so state facts? If we use some sentences to state facts, others to express decisions, others to give advice, issue orders and so on, how are all these things that we do with bits of language related to each other? Earlier I drew a broad distinction between questions about ends and questions about means. Is this distinction as clear-cut as it seems to be? And is this terminology of means and ends adequate to the subject, or are there some questions which stubbornly insist on posing themselves but which cannot be satisfactorily posed in this form?

This set of questions raises another set of an even higher order of abstraction, still more remote it would seem from solving a moral problem. If we distinguish between different types of question or sentence we presuppose that we have some basis for the distinction. What is this basis? Do we discover the difference by inspection? And, if so, of what? Their grammatical form? Or by reflecting on the different jobs that they are used to do?

But, while the first range of questions that I have mentioned has always occupied the attention of philosophers, the more obviously logical questions about words and sentences were, until very recently, largely neglected. This was because it was implicitly held that the logic of every type of discourse must be identical. Grammarians might be interested in verbal forms, statements, questions, commands, wishes, and so on. But the province of philosophy was Truth and the sole vehicle of Truth was thought to be the 'proposition', expressed in an indicative sentence which ascribes a 'quality' to an 'object'. Other moods and sentence-forms and other uses to which sentences might be put, however important they might be in other ways, were irrelevant to the quest for Truth. In the following chapters I shall try to show how adherence to this logical dogma has prejudiced and distorted the accounts which moral philosophers have given of what it is to make a moral decision or judgement. And if this examination involves postponing my own account of the logic of moral words, my excuse is that a philosopher can only make his own views clear by contrasting them with those of his predecessors.

CHAPTER 2

Theoretical Ethics

[1]

In the last chapter I suggested that, to the great moral philosophers of the past, ethics was primarily concerned with answering practical questions. We sometimes find these questions put in what looks like a theoretical form: 'What is the Good for Man?', 'What is the nature of Goodness or of Obligation?'. Their investigations then take on a superficial resemblance to theoretical inquiries, inquiries into the nature of molluscs or carbohydrates or igneous rocks or conic sections. But the disguise is thin. When Plato asks "What is Justice?", it is clear that he keeps his eye continually on the question 'What ought we to do?'.

Moral philosophers were, of course, always partly theoreticians. They claimed to give a true account of what it is to make a moral judgement, to decide, deliberate and choose, as well as to answer moral questions in a more direct way. But they did not, except superficially, represent moral judgements as being themselves theoretical statements, as being descriptions or explanations of a special world of moral qualities and objects. When, for example, they offered definitions of goodness or obligation, they would claim that their definitions truly and faithfully reflected our ordinary use of the words 'good' and 'ought', but they regarded judgements in the form 'X is good' and 'X is obligatory' as practical judgements.

When we turn, however, to the works of some of the best-known twentieth-century moralists we find this conception of moral judgements as practical judgements deliberately abandoned. The direct object of ethics, we are told, is not Practice but Knowledge. And we shall soon see that this knowledge is not theoretical knowledge *about* moral judgements and concepts. Moral judgements are themselves bits of theoretical knowledge about special moral objects. Knowing that this is right or that that is wrong is knowing that something is the case, not knowing what to do.

This contrast between Practice and Knowledge implies the assumption that there is no such thing as *Practical Knowledge*, an assumption that the older philosophers would have rejected if it had ever occurred to them. The moral philosopher's task is now conceived, not to be one of conducting a theoretical inquiry into practical wisdom, but to be one of investigating questions, judgements, doubts, and beliefs that are themselves theoretical. The moral philosopher not only makes theoretical statements about his subject-matter; his subject-matter consists of theoretical statements.

And it is partly in consequence of this change of view as to what sort of a subject moral philosophy is that the intuitionist philosophers whose theories I am about to examine have accused traditional moral philosophy of resting on a mistake. This is a sweeping condemnation and we must now see how it came to be made and whether it is just.

According to Professor Broad "Ethics may be described as the theoretical treatment of moral phenomena".[1] This approach at once assimilates the moral philosopher's task to that of a scientist. The underlying assumption is that there is a special field or subject-matter, a special set of objects, qualities, or phenomena that the moral philosopher is going to study in the way that the chemist studies the chemical properties of matter, the geologist rocks, and the astronomer stars.

It is true that an important distinction is soon drawn between moral philosophy and natural science, and intuitionists have, as we shall see, a special way of marking this distinction. But it is important to insist on the implied analogy; for it is the uncritical use of this analogy that distorts what intuitionist writers have to say about the difference between the two subjects and leads them to their sweeping condemnations of

1. Broad: *Philosophy*, 1946. Reprinted in Feigl and Sellars: *Readings in Philosophical Analysis*, p. 547.

traditional ethics. In the next three chapters I shall argue that the analogy cannot be sustained and that intuitionists fundamentally misrepresent the differences between moral and empirical discourse, differences which they recognize to be genuine and important, by treating moral discourse as if it was itself descriptive and explanatory. They have treated moral discourse as being descriptive of a special world of special objects, qualities, and phenomena, when the real burden of their arguments is to show that moral discourse is not descriptive at all.

What, we must ask, are the objects that ethics studies, the objects that bear the same relation to the moralist as birds bear to the ornithologist or coins to the numismatist? We might in the past have pointed to pleasure and pain, to the various desires, aversions, and motives, that play a part in human conduct. But this will not do. The description, classification, and explanation of these 'phenomena' belong to the empirical science of psychology, and psychology is not ethics. It is a cardinal doctrine of the intuitionists that ethical concepts cannot be identified with or reduced to psychological ones or to the concepts of any other natural science.

According to Broad the special phenomena to be studied are of three kinds, moral judgement, moral emotion, and moral volition. Of these he gives the following examples:

(a) I know or believe that I ought to keep a promise . . . and that it is wrong to inflict useless pain. These bits of moral knowledge or belief are instances of Moral Judgements.

(b) I feel remorse or self-disapproval, as distinct from mere fear of punishment or embarrassment at being found out. These feelings will be instances of Moral Emotion.

(c) In so far as I am influenced in my decision (between two alternative courses of action) by the thought that one of them is right, this is an instance of Moral Volition.[1]

We may concentrate on moral judgement since moral

1. Loc. cit.

emotion and volition owe their place in ethics to their connexion with moral judgement. Remorse seems to me to differ, as an emotion, in no fundamental way from embarrassment; it belongs to ethics solely because this emotion is not called 'remorse' unless it arises from the judgement that what one did was morally wrong. Similarly, volition is expressly said only to be 'moral' if my decision is influenced by the thought (i.e. judgement) that the action is right.

The central phenomenon of ethics is, then, the moral judgement or, as Broad also calls it, the "opinion that something is right or wrong". It should be noticed from the start that moral judgements are said to be, not emotional reactions or attitudes or expressions of approval and disapproval, but *opinions*. This word immediately takes us into the vocabulary in which we talk about questions of fact, in science and in everyday life. Opinions are true or false, correct or mistaken; a man can be convicted of error in holding an opinion in a way that he cannot if he merely expresses his taste. It may be 'wrong' in some sense to like comic strips or the music of Cole Porter; but we could not say that a man who liked them was *mistaken*; and if we did we should have to add that we were using 'mistaken' in a different way from that in which we use it when we say that a man who thinks that New York is the capital of the United States is mistaken.

There is nothing logically surprising in the notion of the whole world being mistaken about a point of fact; indeed we know that for centuries everyone believed the earth to be flat; but the suggestion that if everybody called strawberries 'nice' they might all be mistaken is very odd indeed. The contrast between cases where a man can be said to be mistaken and cases where he cannot is usually put in the form of saying that matters of fact are 'objective', matters of taste 'subjective'. By using the word 'opinion' Broad shows that moral judgements are, for him, judgements of fact, not judgements of taste, objective not subjective.

But if we say that the phenomena studied by the moralist are moral judgements or the reports of the moral consciousness, we are met by a peculiar difficulty. How does the moral philosopher 'theoretically treat' these? It would seem that, if the analogy with the natural sciences is to hold, he must ask such questions as: 'Under what circumstances does such and such a moral judgement occur?', 'What causes does it have?', 'What effects?'. His job must be to classify moral judgements into types and genera and to discover general laws governing the occurrence of these 'phenomena'. But it is obvious that such an inquiry would be a part of empirical psychology and that the moralist is not interested in describing, classifying, and explaining these judgements. He is interested in discovering whether or not they are *true*. Judgements and opinions (usually dignified with the name of 'theories' when they are of a general kind) play an important part in science; and the student of a science must study them in the sense that it would ill beseem him not to be *au fait* with the theories current in his subject. But, in a quite different sense, the student of chemistry studies, not the theories of Dalton and Mendeleev, but the properties of chemical substances; these, and not the theories, are the objects or phenomena that he theoretically treats. And we soon find Broad taking it for granted that the phenomena studied by the moralist are not moral *judgements* at all, nor even moral emotions and volitions, but a special set of objects, namely the Right, the Wrong, the Good, and the Bad.

If we took Broad's opening paragraph literally we should have to regard the moral philosopher as an historian of moral opinions analogous to the historian of natural science whose objects of study are indeed the theories held at different times by scientists. Professor Westermark does in fact take this line; he believes that the purpose of ethics "can only be to study the moral consciousness as a fact".[1] But he does this frankly as an historian of morals because he believes that there is nothing to study but the psychological and sociological phenomena involved.

Sir David Ross also takes as his starting point "the exist-

1. *Ethical Relativity*, p. 61.

ence of what is commonly called the moral consciousness, . . . the existence of a large body of beliefs and convictions to the effect that there are certain kinds of acts that ought to be done and certain kinds of things that ought to be brought into existence".[1] But it is clear that, for him, we 'start from' these beliefs not in the sense that they are the phenomena that we study first, but in the sense that the student of any subject 'starts from' the opinions of his teachers. There is, however, a difference between ethics and a natural science which Ross notices without, I think, realizing its crucial importance.

In the natural sciences, he says "it would be a great mistake to take as our starting point either the opinions of the many or those of the wise. For in them we have a more direct avenue to truth; the appeal must always be from opinions to the facts of sense-perception".[2] Clearly Ross does not mean that it would be a mistake for a student to start from the opinions of his teacher. How else could he start? Nor does he mean that it would always be a mistake for a layman to prefer the verdict of an expert to his own untutored observation. He means that in the natural sciences and, indeed, wherever the question is one of fact there is a test of truth superior to the appeal to authority. This is a consequence of the logic of the word 'fact'. It would be foolish for the young scientist to ignore the opinion of the expert and foolish for a traveller to ignore the information contained in Bradshaw. But Bradshaw's statement that the train leaves at ten o'clock is not true because Bradshaw says it; it is true because the train leaves at ten o'clock. The opinions of eminent scientists are ignored at our peril; but if they are true it is because they correspond with the facts, not because eminent scientists hold them.

Ross goes on to say that in ethics we have no direct avenue to truth such as that which observation provides in empirical matters, and must therefore be content with the opinions of the many and the wise. But our inability to observe ethical truth has far-reaching consequences. It must raise a doubt

1. *The Foundations of Ethics*, p. 1.   2. Op. cit., p. 3.

about the propriety of taking over into ethics the concept of truth and its attendant concepts such as 'fact', 'false', 'mistaken', 'correct' and so on. For, in empirical matters, our use of these concepts is, as Ross says, bound up with our having the direct avenue of observation.

Now it is a fact that we do talk of truth and falsity in moral matters, of opinion and knowledge (not just emotion and taste), of being correct and mistaken; and this is a fact that must be accounted for. But the logic of this talk is now seen to be different in an important way from its logic in empirical discourse. The two uses are analogous; but the analogy is not exact. And this should make us cautious about applying to ethics logical concepts that we customarily apply to empirical discourse. When, in an empirical case, I have not observed something myself but accept someone else's opinion as true, I do so because I believe that it corresponds with the facts and that he has observed this although I have not. But, if Ross is right, in ethical matters the many and the wise are, like me, debarred from the direct access to truth that we have in empirical matters.

And this leads us to ask what it is in ethics that makes one man's opinion true and another's false, when there is nothing analogous to the scientist's appeal from opinions to the facts of sense-perception. The question is a crucial one, but what Ross has to say on it seems to me obscure. "We must start with the opinions that are crystallized in ordinary language and ordinary ways of thinking, and our attempt must be to make these thoughts, little by little, more definite and distinct, and by comparing one with another to discover at what points each opinion must be purged of excess and misstatement till it becomes harmonious with other opinions that have been purified in the same way."[1] Part of this programme is not difficult to understand. We can see how careful thinking will make our thought definite, distinct, and harmonious. But how are we to detect a *mis*-statement? How are we to tell when the rejection of an opinion is really the purging of a

1. Loc. cit.

falsehood and not the rejection of a truth? Ross seems to be advocating a Coherence theory of ethics in which the truth of a moral opinion would depend on its coherence with other opinions. But this is not really so. For we soon find that an appeal analogous to the scientist's appeal to sense-perception is introduced and the test of truth remains one of correspondence. A direct avenue is discovered and it turns out to be a very short one. We are directly aware of the moral phenomena to which true moral opinions correspond.

The method actually practised by intuitionist philosophers is partly that described by Ross in this passage. They take the tangled web of our ordinary moral discourse, which they believe to be often obscure and muddled, and subject it to careful analysis. Vague and general statements expressed in loose terminology are split up into a number of different and precise things that they could possibly mean and these products of analysis are submitted for our inspection. But how do we know which of them is true? We may compare them with similar products presented by rival moralists; but which are we to accept?

In the course of the intuitionist's argument a crucial, but unnoticed, shift of interest has occurred. The 'phenomena' to be studied were originally said to be men's moral volitions, emotions, and opinions, of which opinions were the most important. But they are now seen to be, not the opinions, but what these opinions are about, the special objects or properties denoted by the words in our moral vocabulary, the Right and the Good. The belief that ethics is a theoretical science, that its task is the description, classification, and explanation of special phenomena, objects, and qualities, is maintained in spite of the fact that the intuitionist has noticed a crucial difference between ethics and the other theoretical sciences. The difference was that, while in the sciences opinions are checked by reference to facts, in ethics the opinions themselves are the only facts available. Yet this conversion of ethics into a sort of empirical psychology is so unplausible that the intuitionist abandons it from the start and, to save the analogy with science, draws our attention to (or postulates) a special set of objects which are to the moralist what rocks, stars, and birds are to their respective scientists. The appeal is made to observation; but it is observation of a very special kind.

[2]

In rejecting the evolutionary theory of ethics, (according to which 'right' means 'more evolved') Ross says: "There is really no *resemblance* between the *characteristic* which we *have in mind* when we say 'right' or 'obligatory' and that which we have in mind when we say 'more evolved'. . . . If we ask ourselves what 'more evolved' means, we shall find in it, I think, two main elements: (1) that conduct so described comes, in time, after a process of evolution of more or less duration, and (2) that it has a characteristic which usually emerges in the course of evolution, that of being complex, in comparison with the simple activities which appear in an early stage of evolution. And it is surely *clear* that neither temporal posteriority nor complexity, nor the union of the two, is *that which we mean to refer to* when we use the term 'right' or 'obligatory'." [1]

Ross's criticism of the attempt to define 'right' in terms of appearing at a later stage of evolution is surely correct; but I have italicized certain phrases in order to draw attention to the fact that Ross's way of putting his point involves certain assumptions about the logical behaviour of moral concepts.

(a) The words 'right' and 'obligatory' refer to certain characteristics. (Other philosophers use 'denote' and 'stand for' as synonyms for 'refer to', and 'property' and 'quality' as synonyms for 'characteristic'.)

(b) Clarifying the meaning of a word is represented as examining our moral consciousness and discovering therein the characteristic to which the word refers. We have this

1. Op. cit., p. 13 (my italics).

characteristic 'in mind' and, if we are careful, we can see it clearly.

(c) Discovering whether or not two words mean the same thing is a matter of examining the characteristics for which they stand and just *seeing* whether or not these characteristics are identical.

(d) In other passages Ross represents apprehending a moral truth as 'seeing' whether or not a certain object has a certain characteristic.

Putting these points together we find that in ethics the test of truth is no longer the opinions of the many and the wise, but is, as in science, the perceived attributes and relations of things.

The same assumptions, that moral words denote characteristics and that truth in ethics is discovered by observation, occur in the writings of Professor Moore. "My business", he says, "is solely with *that object or idea*, which I hold, rightly or wrongly, that the word 'good' is generally used to *stand for*." [1] Moore's argument against the Naturalistic Fallacy is accepted in outline by all the intuitionists and is the basis of their belief that traditional moral philosophy rests on a mistake. It is too well known to require exposition in detail; but a brief summary will help to bring out the logical points to which I wish to draw special attention.

Moore distinguishes sharply between 'analytic' statements, which are statements about the meanings of words, and 'synthetic' statements, which are about the facts of the case. Hedonists, for example, must make up their minds whether they want to say that 'good' just *means* 'pleasant' or to say that *in fact* pleasure alone is good. He then refutes each of these alternatives and shows how hedonism derives its plausibility from a confusion of the two. Besides the distinction between analytic and synthetic statements Moore's logical apparatus contains the following points:

1. *Principia Ethica*, p. 6 (my italics). The full argument against the Naturalistic Fallacy is given in chapters 1 and 2.

(a) Words 'stand for' objects or ideas, and these are either simple or complex.

(b) Definition is the analysis of a complex idea into the parts of which it is composed. Thus a chimaera is an animal with a lioness's head and body, with a goat's head growing from the middle of its back and with a snake in place of a tail. Similarly, when a word stands for a complex idea, explaining its meaning is a matter of enumerating and describing the simpler ideas of which the idea it stands for is composed.

(c) Words which stand for simple ideas cannot be defined, since the ideas for which they stand cannot be split into parts. 'Yellow' is given as a typical example of such a word. Moore holds that 'good' also stands for a simple, and therefore indefinable idea; and the analogy with 'yellow' strongly suggests that we learn both what 'good' means and also what things are good by a process analogous to sense-perception.

(d) Simple ideas are either 'natural' or 'non-natural'. In *Principia Ethica* this distinction is not expounded and we shall see that it gives rise to certain difficulties. Later, Moore was inclined to accept Broad's definition of a 'natural' object or characteristic as one which "either (a) we become aware of by inspecting our sense-data or introspecting our experiences, or (b) is definable wholly in terms of characteristics of the former kind together with the notions of cause and substance".[1]

The Naturalistic Fallacy consists in identifying certain ethical properties, such as rightness and goodness, with natural properties, whether simple or complex, such as 'pleasant', 'normal', 'more evolved', or 'according to God's will'. And the argument which refutes it is that, on reflection, we just *see* that the ethical properties are not identical with any of these natural ones. But in order to be able to see this we must first be able to see what goodness and rightness are. We do not literally see these properties with our eyes; but the faculty concerned is called 'non-sensuous intuition',

1. *The Philosophy of G. E. Moore*, p. 62 and p. 592.

'awareness', 'apprehension', 'recognition', 'acquaintance', words which all strongly suggest an analogy with sight or touch.

This analogy comes out well in the following passage: "But whoever will attentively consider with himself *what is actually before his mind* when he asks the question 'Is pleasure (or whatever it may be) after all good?' can satisfy himself that he is not merely wondering whether pleasure is pleasant. And if he will try this experiment with each suggested definition in succession, he may become expert enough to *recognize* that in every case *he has before his mind a unique object. . . .*" [1]

The same faculty that reveals to us the identity or non-identity of the objects for which words stand is also called into play to decide questions of ethical fact, namely what things are good. Moore holds that, once the meaning of this question is clearly understood, the answer to it is just *obvious*.[2] Thus the final touchstone turns out to be analogous to that used in chemistry. Just as, in the last resort, we know that the stuff in the bottle is sulphuric acid because it looks, smells, and tastes like sulphuric acid; so, in ethics, we know both that one property is or is not identical with another and also what things have what properties by inspection.

Professor Prichard represents the intuitionist thesis in its clearest and most uncompromising form. He uses the analogy with mathematics rather than that with empirical discourse; but this makes little difference since he thinks of mathematical knowledge as an affair of 'seeing' or 'apprehending' and thus appeals to the analogy with sight and touch at one remove. It is in Prichard's writings also that we see most clearly how this analogy leads to the rejection of traditional moral philosophy as resting on a mistake.

It is not a mistake in detail; but a mistake in principle. It is that of supposing that when we are confronted by a duty it makes sense to ask why we ought to perform it. Moral philosophers have tried to answer this question; they have indeed made it the central question of ethics. But they have

1. *Principia Ethica*, p. 16 (my italics)   2. Op. cit., p. 188.

failed to find the answer because the question itself is a mistaken or absurd one. It is absurd because our obligation to perform a duty is immediate and direct, neither requiring nor capable of supporting reasons. Our knowledge that we have a duty to perform is in the same way direct and immediate. If a man says that he does not see why he should do something that is in fact his duty we can only tell him to think again; and 'think' does not mean 'work it out'; it means '*look*'.[1]

There are three points in Prichard's thesis to which I wish to draw attention. (a) Difficulties in the solution of a moral problem are all concerned with the non-moral facts of the situation. Once the "general and not moral" thinking has been properly done no further question can arise, since the recognition of the obligation is immediate and direct. There is really no such thing as *moral thinking* or wondering what I ought to do in this situation. We can only wonder whether the situation is really such as to give rise to a duty.

(b) Although Prichard speaks mainly in terms of 'appreciating' a moral truth, he also speaks of 'recognizing' one; and although he avoids, perhaps deliberately, the word 'seeing', the whole tenor of his argument requires us to take 'appreciating' as analogous to 'seeing'.

(c) Not only is moral knowledge the direct and immediate awareness of a datum; we also know with a similar immediacy that we are knowing and not believing. Genuine knowledge (as opposed to belief) is infallible. A man who really knows cannot be mistaken; and since he knows that he knows, he also knows that he cannot be mistaken. It is on this that Prichard's rejection of a criterion for either mathematical or moral knowledge rests. A criterion is both impossible and unnecessary; impossible because it would be subject to the same sceptical doubts to which the knowledge it is used to test are subject, and unnecessary because the knowledge it is used to test is not subject to any genuine doubts at all.

1. *Does Moral Philosophy rest on a Mistake?* Reprinted in *Moral Obligation*, pp. 7 and 15.

CHAPTER 3

Intuitionism

[1]

In this and the following chapter I shall criticize the intuitionist theory; but my purpose is not to show that it is wholly mistaken or that its attacks on the Naturalistic Fallacy are misplaced. Rather I shall try to show that, on the negative side, the points which the intuitionist makes against the naturalist are correct; but that his way of making these points, the logical terminology in which he couches his arguments, misrepresents the very truths that the arguments are designed to bring out and makes his positive thesis in its own way as misleading as an account of moral discourse as were the earlier, naturalistic theories. The intuitionist has noticed important differences between moral and empirical discourse; but he has marked these differences in the wrong way.

The strength of intuitionism lies in its uncompromising insistence on the autonomy of morals. To put the point briefly and in my own way, practical discourse, of which moral discourse is a part, cannot be identified with or reduced to any other kind of discourse. Ethical sentences are not, as Moore so clearly shows, psychological or metaphysical or theological sentences. Almost all earlier theories had tended to reduce ethical concepts and sentences to those of some other subject, usually psychology; they tried to define words such as 'good' and 'ought' in terms, for example, of the satisfaction of desire or of pleasure and pain. Against all such attempts the intuitionists produce a crushing argument which is derived (surprisingly) from Hume.

In a celebrated passage Hume says: "I cannot forbear adding to these reasonings an observation which may perhaps be found of some importance. In every system of morality which I have hitherto met with I have always remarked that the author proceeds for some time in the ordinary way of reasoning, and establishes the being of a God, or makes observations concerning human affairs; when of a sudden I am surprised to find, that instead of the usual copulations of propositions, *is* and *is not*, I meet with no proposition that is not connected with an *ought*, or an *ought not*. This change is imperceptible; but is, however, of the last consequence. For as this *ought* or *ought not* expresses some new relation or affirmation, it is necessary that it should be observed and explained; and at the same time that a reason should be given for what seems altogether inconceivable, how this new relation can be a deduction from others that are entirely different from it." [1]

Freely translated into modern terminology, what Hume means is this. In all systems of morality we start with certain statements of fact that are not judgements of value or commands; they contain no moral words. They are usually statements about God or about human nature, that is to say about what men *are* and *in fact do*. We are then told that *because* these things are so we ought to act in such and such a way; the answers to practical questions are deduced or in some other way derived from statements about what is the case. This must be illegitimate reasoning, since the conclusion of an argument can contain nothing which is not in the premises, and there are no 'oughts' in the premises.

We are not concerned with the validity of this argument as a criticism of traditional ethics. It might be argued that Aristotle and certain Christian writers did not make this mistake, since their premises were really disguised value-judgements or 'ought'-judgements from the start. But some philosophers, notably the hedonists, certainly did make this mistake, and of them Hume's criticism is an unanswerable refutation. [2]

---

1. *Treatise*, Book III, Part 1, Section i.
2. Cf. Bishop Mortimer: *Christian Ethics*, p. 7. "The first foundation is the doctrine of God the Creator. God made us and all the world. *Be-*

In their various ways the writers of the intuitionist school have but repeated Hume's argument. I may know that a certain action will please God or maximize my own pleasure or produce the greatest happiness of the greatest number; but this is all knowledge of what *is* or *will be* the case. It still makes sense to ask whether I *ought* to do the action. As Prichard points out a 'link' is required to connect the statements of fact with an injunction to do or not do something or, in my terminology, to connect the answer to a theoretical question with the answer to a practical one. We must now see whether the intuitionist is in a better position to provide this link, to bridge the gap between 'is' and 'ought' than his naturalistic predecessors.

At first sight it seems that he is; for he has so arranged matters that no gap exists. Earlier moralists tried to derive obligation-statements from statements of other kinds; but, for an intuitionist, obligations are immediately and underivatively known and require no deduction. The demand for a bridge, for an argument connecting 'ought' to 'is' is senseless because we are directly confronted by 'oughts'. But a closer examination will show that this way out of the difficulty is a spurious one. I shall argue later that the intuitionist cannot both maintain the immediate and underivative character of moral knowledge and also the analogy with empirical discourse which justifies his use of such terms as 'see', 'recognize', 'true', 'mistaken', 'know', 'fact', and 'objective'.[1] In this chapter I shall try to show that his way of representing moral knowledge as theoretical knowledge still leaves him with a gap to be bridged.

cause of that He has an absolute claim on our obedience. We do not exist in our own right, but only as His creatures, who ought *therefore* to do and be what He desires." This argument requires the premise that a creature ought to obey his creator, which is itself a moral judgement. So that Christian ethics is not founded solely on the doctrine that God created us.

1. Chapter 4, below.

[2]

Moral knowledge is represented by intuitionists as knowledge that a certain object has a certain characteristic. To learn a moral truth is like learning that Henry VIII had six wives or that α Centauri is $4\frac{1}{2}$ light years away. The difference between moral characteristics and those that we learn about in science and in history is marked by calling them non-natural. But moral judgements are treated as descriptions of features of the universe, and the fact that these features are so peculiar as to merit the epithet 'non-natural' in no way affects the status of moral judgements as descriptions.

Yet in spite of this the core of the intuitionist argument against naturalism is that normative or evaluative propositions cannot be deduced from descriptive ones. Intuitionists recognize the importance of moral approval and disapproval and of moral sentiments such as remorse; and it might seem that a philosopher who was prepared to assert that there are special, non-natural, moral emotions is not guilty of the naturalistic fallacy. At least he would not be guilty of trying to reduce something specifically moral to some non-moral thing. But this concession to the non-natural status of moral concepts is not enough to satisfy the intuitionist. In criticizing 'approval' and 'emotive' theories of ethics Ross says: "For as of moral approval, so of the emotion of obligation, we must say that it is not a blind feeling that arises in us, we know not why, on contemplating a possible act. It is an intellectual emotion which arises only when we judge the act to have a certain character, say that of producing a maximum of good, and to be on that account obligatory." [1] Moral emotions could not occur unless we were aware of moral facts.

The intuitionist's answer to the question 'why should I be moral?' – unless, like Prichard, he rejects it as a senseless question – is that, if you reflect carefully, you will notice that a certain act has two characteristics, (a) that of being obligatory and (b) that of producing a maximum of good or of

1. Op. cit., p. 26. cf. p. 23.

being a fulfilment of a promise or the payment of a debt, etc. There are a certain number of these 'right-making' characteristics and they are related to obligation in the following way. An act which has one of the right-making characteristics would always be right; but these characteristics might conflict and we cannot be obliged to do conflicting actions; so an action is obligatory only when the balance of rightness is on its side. You decide which action has the balance of rightness on its side by estimating the stringency of the various 'claims' or '*prima facie* rightnesses' concerned.

Moreover, if you have noticed these characteristics you will feel a special moral emotion of obligation; and you will not feel this special emotion if you have not noticed the characteristics.[1]

But suppose all this has taken place. I have noticed the right-making characteristic and the rightness; and I feel the emotion of obligation. Does it follow that I ought to do the action towards which I feel the emotion? If Hume's argument is valid at all, is it not equally valid against this deduction? It cannot be evaded by merely calling the characteristic and the emotion 'non-natural'; copious use of this epithet serves only to disguise Hume's gap, not to bridge it.

In representing moral knowledge as theoretical, an affair of being aware of or noticing 'phenomena', albeit of a very special kind, the intuitionist is drawing our attention to an analogy between ethics and empirical science. We learn some things, he says, by *inspecting* our sense-data, others by *introspecting* our experiences; and a third world, a world of non-natural characteristics, is revealed to us by a third faculty called '*intuition*'. (Perhaps there is a fourth world in which the Beautiful and the Ugly reside, which is revealed by a fourth faculty. Intuitionists are divided on this point, some claiming that there is, others that there is not. Surely this in itself is suspicious.)

---

1. It is not quite clear what the connexion between noticing the characteristics and feeling the emotion is supposed to be. Is it logically or causally impossible for a man to feel just this emotion if he has not noticed the characteristics? Or is it impossible in some other way?

It is only in this way that moral knowledge can be represented as theoretical. For what is it to call something 'theoretical' but to draw an analogy between it and something that is theoretical in a straight-forward sense, such as empirical science, and to treat the logical terminology that we use when talking about the latter as equally applicable to the former? But, if the analogy is just, are we not simply confronted with a new set of data or phenomena or characteristics? And from statements to the effect that these exist no conclusions follow about what I *ought to do*. A new world is revealed for our inspection; it contains such and such objects, phenomena, and characteristics; it is mapped and described in elaborate detail. No doubt it is all very interesting. If I happen to have a thirst for knowledge, I shall read on to satisfy my curiosity, much as I should read about new discoveries in astronomy or geography. Learning about 'values' or 'duties' might well be as exciting as learning about spiral nebulae or waterspouts. But what if I am not interested? Why should I *do* anything about these newly-revealed objects? Some things, I have now learnt, are right and others wrong; but why should I do what is right and eschew what is wrong?

"But", you will say, "all this is monstrous. It is regrettable, perhaps, that you are not interested in nebulae or waterspouts, – regrettable, but not blameworthy. But not to be interested in the difference between right and wrong! Not to be able to *see* the difference, not to feel the obligation to do the one and eschew the other! This is not regrettable; it is wicked, immoral, sinful, inhuman. And anyhow I just don't believe you. You are propounding a philosopher's paradox, playing with words."

And of course you are right. Of course the question 'Why should I do what I see to be right?' is not just an immoral question, but an absurd one. In ordinary life we should be puzzled by a man who said "Yes, you have convinced me that it is the right thing to do; but ought I to do it?". We shouldn't know how to answer him, not because we could not think up any new arguments, but because, in conceding that it is the right thing

41

to do, he has already conceded that he ought to do it. Our puzzle is to understand the distinction he seems to be making between what it is right for him to do and what he ought to do. He must be able to see a distinction here, since he grants that something is right but still wonders whether he ought to do it. He has really solved his practical problem; but he seems to think that there is an extra step to be taken. What could this step possibly be?

But the argument I have used is not designed to convince the ordinary man that there is really no difference between right and wrong or to prove to him that he has no obligations or even to insinuate doubts about the propriety of passing from 'this is right' to 'I ought to do this'. It is a philosophical argument designed to refute a special, philosophical account of what obligation and our knowledge of obligations are.

These questions, which are absurd when words are used in the ordinary way, would not be absurd if moral words were used in the way that intuitionists suppose. For in ordinary life there is no gap between 'this is the right thing for me to do' and 'I ought to do this' into which a sceptic might insert a wedge. But if 'X is right' and 'X is obligatory' are construed as statements to the effect that X has the non-natural characteristic of rightness or obligatoriness, which we just 'see' to be present, it would seem that we can no more deduce 'I ought to do X' from these premises than we could deduce it from 'X is pleasant' or 'X is in accordance with God's will'. A gap of which ordinary language knows nothing has been created between 'X is obligatory on me' and 'I ought to do it'; and this gap requires to be bridged.

To escape from this argument the intuitionist might reply that his talk about recognizing non-natural qualities in actions and things has been taken far too seriously. There is really, he will say, no such characteristic as 'obligatoriness'. Saying that an action is obligatory on me is a convenient but *strictly an incorrect* way of saying that I ought to do the action.

This line of argument does indeed eliminate the unbridgeable gap between what is obligatory and what I ought to do, but it does so only by conceding that the characteristic of 'obligatoriness' is a myth. And he might deal with 'rightness' in the same way – and at the same cost. He might say that calling an action *'prima facie* right' is a convenient, but *strictly an incorrect* way of saying that I ought to do it if there is nothing that I ought to do more. But he still has on his hands the task of explaining the fact that no action is merely right, but always 'right as being of a certain character', for example as being the payment of a debt or the fulfilment of a promise.

And what, meanwhile, has happened to the intuitionist theory? The account of obligation as a non-natural characteristic of actions was designed both to tell us what obligation is (not to tell us what our obligations are) and to explain how we know what we ought to do. It fails in both tasks; and for the same reason. For it turns out to be, not an explanation, but a restatement in technically convenient, but *strictly incorrect* language of the facts to be explained. We are no nearer to knowing what obligation is, because it is now conceded that 'X has the characteristic of obligatoriness' is just another way of saying 'I ought to do X'. And the intuitionist's reply to the question 'How do I know what I ought to do?' is equally unenlightening. For it turns out to be: "You know what you ought to do by intuiting the non-natural characteristic of obligatoriness that inheres in certain actions. But, my dear sir, do not be alarmed by this mysterious phrase. It is only another way of saying that you know that you ought to do those actions." We know what we ought to do by knowing what we ought to do. Opium sends us to sleep because it has a *virtus dormitiva*.

[3]

The authors so far considered would not claim that their talk about objective, non-natural properties was intended to help us to solve practical problems. They claimed to show how the words in our moral vocabulary, 'good', 'right', 'obligatory', and 'ought' are to be construed. What they offer us is in effect a translation of ordinary moral sentences into a new terminology. And such a translation might well be enlightening. We might, for example, wonder whether moral judgements were more like statements of empirical fact or like expressions of taste; and, by showing that they can be translated into the language of objective properties, by making out a case for the analogy with empirical discourse, they might settle this old dispute in favour of Reason, not Sentiment.

But how would we discover whether such a translation can profitably be made? The new way of saying what a moral decision or conflict or judgement is ought to make these notions clear. I shall now try to show that, even if the objective-property theory is correct, it throws no light on one of the most important and difficult problems of ethics which it ought to be able to elucidate.

THE RECONCILIATION OF CONFLICTS

For the extreme intuitionist there is no problem about reconciling the conflicting moral insights of different people. If I clearly apprehend the truth I may grieve at your inability to see it; but I cannot be troubled by any anxiety that I may have failed to see it myself. But if once this possibility is admitted, if I can wonder whether what I took to be a genuine intuition might not have been a spurious one, the problem becomes serious. How does the appeal to intuition help us to settle radical differences that cannot be attributed to disagreement about the non-moral facts of the case?

Let us see first of all how a subjectivist would describe such disagreement. If I disagree with you about the rightness of an action or the goodness of a person or the morality of some general line of conduct, my arguments, he would say, must be of one of two kinds.

(a) I might try to convince you that you were mistaken about some non-moral fact. For example you thought it wrong of me to have refused money to that blind beggar, and the dispute ceases when I point out that I happen to know him to be a fraud. There was never any *moral* dispute between us, since we both wished to advocate charity towards genuine beggars, not frauds.

(b) I might try to convince you that my moral judgement follows from or is a special case of some more general moral judgement which I know that you accept. For example you might approve of giving money to beggars because it relieves distress – and we both approve of relieving distress. If I convinced you that your sort of charity creates more distress than it alleviates, which is a question of empirical *fact*, then you must withdraw your censure and the dispute ceases.

Both these forms of argument presuppose that there is some common moral ground between us, if only we can find it. Many disputes, say the subjectivists, turn out to be disputes about the facts or about the validity of deductions made from those facts and our common ethical premises. But, they say, a point may be reached when there is no disagreement of a factual or logical kind; and yet a *moral* disagreement remains. You approve of one thing and I approve of another. And when this point is reached it is tautological to say that the dispute cannot be settled by *rational* argument. We must either agree to differ or resort to flattery, cajolery, bribery, or other non-rational methods of persuasion. Or I must use force or submit to your using force on me.

Now this is not a palatable conclusion, especially when it is erroneously believed to lead to the doctrine that Might is Right.[1] And one of the most important claims that has been made for 'objective values' is that they enable us to escape from it. We do not think it necessary to resort to force where logical, mathematical, or empirical truths are concerned. And if moral truths can be apprehended in the same sort of way, if

1. The conclusion that Might is Right does not in fact follow from the subjective thesis, though it is surprising how often it has been thought to do so. Subjectivism is a theory about the nature of moral judgements. To put it crudely, it is the theory that they are expressions of a man's personal attitudes, his approvals and disapprovals. It does not imply the theory that most men approve of trampling on their neighbours; nor need the subjectivist himself approve of this.

there are criteria that anyone can use to discover them, it ought to be possible to settle moral disputes without recourse to force, by rational argument.

But does the notion of objective values in fact help us to reconcile conflicts without recourse to force? Clearly it cannot. For I will claim this status for the values that I intuit, and you will claim it for yours. If the empirical analogy is used, it will make sense for me to say that my view is 'true' and yours 'mistaken', terms which the subjectivist must deny himself; but we are no nearer a solution of the conflict, which still remains exactly what it was before, a conflict between the moral facts that I claim to descry and those that you claim to descry. If I do not recognize the truth of your statements of objective moral fact, you can do nothing to convince me by argument but are, like the subjectivist, thrown back on force or acquiescence. Wars are not fought over logical or empirical issues, just because men do in the end agree about what they see to be the case or 'see' to be logically valid. But wars are fought over moral issues, and the only difference between the subjectivist and the objectivist is that to the former this fact is not surprising.

Theoretically the objective theory cannot help us to reconcile conflicts, since it conceals a difficulty endemic in all theories involving 'intuition'. Intuitions of objective properties are either infallible or they are not. If they are fallible, the mere *existence* of an objective property or value is no guarantee that anyone has apprehended it properly. However convinced you may be that you are right, it is still open to me to deny the genuineness of your intuition. If, on the other hand, intuitions are infallible, then disputes cannot be genuine. If I disagree with you, you must charge me either with insincerity or with moral blindness. And that this account of the matter is false is shown by the fact that we do often allow others to be sincere when their moral views differ from our own.

And in practice the objectivist is, as we should expect, in a far worse position for solving moral conflicts. He necessarily attributes his opponent's denial of the truth to wilful perversity; and, holding as he does that in spite of his denials his opponent must really see the truth all the time, he realizes that what his opponent needs is not argument but castigation. For arguments cannot convince a man who already sees the light. The objective theory, so far from minimizing the use of force to settle moral conflicts, can be, and constantly has been used to justify it. It is no accident that religious persecutions are the monopoly of objective theorists.

The theory underlying persecution is admirably explained by Samuel Clarke. "These things are so notoriously plain and self-evident, that nothing but the extremest stupidity of mind, corruption of manners or perversity of spirit can possibly make any man entertain the least doubt concerning them. For a man endued with Reason to deny the truth of these things, is the very same thing, as if a man who has the use of his sight should, at the same time that he beholds the sun, deny that there is any such thing as light in the world; or as if a man that understands geometry or arithmetic, should deny the most obvious and known proportions of lines or numbers, and *perversely* contend that the whole is not equal to all its parts. . . . And 'tis as *absurd* and *blameworthy* to mistake negligently plain right and wrong . . . as it would be absurd and ridiculous for a man in arithmetical matters ignorantly to believe that twice two is not equal to four or wilfully and obstinately to contend, *against his own clear knowledge*, that the whole is not equal to all its parts."[1]

If the analogy between moral knowledge and sight or mathematics is as close as Clarke makes out those who disagree with us on a moral issue must be insincere. It is force, not argument that they need. It is hardly necessary to add that this theory has had the most tragic consequences in international affairs. To suppose that people whose professed moral principles differ from ours do not really hold them is to invite disaster.

1. *On Natural Religion.* Selby-Bigge: *British Moralists*, Vol. II, pp. 6 and 13 (my italics).

CHAPTER 4

The Analogy between Ethics and Science

[1]

H o w are we to interpret this talk of a special 'world' or 'order' of values which man's moral consciousness apprehends or of special 'qualities' (like yellow, yet so unlike yellow), that we are aware of, but not by means of the senses? We have seen that if we take it quite literally ethics becomes the geography of a special world out of space and time and that moral knowledge, in being represented as knowledge of what is the case, becomes cut off from practical knowledge, from doing, deciding, choosing, advising, and exhorting in such a way that special intuitions are required to fill the gap. And if we take it less literally it turns out that all these mysterious phrases are only a rather pretentious way of saying – what we all know – that some things are right and others wrong, whereas they were intended to explain how we know this.

The intuitionist thesis cannot really be taken in this straightforward way and it is obviously unfair to take it so. The intuitionist is not drawing our attention to the obvious fact that we have moral experience; he is inviting us to construe this experience in a special way. To be specific, he is inviting us to construe this experience as being analogous to *seeing*. Moral judgements are reports of what we see when we look at the non-natural world in the same sort of way that empirical statements are reports of what we see when we look at the natural world. This point comes out clearly in the passage quoted from Clarke. But much has happened in philosophy since Clarke's day and the analogy must now be put more warily. We must guard against the accusation of naturalism at every step by insisting that the moral world and all that is in it is 'non-natural'. This will remind us that moral qualities are not ordinary qualities, moral judgements not ordinary statements and moral insight not eyesight.

I have already suggested that this analogy fails to explain at least one of the most important problems of ethics, the problem of reconciling moral conflicts; and I shall now try to show that the analogy is mistaken in principle. It is not that the analogy is wholly false. The very fact that we use objective terminology in moral matters, that we say 'this is good' rather than 'I approve of this', that we call moral judgements true or false, shows that there is some analogy between moral and empirical discourse. I shall try to show that the analogy breaks down at a crucial point; but it does not follow, as some philosophers have thought, that we must then say that moral judgements are mere matters of taste or of what I happen to like.

To believe this is to take a mistaken view of the part played by analogies in philosophy. Suppose that a man were told that a piece of music was either by Haydn or by Mozart and asked to guess which. He might notice many Haydnesque and many Mozartesque features and he would decide in favour of the composer to whose other works he found the best analogies. He uses these analogies to decide which answer is correct, knowing that the composer must *be* one or the other and not both.

But philosophical analogies are not like this. We find that moral judgements are in some ways like empirical statements and in other ways like expressions of taste; but it is not incumbent on us to say that moral judgements must *be* the one or the other. In fact they are obviously neither. We use analogies, not to help us to decide which they are, but to elucidate what a moral judgement is by showing in what ways it is like an empirical statement and in what ways it is like an expression of personal taste.

The analogy with empirical discourse is designed to bring out the fact that moral judgements are like empirical statements in the following ways. They describe or refer to *facts*. Facts are discovered, not created by thinking. If the facts are such and such anyone who believes them to be so is *correct* and his belief is *true*; anyone who believes them to be something different is *mistaken* and his belief is *false*. It is a cardinal point that the truth or falsity of an opinion depends wholly on what the facts are, not on whether anyone holds it. However unlikely it might be, it is always possible for everyone to be mistaken on a certain point of fact. This is the sort of language that we must be prepared to use if we call something 'an objective matter'; and the thesis that moral judgements are objective is, in effect, the thesis that this sort of language can properly be used about them.

By the test of ordinary usage objective language is, as I have said, appropriate to moral discourse. But it is in empirical discourse that these objective expressions have their most typical standard application and, when we apply them elsewhere, we are apt to have empirical discourse in mind. And we must now see whether we can find in moral discourse just those features that lead us to use objective language in empirical discourse.

We have seen that the intuitionist represents moral knowledge as an affair of immediate insight into, or apprehension of a 'datum' that is directly presented to us. This might do as an account of moral knowledge in a case in which we can have no serious doubts. There is point in Clarke's analogy between a man who denies a plain moral truth and a man who, having the use of his sight, denies that he can see the light. It is in cases where there is doubt about the moral 'facts' that we are involved in difficulties.

It is curious how little attention has been paid by intuitionists to the problem of conflicting obligations, which seems to be one of the most important in ethics, except by way of criticism of those writers who have thought to solve it in terms of the intensity or quantity of pleasure which different actions would bring about. Ross says of it: "In this region our knowledge is very limited. While we *know* certain types of action to be *prima facie* obligatory, we have only opinion about the degree of their obligatoriness. . . . While we can see with certainty that the claims exist, it becomes a matter of individual and fallible judgement to say which claim is in the circumstances the overriding one. In many such situations, equally good men would form conflicting judgements as to what their duty is. They cannot all be right, but it is often impossible to say which is right; each person must judge according to his individual sense of the comparative strength of various claims."[1]

Broad speaks of "allowing due *weight* to the relative urgency of each claim" and he also compares "the claims which arise from various right-tending and wrong-tending characteristics to forces of various magnitudes and directions acting on a body at the same time."[2] The empirical analogy has seldom been so clearly put. Deciding whether I ought to do this or that in a case where I am confronted by conflicting obligations is like estimating the magnitude of a force or like estimating the relative weights or temperatures of two different bodies. I shall try to show that the analogy between estimating the stringency or urgency of various moral claims and estimating the magnitude or intensity of an empirical property is fundamentally misleading, and that we cannot both maintain this analogy and maintain that "each person must judge according to his individual sense of the comparative strength of the claims". The concession to subjectivism which is, as we shall see, involved in representing moral experience as the awareness of a datum is fatal to the attempt to treat moral qualities or 'phenomena' as objective.

[2]

It is a truism that we detect the presence and estimate the degree of empirical properties 'by means of the senses', by looking, feeling, tasting, and smelling; since 'empirical properties' are just those properties of which the presence and degree are discovered in this way. The language of 'awareness', 'perceiving', 'observing', and 'apprehending' has its standard

1. Op. cit., pp. 188–9 (author's italics).   2. Op. cit., p. 552.

application here and cannot, therefore, significantly be called in question. Many empirical properties are not directly perceived; but even though estimating their degree involves indirect methods, the appeal must, in the end, be to observations.[1]

The logic of the language that we use in empirical discourse reflects the conditions under which such language is used, and it is these conditions that make possible and give point to the objective-subjective distinction and all that it implies. We must rely on observation; but we also know that our senses sometimes deceive us. Direct observation often gives different results when there is no reason to suppose that the object observed has changed. The suitcase that felt light when I left the station feels heavy after I have walked a mile; yet no one has put anything in it. In one of the standard examples of optical illusion a certain line appears to be curved but when a ruler is put against it it appears to be straight; yet no one has altered the position of the ink on the paper. A piece of paper that looked white before looks red under a red light; yet no one has painted it.

We could cope with these situations without the objective-subjective contrast. We could say that the suitcase was light and is now heavy, the line was curved and is now straight, the paper was white and is now red. But this way of putting things has an obvious disadvantage; it makes all our talk about the properties of things dependent on the conditions of observation and, above all, on the position and condition of the observer's body. And in fact we adopt a different method. We make use of a double language in which 'is' is contrasted with 'looks' and 'feels'.

The double language operates in two ways. (a) In some cases, for example that of colour-words, the test of whether a thing really has a property or not is whether it appears to a normal observer to have it under certain standard conditions; thus the test for whether something is red is whether it appears

1. The subject of empirical estimating and the contrast between 'directly-perceived' and 'scientific' properties is more fully discussed by S. E. Toulmin: *The Place of Reason in Ethics*, chapters 7 and 8.

to be red to a normal observer in ordinary sunlight; and it is important to notice that both the normal observer and the standard conditions can be defined without circularity.

(b) But in many cases, especially where scientific properties are concerned, the test is more indirect. 'This feels heavier than that' corresponds to 'this looks red'; but we do not decide the real relative weights of things by reference to the sense of muscular strain of a normal person in standard conditions. We appeal, as in many other cases, to the sense of sight. We put the objects on a pair of scales and *see* which scale is depressed or put them in turn on a spring balance and see how much the spring is stretched. Similarly we test the 'real' temperature of a bowl of water, not by putting our hand into it, but by seeing the height to which the mercury in a thermometer immersed in it rises.

Now it is an essential feature of the double language of 'looks or feels' and 'really is' that, while the observer himself is allowed to be the best judge of how a thing looks or feels to him, he is not allowed to be the best judge of what it really is. If two cakes feel equally heavy to me but the balance shows one to be heavier than the other, I must say that one of them was really heavier all the time; but I am not compelled to say that it must have *felt* heavier. Obviously it did not. There is something about the first observation that I stubbornly wish to retain, since to abandon it would be to cast doubt on all observation; and it is a truism that we must rely on observation in the end. But I also want to admit that I was mistaken, since the balance shows that the cakes are not equal in weight and I have no reason to believe that anything has happened to either of them. The double language enables me to deal with this sort of situation. "They both *felt* the same to me", I shall say, "but one of them must really have *been* heavier all along."

There is no need to investigate the philosophical problem whether looks and feels are absolutely incorrigible, whether there are what some philosophers call 'bare sense-data' in reporting which I cannot be mistaken. It is enough to notice that the language of 'looks' and 'feels' is relatively incorrigible, a language into which we can retreat if we do not want to commit ourselves to the hazards of saying what a thing really is. And I am safer here than in the 'is' language just because I am the best judge of how a thing looks or feels to me, though not of its real properties.

But there is an important condition that must be satisfied if any particular test is to be used as a test for a 'real property'. There must be a very wide measure of agreement in its application. If balances and thermometers did not give a greater measure of agreement than the felt heft or warmth of things, we could not appeal to them from feeling in the way that we in fact do. Now it is an empirical fact that there are indirect tests, loosely correlated with felt weight and temperature, which are such that their application gives more accurate, more stable, and better agreed results than does the application of the direct tests. But it is a logical fact that nothing could be used as an indirect test unless it fulfilled these conditions. If, for example, people disagreed as much about the readings of thermometers as they do about felt temperature and if the thermometer reading were liable to fluctuate when there was no reason to suppose that any change had occurred in the object, we could not (logically) use thermometers as tests for real temperature. And if no devices had been discovered which had these logical properties of loose correlation with feeling and a high degree of stability and agreement we could not (logically) treat temperature as a real property at all. 'Hot' and 'cold' would be wholly subjective words.

If these conditions were not fulfilled we should have, in short, no use for the double language of 'feels' and 'is'. We are able to contrast real weight with felt weight, not because we have some mysterious insight into an unobservable real property that somehow underlies or causes the felt and seen weights of things, but because there is a marked contrast between the balance test and the feeling test. There is no more need to claim universal agreement in the application of tests for real properties than there was to claim absolute incorrigibility for looks and feels. Some people are notoriously bad experimenters; but this fact does not tempt us to deny that there are real properties. It is enough that the contrast should be marked.

It should be noticed that I am not arguing that general agreement is a conclusive test of the presence or degree of a real property. Our ordinary objective language makes truth independent of opinion and allows for the possibility, however remote, of everybody being mistaken. A Gallup Poll could not settle the question whether the earth is round. General agreement is not a test of truth; but is a necessary condition of the use of objective language. We could not treat roundness as an objective property, we could not talk about things *being* really round or say that statements about roundness were objectively true or false, unless two conditions were fulfilled: (a) We must agree about the tests for roundness, what observations would strengthen and what would weaken the case for the earth being round, and (b) the tests used must be such as to give a high degree of agreement in their application over a wide field. It is not necessary that there should be agreement in a particular case or that the agreed opinion should be correct. If everyone agreed that the thermometer reading was 100° F, everyone could (logically) be mistaken; but it would be impossible to speak of people being correct or mistaken in their readings of thermometers or of statements about these readings being true or false if such disagreement were common.

This last point has an important bearing on the relevance of the existence of moral disagreement to the objective-subjective controversy. Subjectivists point to the fact of disagreement as conclusive proof that moral properties are not objective. To this it is replied that the conclusion does not follow because people often disagree where objective, empirical properties are concerned. Moreover there is no reason to suppose that there ought to be as much agreement in the reports of moral intuition as there is in the reports of what we see. Moral intuition might be a very imperfectly developed faculty and better developed in some men than in others. But this reply misses the point of the objection. If people really do disagree much more widely and violently in their reports of moral 'data' than they do about empirical data, the conclusion must be, not that moral opinions are subjective or that one party must be mistaken, but that the language of 'correct' and 'mistaken', which is an essential part of the objective terminology, cannot be applied. For there are no tests for deciding which party is correct and which mistaken.

If we are to justify the analogy between moral properties and empirical properties, which is implied by the use of objective terminology, we must show that there is a contrast in moral matters between 'is right' and 'seems right', which corresponds to the contrast between 'is red' and 'looks red' or between 'is heavier' and 'feels heavier'. But this is exactly what the intuitionist cannot do; for in making direct awareness the test of real ethical properties he eliminates the whole point of the objective-subjective contrast. It is not that ethical properties are subjective or even that the objective-subjective contrast is wholly misplaced in ethics, but that the use of this contrast is quite incompatible with intuitionism.

[3]

From their talk about estimating the strengths of claims or the stringency of obligations and from Broad's comparison of these properties to forces in mechanics it would seem that intuitionists have in mind mainly the analogy with type (b) properties. But this can hardly be the case. For in type (b) cases the real and the apparent property are detected by different senses; and no one supposes that 'apparent stringency' and 'apparent moral value' are revealed to one moral sense while their 'real' counterparts are revealed to another. It is therefore to type (a) properties that the analogy is drawn; and I shall now try to bring out an important difference between recognizing a moral property and discovering what colour a thing really has.

We have seen that the double language only has point if we allow that the observer himself is the best judge of looks and feels but not of what a thing really is. And this enables us to admit ourselves consistently wrong in empirical cases. If a man finds that his judgements about colour differ consistently from those of others, he will admit himself to be colour-blind. He might start by saying that two things were the same colour; but if he finds that everyone else says that they are different he will retreat into the language of 'looks to me'. In the same way a man who finds that his readings of scales and meters differ from other people's does not immediately write to *Nature* to claim that his observations upset some well-known scientific law; he recognizes that he is a bad experimenter and probably takes up some other career. The existence of colour-blind persons and bad experimenters does not prevent our using objective language; for the dissentients are willing to allow that the common opinion is correct, however much it may conflict with their own experience. If each man had to judge the real colour of an object by his individual sense of colour, the very distinction between 'is red' and 'looks red to me' would have broken down and we should have no use for redness as a real property at all. For, where real properties are concerned, general agreement is admitted, even by a dissentient, to be the criterion for the property.

But, according to the intuitionist, immediate insight is the test of the presence and of the degree of stringency of an obligation. "Each person must judge according to his individual sense of the comparative strength of the various claims." It is admitted that, at least as far as questions of stringency are concerned, "equally good men would form conflicting judgements". But this admission is fatal to the empirical analogy. For, in the first place, if the appeal is to each person's individual sense, it is impossible to know whether those who disagree are really "good men". We cannot, as we can in empirical cases, define the normal or standard observer without circularity.

Secondly, even if we have somehow been able to select our panel of experts, the disagreement that arises between them is of a kind that could not possibly occur in the case of objective empirical properties. No doubt the greatest experts can disagree about *theories*, whether in science or elsewhere; but theories are not 'data' or reports of observation. The disagreement which Ross has in mind is not that between rival moral theorists, for example Hobbists, Kantians, and Utilitarians, but disagreement about something which is represented as analogous, not to scientific theories, but to reports of observations. The parallel case would be that in which a number of scientists failed to agree about the reading of a scale or a meter or about the colour of an object. And we have seen that, if this sort of disagreement were of frequent occurrence, the property in question could not be treated as a 'real' or 'objective' property at all.

If there really is widespread disagreement about the relative stringency of two claims, it is logically impossible that stringency should be a real property analogous to the real properties of empirical discourse. It is not just that we cannot say which view is correct; for this presupposes that we have a test *other than immediate awareness* for deciding which view is orrect and that our predicament is one of not being in a position to apply the test. But our predicament in moral cases is that we d o not know what other test there is to apply and that we are de barred from using the objective-subjective contrast because one of the conditions essential to its use is absent.

The intuitionis ts are, in fact, trying to combine in one form of judgement two assets, objectivity and relative incorrigibility. But these cannot be combined since the objective-subjective contrast loses its point if objective judgements are made relatively incorrigible. They use the language of 'really is'; but the test that they apply to discover whether something really is right or wrong is the test of immediate insight, which is analogous to the test for 'looks' and 'feels'.[1]

1. A similar point can be made in connexion with the intuitionists' treatment of 'knowledge'. They represent knowledge as incorrigible because it is the immediate awareness of a datum which no further observation could (logically) upset. But, in fact, a claim to knowledge is not of this kind. If I claim to know something as a 'matter of objective fact', I shall be amazed or amused or bored if someone proposes to

If we compare the position of the colour-blind man with that of the man whose moral views conflict with received opinions the contrast comes out clearly. The colour-blind man is willing to admit his own deficiency; but we cannot admit ourselves to be morally blind in the same sort of way. The colour-blind man will say "It still looks red to me; but it must really be brown, since everyone else says that it is brown". But there is nothing analogous to this that a moral dissentient can say.

If I think that a certain type of conduct is wrong when other people think it right, there are two things I can do. (a) I can say: "I still think it is wrong; everyone else must be mistaken". This is the line taken by the moral reformer and must be the line taken by an extreme intuitionist to whom conscience is an infallible guide. (b) A less extreme intuitionist might say: "I *used to think* it wrong; but now that I have discovered that many good and wise people think it right I no longer do so; I was formerly mistaken". This is the line that would be taken by a man who was not confident about his own moral judgements and was prepared to change them.

But the one thing I cannot say is (c): "This type of conduct still seems to me to be wrong; but it must really be right, since everyone says so". And this is precisely what the colour-blind man does say in such a case.

The reason why (c) is impossible cannot be made clear until I have given a positive account of what a moral judgement is; but to say that it is impossible may seem surprising. We can, of course, admit ourselves to be miserable sinners and also admit ourselves to have been mistaken in the past on a moral point. We might also admit ourselves to be morally blind in a dispositional sense, to recognize a general incapacity to see moral truths until someone else points them out to us. We may also admit the possibility that our present moral view may be mistaken in the sense that we might in the future be

submit the matter to further tests, since my claim expresses complete confidence that such testing can only corroborate my view. But further testing is not logically irrelevant. Knowledge claims to be *valid;* and what cannot be tested is neither valid nor invalid.

led to change it. But what we cannot do is admit that our present moral view *is* in fact mistaken. For to admit this would be to abandon the moral view in question. A moral view is, as we shall see, a principle that we adopt, an affirmation that we are prepared to make; and to make an affirmation and at the same time to admit it to be false is a contradiction-in-use like 'It's a horse, but I don't believe it is' or 'It's a horse but that isn't true'.

There is one way in which it might appear to be possible to admit one's own present lack of moral insight. If a man has been strictly brought up in a certain code of morals, he may come to reject some article in this code. Thus a Christian, converted to Islam, might once have believed it wrong to have four wives but now no longer does so. But the strength of his upbringing might be so great that, even after his conversion, it still 'feels' wrong to him. He has an emotional aversion to the practice that cannot be called 'genuine moral disapproval' – for he does not disapprove morally any more – but might be called 'quasi-moral repugnance'.

In the same way a reformed teetotaller might still feel very uncomfortable about having a drink. He might say to himself: "Drinking in moderation is really quite blameless; there *is* really nothing wrong in it, but it still *feels* wrong to me. My moral sense is therefore deficient in this particular; it does not correspond to the real rightness and wrongness of things." He contrasts his feeling of repugnance, which is a 'subjective' feeling in that he himself is the best judge of whether he feels it, with the 'objective' rightness with which it conflicts. And this seems to make his case analogous to that of the colour-blind man.

But the appeal to this type of case does nothing to help the intuitionist's thesis. For it is not to mere feelings of repugnance that he refers when he talks about immediate awareness of or insight into objective properties. These are mere emotions, not even genuine moral emotions, and they cannot play the part which the theory assigns to the apprehension of non-natural qualities.

CHAPTER 5

The Logic of Adjectives

[1]

THE study of ethics seems to end in a blind alley. The older philosophers set out confidently to "erect schemes of virtue and of happiness", to discover what the Good Life is or what our duties are; but we end with an argument the burden of which is to show that all their efforts rested on a mistake. In place of the old, often laborious and sometimes exciting road we are offered the short cut of immediate insight. But our new guides not only fail to lead us where we want to go, they do not seem to understand where this is. We ask for help in the solution of practical problems and they offer us a description of a non-natural world. It is not surprising that this has led to a radical scepticism in the writings of otherwise very different philosophers. Both Logical Positivists and Existentialists tend to deny the possibility of knowledge or rational opinion in ethics and to doubt whether we can ever give good reasons for doing this rather than that.

What has been the cause of this failure? We have been dogged all along by certain assumptions which belong to logic and are implicit in the use of the logician's technical vocabulary. In this and the following chapter I shall try to show how the nature and purpose of practical discourse has been made unintelligible by the attempt to elucidate it by means of a logical apparatus unsuited to the purpose and to substitute a new logical apparatus that may be more successful. The first two assumptions that I shall question are concerned with the logic of single words, especially adjectives; in Chapter 6 I shall consider the use of sentences and arguments in practical discourse.

(a) The first assumption is that adjectives are the names of properties (or qualities or characteristics), that their logical role is that of denoting, referring to or standing for something.[1] It is a corollary of this that questions about the meaning of a word are to be answered by inspecting the idea, concept, or object which it denotes and comparing this with the objects denoted by other words. It is as if we discovered the meaning of an adjective in the way that a man might discover the meanings of the names of animals, that is to say by walking round a zoo, inspecting the animals in their cages and reading the label on each cage.

(b) A second assumption, intimately connected with the first, is that we can ask what a certain word means instead of asking 'What does So-and-so mean by it ?'.

The logician's task is to map the words, phrases, sentences, and arguments that we use in theoretical and practical discourse. And, to perform this task, logicians have elaborated a special vocabulary of technical terms such as object, quality, property, relation, class, denote, proposition, entail, contradict, analytic, synthetic, and so on. Like other theoreticians, the logician is interested in classifying the objects that he studies and discovering what is common to all objects of the same type. Text-books of logic usually begin with the assumption that such statements as 'All delphiniums are blue', 'All men are mortal', and 'All bishops wear gaiters' are examples of a single type which they represent by the formula 'All S is P'. And they give to these statements the technical name 'Universal Affirmative Propositions'.

Now this procedure of classifying types of word, sentence, and argument and giving names to each type presupposes that the logician has some method of discovering what words, for example, 'stand for properties', what sentences express 'propositions' and what strings of sentences constitute 'arguments'. But logicians seldom have anything to say about this method. More often they simply assume that all adjectives – (a grammarian's classification) – play the same role and they give to this role the technical name 'standing for a property'.

1. Cf. pp. 31–33, above.

But we can only understand what this technical phrase means if we study the examples that logicians give when they introduce it. And the examples they give are very rarely drawn from practical discourse; for they have devoted almost all their attention to the logic either of mathematics or of the natural sciences. "The various sciences are the best examples of human thinking about things, the most careful, clear, and coherent that exist. In them therefore the logician can best study the laws of men's thinking."[1]

If the logician has done his work well the technical terms he uses will elucidate the logic of mathematics or of natural science. But it is by no means obvious that the technical apparatus he uses will help to elucidate a realm of discourse quite different from that from which he chose his examples. The making of a decision to do something or of a moral or aesthetic judgement often requires careful, clear, and coherent thought; but is there any reason to suppose that the logic of this thought can fitly be described or criticized by means of a technical vocabulary which was not designed to describe and criticize it? Must practical thinking be like the thinking that goes on in mathematics or the natural sciences?

[2]

(a) *Do all adjectives stand for properties?* Suppose someone were to ask whether or not goodness was a property. How could this question be answered? 'Good' is certainly an adjective; and if to say that goodness is a property is only another way of saying that 'good' is an adjective, it is easy to see that goodness is a property. But the doctrine that goodness is a property is clearly intended to assert more than this triviality. It is intended to assert that the logical behaviour of 'good' conforms to the same standard pattern to which the logical behaviour of other names of properties conform. But we only know what 'standing for a property' means because we already

1. H. W. B. Joseph: *Introduction to Logic*, p. 3.

know how the typical logician's examples, such as 'blue', 'loud', and 'round' behave. To say that goodness is a property commits us to the very debatable assertion that the logic of 'good' is like that of 'blue', 'loud', and 'round'.

The word 'property' is a technical, logician's word and we cannot answer the question 'Is goodness a property?' in the same sort of way that we would answer the question 'Do cats eat mice?', by observation. It is more like 'Is a gong a musical instrument?', 'Is dancing exercise?', 'Are limericks poetry?', 'Is medicine a science?'.

To answer this last question we should have to start with certain typical examples that everyone would admit to be sciences, chemistry, physics, botany, astronomy, and the like, and to compare each in turn with medicine. These standard sciences differ from each other in many ways; but they also have certain points in common in virtue of which we call them all 'sciences'. Since medicine has important points in common with the standard sciences and also important differences, a straight yes-or-no answer could not be given. Our task would be to discover whether medicine is, on the whole, sufficiently like the standard sciences to make it more enlightening than misleading to call it a 'science'. And this will depend on the associations of the word 'science' for the questioner. If I tell him that medicine is a science, will he expect to discover in it Newtonian laws and so come to misunderstand the special nature of the doctor's skill? If, on the other hand, I tell him that it is not, will he go away with the impression that medicine is 'unscientific' and that medical men are on a par with quacks and astrologers? The only safe course seems to be to give a longer answer which brings out both the similarities and the differences.

In the same way we can only hope to answer the question 'Is goodness a property?' by exhibiting the similarities and differences between 'good' and those adjectives that most typically fit what the logician has to say about properties; and these are the names of empirical, descriptive properties. Moore partially adopts this method. He discovers both similarities and differences between 'good' and 'yellow'. They are alike, he thinks, in being simple and indefinable; but they are also so unlike that we must mark the difference by calling one a 'natural', the other a 'non-natural' property.

Later writers were not content with the vague, negative word 'non-natural' and tried to bring out the differences between 'good' and the natural properties by calling it a 'gerundive property'. This was a move in the right direction; for the phrase 'gerundive property' begins to bring out the intimate connexion between 'good' and overtly gerundive words such as 'laudable', 'praiseworthy', 'admirable'. But the question they failed to ask was "Why call goodness a *property* at all?". If our previous interpretation of the non-natural world theory was correct, Moore intended to mark an important difference in logical status and behaviour between 'good' and 'yellow'. Yet this is precisely the sort of difference that is denied by calling goodness a property. For what is it to call goodness a property but to say that the logic of 'good' is like that of other property-words? The terminology that Moore used to mark an important difference that he noticed between 'good' and other adjectives was singularly ill-adapted to bringing out just this difference.

But, even if goodness is a property, are we justified in assuming that the logical role of 'good' is that of standing for or denoting that property? "In fact, if it is not the case that 'good' denotes something simple and indefinable, only two alternatives are possible: either it is a complex, a given whole, about the correct analysis of which there may be disagreement; or else it means nothing at all, and there is no such subject as ethics."[1] Moore devotes a considerable space to the refutation of the first alternative and rightly regards the second as unworthy of refutation. But his proof that 'good' denotes something simple rests on the assumption that, if 'good' has any meaning at all, it must *denote* something.

Meaning and Naming. Do all meaningful words and symbols

1. *Principia Ethica*, p. 15.

denote? Sharps and flats in music do not denote anything, nor indeed does any other bit of musical notation. We might toy with the idea that C♯ 'denotes the fact that' the performer is to play C♯. Or does it denote the fact that the composer had C♯ in mind? But 'denoting the fact that the performer is to play C♯' is already an odd circumlocution for 'instruction to play C♯' and the facts denoted are a strange sort of facts. Nothing but the assumption that what has meaning must denote could lead us into playing such tricks. This assumption is obviously false in the case of musical notation. But notes are not words and we must see whether there is any more justification for it in the case of words.

To say that a word has a meaning is not to say that it denotes something and to say what its meaning is is not to say what it denotes. The word 'meaning' itself is both vague and ambiguous and depends more than is usual on the context and purpose of the speaker. If someone asks what the meaning of a word is, he is usually asking for an explanation of the way in which it is used. Now the temptation to say that he is asking what the word *refers to* arises from the fact that the job of a great many words is that of referring to something, so that to ask how the word is used and to ask what it refers to come to the same thing.

If the word is the name of an ordinary physical object, for example 'table', 'mountain', or 'dog', or of an ordinary empirical quality, 'yellow' or 'round', the easiest way to explain its use is to point to the objects concerned or to objects that have the quality. But, although this pointing is a way, and a very good way, of explaining the meaning of a word, it does not follow that *what is pointed at is the meaning*.

The typical case of a word of which the job is to refer to something is the proper name; and the typical cases of things to which we give proper names are people, animals, ships, and geographical features. These are all 'things' in the least philosophical sense of that vague word, visible, tangible, spatio-temporal things that you can meet again and again and recognize as being the same thing each time. They are also things in which we are interested as individuals and not just as instances or examples of a general type. Sticks and stones could have names too, and would have them if we were interested in them as individuals. Some actually do have such names; for example the Rosetta stone, the Rufus stone.

To equate 'meaning' with 'naming' or 'denoting' is to use as a model for all elucidation of meaning the special cases in which we should naturally say that a word was the name of or denoted something; and the standard case of this is the proper name. But the inadequacy of this model is shown by the fact that when a word is a proper name we hesitate to talk about its 'meaning'. Suppose that we were helping a foreigner to translate a leading article and explained to him the meanings of the words 'government', 'statesman', 'constitutional', and so on, and that he then asks "What does the word 'Churchill' mean?". I think we should reply: "It doesn't exactly *mean* anything; it's a man's *name*." To say this, with the accent on 'mean' rather than on 'anything' is not to say that it is meaningless in the way that an accidental blot of ink is meaningless. The word has a linguistic job to do; but its job is one of naming, not of meaning; and words of which the job is meaning are not names of what they mean.

(b) *Meaning and Context.* Elucidating the meaning of a word is explaining how the word is used, and it is only in the exceptional case in which a word is the name of something, either a proper name which is used to refer to just one thing or a 'general' or 'common' name that is used to refer indifferently to a number of things, that explaining how it is used can be identified with saying or showing what it refers to. To treat all words as names of what they mean is to presuppose that 'meanings' have just those characteristics that a thing must have to fit properly into the name-thing situation. 'Meanings' come to be regarded as identifiable individuals which crop up every now and again, as distinct and self-identical as the boys in a class. And it is because philosophers have unconsciously modelled their accounts of meaning on the name-thing situation that they have represented understanding the meaning of a moral word as an affair of inspecting (with the inward eye) the object or quality of which it is the name.

And this use of the name-thing situation as a model for meaning has had a further consequence of the greatest importance. It has led philosophers to ask the question 'What does the word . . . mean?' as if it must mean the same thing in all contexts. But is it safe to make this assumption? Ought we not rather to ask 'What did So-and-so mean by that word on that occasion?' Clearly, if it were never safe to abstract a word from its context and to say what *it* means the writing of dictionaries would be impossible. But this assumption is only safe in the case of two types of word.

(i) It is safe if the word is a technical one; for a technical language is relatively precise and those who understand and use such a language all mean the same thing by the words they use. The word 'engine' does not mean the same thing for a schoolboy, an engine-driver, and an engineer, but 'kinetic energy', 'erratic block', 'asteroid', and 'differential equation' do mean the same thing for the experts who alone use these expressions. There is therefore little danger in abstracting these words from the context in which they are used and in talking about what they mean as opposed to what some particular person means by them on a particular occasion. As usual, mathematics is at one end of the scale, since mathematicians insist on a rigour of definition superior to that found elsewhere; poetry and other forms of literature are at the other end of the scale, where it is most obviously the case that we cannot understand what a writer means by a word except in the context of his thought as a whole.

(ii) In the case of common objects, which, as we have seen, supply the model which philosophers have used for meaning, there is little disagreement about the meanings of words and such doubts as arise are mainly doubts about borderline cases. But with words that are not the names of common objects difficulties of a very different sort arise. For the same word can be used on different occasions, not merely as the name of slightly different objects, but to do different jobs, some of which are not naming jobs at all. With which of these jobs are we to identify the meaning?

[3]

As soon as we abandon the assumption that all adjectives 'stand for properties' we are able to see that there are different sorts of adjectives that operate in logically different ways; and our problem will be to classify these sorts and to explain how they are connected with each other. To say that every adjective has its own logic would be to leap from the frying-pan into the fire and to confess our inability to make any logical generalizations whatever. But this is in fact not the case. 'Blue' does not mean the same as 'green'; but there are no logical differences in their behaviour and we could classify them both as 'colour-words'. Our task will be to examine the adjectives used in practical discourse, of which the most important are 'right' and 'good', and this must be done with as little recourse to the technical terms of traditional logic as possible. For a logical apparatus that leads us to say that practical discourse is either meaningless or descriptive of a special non-natural world must be inadequate.

For the question 'What does the word . . . mean?' I shall therefore substitute the two questions 'For what job is the word . . . used?' and 'Under what conditions is it proper to use this word for that job?' The importance of separating these questions will emerge later[1]; for the present I shall simply abandon the familiar model of words as labels attached to things and treat them as tools with which we do things. Talking is not always naming or reporting; it is sometimes doing.

1. Pp. 90, 95, and 178, below.

A-WORDS AND G-WORDS

If we examine the adjectives used in ordinary discourse we find that they exhibit a great variety of logical behaviour. The grammatical form of an adjective sometimes gives us a clue to its logical behaviour; for example adjectives in -ent, -ible, -ous, and -ic fall into families which differ logically from each other, and we can often tell something about the meaning of a new adjective from its termination in the same sort of way that a chemist could deduce something about a compound unknown to him from the fact that its name ended in -ite, -ate, or -ide. But termination is not an altogether reliable guide to logical behaviour. In the first place words that are not derived from Latin or Greek sources seldom have special terminations, but they do nevertheless fall into logical families; and secondly it is notorious that words in -ible and -able function in at least two different ways. To say that a man is eligible for parliament is to say that he can (constitutionally) be elected, that his election would not be barred by any disqualification such as insanity or a peerage; it is not to say that he ought to be elected or is worthy to be elected. On the other hand an eligible bachelor is not someone who can legally be married but someone worth marrying.

The classification of adjectives is necessarily a tentative and inexact business, especially in a field where it has never been attempted by people whose interests are philosophical rather than philological; and for a start I shall distinguish three main types. Consider, for example, the following sentences:

The view from the top was extensive.

The view from the top was sublime.

The adjective 'sublime' does not form part of a description of the view, unless we insist on making all adjectives descriptive and thereby reduce the force of 'descriptive' to vanishing point We could give an exhaustive description of the view by enumerating its contents, and if the list contained a large number of large objects this would entail that the view was extensive. The question whether the view was extensive or not is a question of empirical fact.[1] But the sublimity of the view is not part of its contents and no description of the view would logically entail the truth or falsity of 'the view was sublime'. It is just this that the argument against the Naturalistic Fallacy shows so clearly. Some philosophers have said that goodness is a 'consequential property', by which is meant that it is a property that something can have only if it has certain other properties. But we have already seen that the link between goodness and the good-making properties is not a logical one; a special act of awareness is needed to apprehend it. The relation between 'sublime' and those features of a landscape in virtue of which we would call it sublime is of the same type.

Consider the following conversation:

A. When I got to the top, I saw the whole plain spread out beneath me and Nanga Parbat towering above it. A waterfall that must have been at least five hundred feet high cascaded down from near where I stood into the swirling waters of the Indus.

B. What a sublime (magnificent, stirring, awe-inspiring, wonderful, etc.) sight that must have been.

B uses the phrase 'must have been' to indicate that the sight was sublime *because* of the items in A's description; and A would have been surprised and hurt if B had said: "I don't think much of that". The connexion between their remarks is obviously not logical entailment; yet we feel that B's comment was the natural and appropriate one to make. And this is because he is evincing the natural, appropriate emotion. Most people would react to the description in the same way and not say that the view was mean or sordid or squalid.

Taking a cue from this situation I shall refer to words of

1. 'Extensive' is not strictly a 'descriptive' word; for to say that a view is extensive is not to describe it. But it belongs to descriptive discourse and will do as an example as I am not interested in the logic of descriptive discourse for its own sake.

the same family as 'sublime' as Aptness-words (A-words), because they are words that indicate that an object has certain properties which are apt to arouse a certain emotion or range of emotions. I use the word 'indicate' with deliberate vagueness and do not say, for example, that 'terrifying' could be *defined* in terms of 'causing fear'. Nor, for reasons that will appear later, can we say that 'sublime' or 'terrifying' just express the emotion of the speaker. A-words have a logic of their own which is different both from that of Descriptive-words (D-words) and from that of exclamations or reports of one's feelings.

Consider, again, our use of the word 'weed'. The ordinary man (who is not a Berkeleian philosopher) takes, rightly or wrongly, an uncompromisingly realistic view of D-words, such as 'dandelion' and 'yellow'. He believes that even if there were no gardeners there would still be dandelions and that they would still be yellow. But, if there were no gardeners, would there still be weeds? To say that a dandelion is a weed is not like saying that it is a member of the order Compositae; and the difference does not lie only in the fact that 'weed' is an ordinary-language word. To say that dandelions are weeds is not to *classify* them at all. For the contrast between weeds and flowers (in that sense of 'flowers' in which flowers are contrasted with weeds) depends on the interests of gardeners. If there were no gardeners we should have no use for this contrast; and if the interests of gardeners changed, if, for example, dandelions came to be admired for their beauty, rarity, or medicinal properties, dandelions would cease to be weeds. A weed is, roughly, a plant that we wish to eradicate rather than to cultivate. If a man said that he liked cultivating groundsel we might think him odd; but if he said that he liked cultivating weeds, this would be *logically* odd and we should have to take him to mean that he liked cultivating those plants that others usually wish to eradicate. In this way we could remove the logical (but not the horticultural) oddness from what he says by making 'weed' into a descriptive expression.

For amateur and self-employed gardeners 'weed' is an A-word. But for a gardener who is employed by someone else its logic is quite different. He may have no interest in his job at all or he may *like* having plantains and dandelions on the lawn. For him, a weed is, roughly, any plant that he *ought* to eradicate, that it is his duty to eradicate whether he likes the plant or not, and the word 'weed' is a Gerundive-word (G-word), roughly analogous to 'praise-worthy', 'note-worthy', 'laudable', 'damnable', etc.[1]

The logical relationships between A-words, D-words, and G-words will be examined later. The present account is over-simplified and schematic since it is intended only to throw light on the question whether all adjectives 'stand for properties'. We might mark the differences by saying that they stand for different sorts of properties, aptness-properties, descriptive-properties, and gerundive-properties. But what is gained by this? 'Red', 'sublime', and 'laudable' are all adjectives and all obey the same grammatical rules; but we have seen that to say that they all stand for properties is to say more than this. It is to say that they fit in the same way into the same prescribed scheme of categories containing substances, properties, states, events, processes, and so on; and this in turn is to say that their logical behaviour is similar. But this is just what it is not. There is a logical oddness about cultivating weeds or being bored by a sublime view that is not present in cultivating dandelions or being bored by a view of St Paul's. To mark the differences by saying that all adjectives stand for properties, but properties of different sorts, is to mark it in the wrong way. The intention is to mark logical differences, the method is that appropriate to marking logical similarities.

One of Moore's most important arguments seems to depend on ignoring the distinction between A-words and D-words. "Let us imagine one world exceedingly *beautiful*. Imagine it

1. A few more examples: A dress may be red, comfortable, and in-decent. A ball may be a leg-break, tempting, and over-pitched. A man may be blue-eyed, amusing, and admirable.

as beautiful as you can; put into it whatever on this earth you most admire. . . . And then imagine the *ugliest* world you can possibly conceive. Imagine it simply one heap of *filth*, containing everything that is most *disgusting* to us. . . . The only thing we are not entitled to imagine is that any human being ever has or ever, by any possibility, can, live in either, can ever see and enjoy the *beauty* of the one or hate the *foulness* of the other." [1] The conclusion that Moore thinks we must admit is that it would be better for the beautiful world than for the ugly world to exist, even though no one ever lived in either. But the words I have italicized are not purely descriptive and they cannot be understood to mean anything at all if the presence of human beings and their tastes and interests are excluded, as they must be to make Moore's point. If, for example, instead of using the word 'filth' we specified what the second world was to contain in the neutral language of chemistry it is not so obvious that, if there were no one to see or smell either world, the one would be better than the other. To imagine something as beautiful or ugly, admirable or disgusting, is already to 'react' to it.

1. *Principia Ethica*, p. 83.

CHAPTER 6

The Logic of Sentences and Arguments

[1]

THE second pair of traditional assumptions that I shall question is intimately connected with the first pair and is concerned
with the logic of sentences and arguments. We have seen that
in the case of the names of common objects and of proper
names, the meaning of a word can often be given by pointing.
To understand the meanings of such words it is not necessary
to consider the parts they play in a sentence or the parts that
sentences containing them play in arguments. But in order to
characterize, even roughly, the behaviour of A-words it was
necessary to illustrate their behaviour by means of sentences
and even conversations in which they might appear; and this
will be found even more necessary when we come to give a
more detailed account of their behaviour. We shall find that,
although it is convenient to speak of A-words and G-words to
avoid circumlocutions, it would be nearer the truth to speak of
A- and G-*uses* of words or to say that a word can be used with
an A-force or a G-force. This point is ignored if we make the
following assumptions: (a) that it is always possible to draw
a sharp distinction between questions about what a word means
(or the property it denotes) and questions about the things to
which the word applies (or the things that have that property);
and (b) that statements can be sharply divided into analytic
and synthetic.

These two assumptions together underlie the attack on the
Naturalistic Fallacy and make necessary the recourse to special
intuitions. We have already seen how Moore's refutation of
naturalistic theorists depends on his challenging them to decide
whether they want to say that 'good' *means* ' . . . ' or to say
that only things which are . . . are good.[1] And since he claims

1. P. 32, above.

that goodness is unanalysable, he is led to say that propositions containing the word 'good' must all be synthetic. For they can never be 'analyses' of the meaning of the word.

It is unnecessary to investigate at length the history of the distinction between 'analytic' and 'synthetic', a history which is much older than the words themselves and goes back at least as far as Locke's distinction between trivial and informative statements; nor is it necessary to investigate in detail the distinctions which logicians rightly draw between analytic, tautological, logically necessary, true by definition, and so on. It will be enough to say that two concepts or statements are said to be connected 'analytically' if their connexion can be established by reference to the logical rules of language and require no reference to the facts of the case. Thus it is analytically true that if a man is an uncle he has either a nephew or a niece, and 'Fido is an animal' follows analytically from 'Fido is a dog'. That John Doe is an uncle or that Fido begs are, on the other hand, synthetic truths. We could not establish or refute them by appealing to logical rules; we should have to examine the facts of the case.

This sharp distinction between what a word means and what it applies to is connected to the assumptions examined in the last chapter in the following way. If the role of all nouns and adjectives is that of naming, they play only one role. To give the meaning of a word is always to say what it is the name of. In the case of words that have a complex meaning statements that enumerate the items of which its meaning is composed will be analytic; but all other statements containing this word will be synthetic.

The need for intuitions arises in two ways. Some of our moral knowledge seems to be of a universal kind. Cruelty is always wrong; benevolence is always good. This may have to be modified when right courses of action conflict or when there are two incompatible attributes either of which would be good. This may be done by adopting devices such as saying that cruelty always tends to be wrong or that there is a *prima facie* duty not to be cruel or to be benevolent. But these are still universal propositions. Now it is always agreed that analytic or logically necessary propositions must always be true; but, if we define 'cruelty' as a certain sort of behaviour and do not use the word 'wrong' in the definition, the proposition that it is wrong must be synthetic. Now moral propositions are informative and not trivial and they cannot be established by reference to the rules of language. How, if this is the case, do we know that cruelty always tends to be wrong? This is clearly not an empirical generalization that we might discover by examining a number of cases. It seems that we must have a special faculty of insight into necessary, synthetic connexions.

This is a familiar argument; but the need for such insight also arises in a way that is not so often noticed. When we decide to do something or advise someone to do it or make a moral appraisal we give reasons. "I ought to pay for his education because he is my son." "You ought to do this because you have promised." "He is a bad man because he beats his wife." The standard intuitionist account of this situation is that the moral properties involved, the obligatoriness and badness are 'consequential properties' that we see to be necessarily (but synthetically) connected with the natural or descriptive properties that we mention in giving the reasons. But consider the following conversation:

A. I should choose that one if I were you.
B. Why?
A. Because it's more comfortable.

The rules for the use of 'should choose' and 'comfortable' are not such that once we know that one thing is more comfortable than another it follows logically that we should choose it. On the contrary we ought often to choose what is less comfortable. The connexion between 'should choose' and 'comfortable' must, so the story goes, be synthetic; and the same is true of all the connexions between choosing something and the reasons for choosing it.

Now if this is true it seems that there are only two courses open to us, either a complete moral scepticism – there are really never any good reasons for choosing this rather than that, since the obligation to choose never follows logically from any statement about the nature of the thing – or a proliferation of intuitions connecting choosing, advising, and appraising with the reasons. And there is not so much difference as appears at first sight between these alternatives. For what is it to claim insight into a necessary synthetic connexion but to admit that the connexion is unintelligible?

On the intuitionist theory we need:

(a) an intuition that an action has a right-making characteristic;
(b) an intuition that it is right;
(c) an intuition connecting (a) and (b);
(d) an intuition of relative stringencies;
(e) an intuition that the most stringent obligation is our duty;
(f) an intuition that we ought to do our duty;
(g) an inexplicable leap from 'I ought to do X' to the executive decision to do it.

No doubt some of these steps could be represented as analytic; but they cannot all be, and it is no wonder that people have despaired of being able to give good reasons for doing anything. Yet it is certainly true that we do give good reasons for doing things, if only because the phrase 'giving good reasons' is the phrase used in English for something that we all know we do; and if any argument tends to show that this is impossible there must be something wrong with the argument.

The need for all these connecting links has arisen because we have artificially separated the items to be connected; and the apparent need for this separation arises from the assumption that what follows or does not follow from a given proposition is the same on all occasions. Naturalistic philosophers have often offered definitions of 'good' and in so doing they have not been laying down rules for its use or expressing their intention of using it in a certain way, but claiming to show how it is in fact used. To refute such theories it is only necessary to be able to point to one example of a case in which 'good' obviously does not mean 'pleasant' or 'what I desire', etc., or to point out that if a man calls something pleasant it makes sense to ask him if it is good, which would not make sense if 'good' and 'pleasant' meant the same thing. Both these arguments are frequently used by intuitionists because they are held to show that 'good' and 'pleasant' must be the names of different properties.

But this argument rests on the assumption that 'good' always means the same thing, which is an assumption that we are only tempted to make if we treat it as a name. It shows only that 'good' *sometimes* does not mean pleasant, not that it *never* means pleasant. Since the original theory claimed, by implication, that 'good' *always* meant pleasant, the refutation is fair enough. But it scores only a Pyrrhic victory. While it succeeds in refuting any simple, one-track theory of what 'good' means, it is powerless to refute any theory which allows that 'good' may mean different things on different occasions. Both the original theory and the refutation make the same logical mistake of supposing that the meaning of 'good' can be examined in isolation from its context.

[2]

Consider the following conversation:

    A. What are you doing?
    B. I am having a nice smoke.
    A. Are you enjoying it?

The last question is puzzling. Once B has said that he is having a nice smoke there seems to be no further room for the question 'Are you enjoying it?'. This is not to say that the question is necessarily pointless. Perhaps A has some embarrassing communication to make to B and he simply wants to keep the conversation going because he knows that it will be more difficult to broach the subject if it is allowed to die. Perhaps he wants to get B to consider his answer more carefully. But, in the absence of such special reasons, the question seems otiose because, in this context, 'nice' expresses the enjoyment of the speaker and he has already said that it is nice.

And, if we suppose that 'nice' always functions in this way, we might go on to classify 'nice' as a subjective word and to allow that 'this is nice' is more or less equivalent to 'I like it' or 'I enjoy it'. But this will not do. For there are contexts in which 'nice' has little or nothing to do with the enjoyment of the speaker. Suppose that someone who had never tasted oysters asked if they were nice. A thoughtful person would, I think, refuse to give a direct answer to this question. He would say "Well, I like them very much, but many people don't, especially the first time". If, however, the question had been about strawberries most people would answer 'Yes' without hesitation. And the reason for the discrepancy is not hard to seek. We know that almost everyone likes strawberries and in consequence we have good grounds for predicting that the questioner will; in the case of oysters we have no such grounds. I shall defend the view that the reply 'they are nice' is, in this context, a prediction when I come to discuss A-sentences. For the moment I wish only to make the point that 'they are nice' has different implications in different contexts. In the first context 'nice' was used to express the enjoyment of the speaker; in the second to predict the enjoyment of the hearer. This point is obscured if we suppose that 'nice' must mean the same thing in all contexts and that what follows analytically from the statement 'It is nice' is the same in all contexts.

For the concept of logical implication or analytic connexion between statements I propose to substitute the concept of 'contextual implication', and for the concept of self-contradiction that of 'logical oddness'; and since I shall make much use of these technical phrases they must now be explained.

I shall say that a statement p contextually implies a statement q if anyone who knew the normal conventions of the language would be entitled to infer q from p *in the context in which they occur*. Logical implications are a sub-class of contextual implications, since if p logically implies q, we are entitled to infer q from p in any context whatever. Contextual implication can be most easily illustrated in a case where there is clearly no logical implication.

If Jones says "It is raining", Smith is entitled to infer that Jones believes that it is raining, although 'Jones believes that it is raining' clearly does not follow logically from 'It is raining'. Conversely there is clearly no contradiction between 'It is raining' and 'Jones believes that it isn't raining'; yet it would be logically odd for Jones to say "It is raining, but I don't believe it is".

The following rules of contextual implication are not rigid rules. Unlike the rules of logical implication they *can* all be broken without the speaker being involved in self-contradiction or absurdity.

Rule 1. When a speaker uses a sentence to make a statement, it is contextually implied that he believes it to be true. And, similarly, when he uses it to perform any of the other jobs for which sentences are used, it is contextually implied that he is using it for one of the jobs that it normally does.

This rule is often in fact broken. Lying, play-acting, story-telling, and irony are all cases in which we break it either overtly or covertly. But these are secondary uses, that is to say uses to which an expression could not (logically) be put unless it had some primary use. There is no logical limit to the possible uses to which an expression may be put; in many cases a man makes his point by deliberately using an expression in a queer way or even using it in the sense opposite to its normal one, as in irony. The distinction between primary and secondary uses is important because many of the arguments used by philosophers consist in pointing out typical examples of the way in which the word ' . . . ' is used. Such arguments are always illegitimate if the example employed is an example of a secondary use, however common such a use may be.

Rule 2. A speaker contextually implies that he has what he himself believes to be good reasons for his statement. Once again, we often break this rule and we have special devices for indicating when we are breaking it. Phrases such as 'speaking offhand . . .'. 'I don't really know but . . .', and 'I should be inclined to say that . . .' are used by scrupulous persons to warn the hearer that the speaker has not got what seem to him good reasons for his statement. But unless one of these guarding phrases is used we are entitled to believe that the speaker believes himself to have good reasons for his statement and we soon learn to mistrust people who habitually infringe this rule.

It is, of course, a mistake to infer from what someone says categorically that he has *in fact* good reasons for what he says. If I tell you that the duck-billed platypus is a bird (because I 'remember' reading this in a book) I am unreliable; but I am not using language improperly. But if I tell you this without using one of the guarding phrases and without having what *I* think good reasons I am.

Rule 3. What a speaker says may be assumed to be relevant to the interests of his audience. This is the most important of the three rules; unfortunately it is also the most frequently broken. Bores are more common than liars or careless talkers.

This rule is particularly obvious in the case of answers to questions, since it is assumed that the answer *is* an answer. Not all statements are answers to questions; information may be volunteered. Nevertheless the publication of a text-book on trigonometry implies that the author believes that there are people who want to learn about trigonometry, and to give advice implies a belief that the advice is relevant to the hearer's problem.

This rule is of the greatest importance for ethics. For the major problem of theoretical ethics was that of bridging the gap between decisions, ought-sentences, injunctions, and sentences used to give advice on the one hand and the statements of fact that constitute the reasons for these on the other. It was in order to bridge these gaps that insight into necessary synthetic connexions had to be invoked. The third rule of contextual implication may help us to show that there is no gap to be bridged because the reason-giving sentence must turn out to be practical from the start and not a statement of fact from which a practical sentence can somehow be deduced.

This rule is, therefore, more than a rule of good manners; or rather it shows how, in matters of ordinary language, rules of good manners shade into logical rules. Unless we assume that it is being observed we cannot understand the connexions between decisions, advice, and appraisals and the reasons given in support of them.

Logical Oddness. I shall say that a question is 'logically odd' if there appears to be no further room for it in its context because it has already been answered. This is not to say that the question is necessarily senseless, but that we should be puzzled to know what it meant and should have to give it some unusual interpretation. In the example of the man having a nice smoke it was logically odd to ask if he was enjoying it, because *in that particular context* his previous remark implied that he was.

The task of the moral philosopher is to map the mutual relationships of moral words, sentences, and arguments; and this is a task, not of showing how one statement entails or contradicts another, but of showing that in a certain context it would be logically odd to assert one thing and deny another or to ask a particular question.

Consider the following conversations:

(i)   A. I'll have mutton.
      B. Why?
      A. Because I prefer mutton to beef.
      B. Why? (Meaning, not 'Why do you prefer mutton to beef?' but 'Why is your preference for mutton a reason for choosing it?'.)

(ii) A. (Picking up sides) I'll have Jones.
      B. Why?
      A. Because he's the best wicket-keeper.
      B. Why? (Meaning, not 'In what way is he the best wicket-keeper?', but 'Why is his being the best wicket-keeper a reason for choosing him?'.)

(iii) A. I'll pay the butcher.
      B. Why?
      A. Because I owe him the money.
      B. Why? (Meaning, not 'How did the debt arise?', but 'Why is the existence of a debt a reason for paying him?'.)

In each of these conversations A starts by expressing a decision to do something and when asked 'Why?' he backs up his decision with a reason. B then tries to insert a logical wedge between the reason and the decision. And from the point of view of the formal logician he is right. In no case does the reason which A gives, which is a statement of fact, *entail* the decision to do what he decides to do. Nevertheless in each case B's second question is logically odd. What can he be after? What better reason or further reason could he expect to be given after the one that has already been given?

It should be noticed that, although a reason is given in each case, it is a different sort of reason and we shall see that it is tied to the decision in a different way. In the first case the reason is an expression of subjective preference, in the second an objective, verifiable statement of fact, in the third a sentence about obligation. The remainder of this book will be largely devoted to a discussion of the ways in which these different sorts of reasons fit into each other. For the moment I shall keep away from specifically moral uses of words and try to illustrate the sort of connexions that occur by examining the operation of A-sentences. Since the operation of 'good', 'right', 'ought', and G-words is in many respects similar to that of A-words, the digression is not so irrelevant as it may seem.

[3]

THE ROLE OF A-SENTENCES

Among the typical A-words are: Terrifying, hair-raising, disappointing, disgusting, beneficial, ridiculous, funny, amusing, sublime. There may be a gerundive element in the use of many of these words, especially if they are prefixed by 'truly' or 'really'. Thus, if we call something 'truly disgusting' we are suggesting not only that people are usually disgusted by it, but that they ought to be. A man who is not disgusted by something that is truly disgusting is not just unusual; he is in some way defective, reprehensible. I shall for the moment ignore the G-force of A-sentences.

It is not to be supposed that all the words in the list operate in all respects in the same way. There are logical differences between them; but I have grouped them together because they exhibit an important likeness. Each of them is connected with a specific human 'reaction', being frightened, amused, cured, impressed, and so on. The word 'reaction' must be widely construed to cover many things that would not normally be called 'reactions' at all. It includes attitudes that people might take up, emotions they might feel, things that happen to them and things that they do. I shall call the reaction 'appropriate' if it is the reaction that is logically tied to the A-word in question, for example 'being frightened' to 'terrifying', without any suggestion that the reaction ought to be exhibited in a particular case.

To understand the logic of an A-sentence we must ask, not 'What does it (always) mean?', but 'What does its use in this instance contextually imply?', 'What would it be logically odd to question?'. The following elements seem to be contextually implied in typical uses, although it is not necessary that every element should be present on all occasions and the relative prominence of the different elements will be different on different occasions.

(a) *The subjective element.* In default of other evidence the use of an A-sentence usually implies that the speaker has the appropriate reaction. It would be odd to say that a book was enlightening or amusing and then to go on to say that one was not enlightened or amused by it. Odd, but not impossible. 'It was a terrifying ordeal, but I wasn't frightened'; 'It may be very funny, but I am not inclined to laugh'; 'It may be a very beneficial medicine, but it didn't cure me'. In all these cases the subjective element is expressly withdrawn; and, since these statements are not self-contradictory, we cannot say that 'X is terrifying' either means or entails 'I am frightened by X'. Nevertheless, in default of an express withdrawal, we should always be entitled to infer that the speaker has the appropriate reaction.

A reaction need not express itself in any overt action; but it must do so in the absence of counter-reasons. For a man to maintain that strawberries are nice and never eat them is logically odd unless he can give counter-reasons, such as that they are bad for his health or against his religious principles. If no such reasons can be given he has abused the word 'nice'.

(b) *The predictive element.* An A-sentence is sometimes used to imply that someone would have the appropriate reaction to something if suitable circumstances arose. Thus, if I tell you that there is an amusing film at the Scala, when the question is whether you should go to the Scala or not, I am predicting that you will be amused. Who the person is must depend on the context. In this particular case it would be irrelevant to predict the reaction of anyone but you, so that I should be breaking Rule 3 if I used 'amusing' to mean 'apt to amuse all or most people' or 'apt to amuse me'.

A mountain that is said to be climbable at a meeting of experts would not be rightly called climbable at a meeting of novices. The statement implies that it would not be beyond the powers of those concerned to climb it.

(c) *The generalizing element.* Sensible people do not make predictions (or retrodictions) except on the basis of evidence, so that a man who uses an A-sentence to make a prediction contextually implies (by Rule 2) that he has what he believes to be good reasons for making the prediction. If he does not, he is either lying or abusing language. And what reasons for predicting that you will be frightened by X could there be other than the fact that people like you are usually frightened by Xs? If it could be shown that people were not, in fact, frightened by bulls, the statement that bulls are terrifying would have to be withdrawn. Terrifyingness is not an objective property that bulls would still have even if nobody was ever frightened by them, although a particular bull might still be terrifying even if nobody had in fact ever been frightened by it.

(d) *The causal element.* Things are not just terrifying or amusing or comfortable; animals are terrifying if they are strong, fierce, and malevolent; plays amusing if they contain a high proportion of remarks and situations of a certain sort, and cars are comfortable if they have good springs, a heater, and plenty of leg-room. To be told that something has an A-characteristic is not to be told just what causal properties it has that give it that characteristic; but it is contextually implied that it has such properties. And if the A-word is sufficiently narrow in scope we can often infer what properties it has although the speaker does not mention them.

[4]

THE INTERNAL COMPLEXITY OF A-SENTENCES

In what ways are these four elements said to be 'present in' the use of an A-sentence? Since none of them exhausts the meaning of an A-sentence and since they do not logically imply each other, we are tempted to say that A-words denote special causal properties of bulls, jokes, mountains, cars, and so on in virtue of which they cause people to have the appropriate reactions. And this temptation is reinforced by the fact that we do use A-sentences in an explanatory way. "I laughed, because it was funny." "Of course I was frightened; you would have been too; it was a very terrifying experience." But although A-sentences are used in this explanatory way, the logic of their use requires no special properties which they denote; indeed such properties only make their use unintelligible.

The relation between the predictive and the generalizing

element is clearly inductive and could be expressed without the use of an A-sentence at all.

(1) Most people of type X have been frightened by Ys.
(3) You, being of type X, will be frightened by Ys.

This argument is subject to those doubts (real or imaginary) which infect all inductive arguments. It is not my purpose to discuss the logical gap, if any, between the premise and the conclusion, but only to show that it cannot be bridged by the introduction of an A-sentence:

(2) Ys are terrifying to people of type X.

Such a sentence either does too much or too little. (a) If it is held to be both a logical consequence of (1) and to be a logical implicant of (3) it converts the inductive argument into a deductive one. But clearly your being frightened does not follow logically from the fact of others having been frightened in the past.

(b) If both the steps from (1) to (2) and from (2) to (3) are held to be inductive, we are worse off than we were before. Not only have we now two inductive leaps to make; one of them is such that we could never have any reason for making it. There are no tests for Ys being terrifying other than the fact that people have been terrified by them; hence the fact of Ys being terrifying cannot be tied to the fact of people having been frightened by Ys by the observation of a constant correlation; and such a correlation is of the essence of an inductive step.

(c) It might be said that the step from (1) to (2) is quasi-analytic, as it surely is. But we are still no better off than before. For, on this interpretation, our evidence for the belief that Ys are terrifying is identical with our evidence for the belief that people have been frightened by them. And if we are allowed to pass from (2) to (3) we must also be allowed to pass direct from (1) to (3); so that the introduction of (2) is otiose.

The temptation to construe A-words as the names of special

properties does not arise solely from the general tendency to treat all nouns and adjectives as names. It arises from the fact that, while such words obviously mean something, any single-track analysis of what they mean is bound to fail. A man who says that bulls are terrifying means more than that they frighten him. We think of 'being terrifying' as an objective property of bulls because 'bulls are terrifying' states a fact which can be verified in the way that statements about objective properties can be verified. It is true or false independently of the reactions of the speaker and it is for this reason that we use the impersonal form of speech. Moreover, if I am asked why I was so frightened, I might reply 'because it was terrifying'; and we relax, confident in the belief that the explanation has been found. What better reason could there be than the fact that it was terrifying?

But it is an explanation of a very queer kind. It is not like 'the bull terrified me because it was strong, fierce, and malevolent'; for while this explanation does give the reasons why I was frightened, the earlier one does not. It is not the amusingness of the play that amuses me, but the jokes and situations in it.

Does an A-sentence, then, explain nothing? Is it, like 'Opium sends you to sleep because it has a *virtus dormitiva*', merely a pompous reiteration of the thing to be explained? It does more than this; but it explains only at a very lowly level. The function of an explanation is to remove puzzlement and the first step in any explanation is to show that the thing to be explained is not really puzzling at all, but only to be expected.[1] Hence 'They were (I was) terrified on that occasion', is in part explained by 'because it was a terrifying situation', since the latter implies that most people would have been terrified. Their (my) fear was nothing out of the ordinary.

But A-sentences do more than explain at this lowly level. They imply the presence of causal properties without saying what these properties are. People do not like Jones because he is likeable, but because he is kind, generous, and good-

1. Toulmin, op. cit., p. 87.

tempered; and a man who says that Jones is likeable implies that Jones has a number of those characteristics for which people are usually liked without saying which of these Jones has. In the same way people are not able to climb mountains because they are climbable, but because they are so shaped as to provide sufficient holds for the climber. A-words imply the presence of unspecified causal properties because of which a thing causes the 'reaction' that it does; but they do not name such properties.

Nor do they name 'consequential properties'. For example, being strong is a consequential property of tigers because tigers would not be strong unless they had such and such muscles. But, in spite of the fact that tigers would not be terrifying unless they were strong, being terrifying is not a consequential property of tigers. For 'being strong' is tied to 'having muscles of a certain kind' and to 'being terrifying' in different ways. The first two are empirical properties between which a correlation can be observed to exist. But the last is not an observable property at all. A man who calls tigers 'terrifying' contextually implies that they have certain properties which frighten people. But he does not *state* this; still less does he specify what the properties are.

It is now possible to see why it was important to distinguish the question 'For what job is the word . . . used?' from the question 'Under what conditions is it proper to use the word . . . for that job?'.[1] A-words are used to give explanations and to make predictions, not to give the reasons for the explanation or prediction. But their use for these purposes is only proper if the speaker has reasons of a certain sort which are not stated but contextually implied. They are also used to express reactions; and it is this fact that tempts us to equate 'Xs are nice' with 'I like Xs'. But, even apart from the fact that 'Xs are nice' is used for other purposes, its use to express a reaction is different from that of 'I like Xs'. The use of the impersonal formula would be misleading, and therefore improper, if the speaker knew that his taste was

1. P. 69, above.

peculiar and that this fact was important. He is not expressing a different reaction from that expressed by the personal formula; the difference lies in the contextual background. I shall try to show later that this distinction sheds light on the objective-subjective controversy.[1]

The relation between A-words and the names of causal properties is obscured by the fact that we sometimes have no special name for the property that causes a certain reaction and make the A-word do duty for it. We have, for example, no rich, neutral vocabulary with which to refer to the various smells and tastes that do, in fact, nauseate, offend, or disgust people. Hence we refer to such smells and tastes as 'nauseating', 'offensive', or 'disgusting', even when no A-force is intended. If we wish expressly to withdraw the A-force we make do with a periphrasis that mentions the object that most typically has the smell or taste in question: Reeks of disinfectant, smells like sulphuretted hydrogen, tastes strongly of paraffin, smells of pear-drops. On the other hand, since these smells and tastes do in fact offend people, the neutral expressions can be used with an A- or even a G-force. 'The beer at the Pink Elephant tastes of paraffin' is a sentence that could be used not to 'state a fact' but to issue a warning; we have no need to add that the taste is offensive. But the neutral expressions are also used by chemists, doctors, and detectives in a purely neutral way.

This brings out the fact that it can be misleading to talk, as I have done, of A-words and G-words and, as I shall do, of pro-words and con-words. There are no such classes of words; there are different purposes to which words can be put and, in a special context, almost any word can be put to almost any purpose. This is an important feature of ordinary as opposed to technical language. But since there are some words that are almost always used for a restricted range of purposes I shall continue to talk in terms of special classes of words except where the context requires a more accurate approach.

1. P. 178, below.

PART II

Choosing and Advising

CHAPTER 7
The Purposes of Practical Discourse

[1]

WE must now begin to apply the principles outlined in the last two chapters and try to understand the role of practical discourse by studying the purposes for which it is used rather than by trying to discover (or invent) entities to which the words used in it refer. This method has been adopted by philosophers in recent years and is, indeed, the natural way out of the impasse into which non-natural qualities led us. To say that something is good, we are now told, is not to make a statement about it or to describe it, but to express a desire for or an attitude towards it, to express approval of it, to grade it, to praise it, to commend it, and so on. Philosophers might indeed have learnt as much from the *Oxford English Dictionary*, which defines 'good' not by saying that it is the name of an object or property but by its use. It is "the most general adjective of commendation" in English.

We must, however, be careful not to make a mistake analogous to that of supposing that a given word is the name of just one object or property. The commonest practical words do not have just one use. They have many uses and can be used to do more than one job on any given occasion. But this is not the whole story and we must again make use of the distinction between the question "For what job is the word . . . used?" and the question "Under what conditions is it proper to use that word for that job?".

If we did not make this distinction we might find ourselves compelled to postulate special non-natural uses analogous to the non-natural properties postulated by intuitionists. For there is clearly a great difference between 'I approve of X' and 'X is good'; and if we say that the latter is used to express approval we may be compelled to say also that it expresses a peculiar, non-natural approval. But the new model enables us to bring out this difference without recourse to non-natural approval. For we can now say that, while both sentences express exactly the same sort of approval, the latter is properly used to express this approval only under certain fairly stringent conditions that need not obtain when 'I approve of X' is used.

We have already seen that the difference between 'this is nice' and 'I like it' (when the former is used to express the taste of the speaker) does not lie in the nature of the attitude expressed but in the fact that one must not use the impersonal formula to express this attitude unless certain conditions obtain. And the same point applies to the distinction between 'this is good' and 'I approve of this', a distinction that is all too obvious to the objectivist and quite invisible to the subjectivist. If we distinguish between the purpose for which a sentence is used and the conditions, if any, which limit the use of just this sentence for just this purpose (between what a man means by a sentence and what is contextually implied), the dispute between subjectivists and objectivists becomes clear. Briefly, the subjectivists tend to ignore the contextual background and the objectivists tend to treat this background as part of what a man actually says. I shall discuss this more fully when I come to the word 'good'.[1]

Looking at words as tools with which we do things rather than as names or labels which we attach to things has two advantages. In the first place it helps to remind us how close the connexion is between doing things with words and doing them with smiles, nods, winks, and gestures and of the importance, in ordinary speech, of emphasis, tone of voice, and manner. All these things are more or less irrelevant to the dry, precise, and 'objective' uses to which mathematical language and the language of empirical science are put, but they are exceedingly important in ordinary, and especially in practical discourse.

1. Pp. 178–80, 222–5, below.

Ordinary language, well used, is extremely flexible and precise; but the difference between its flexibility and precision and that of scientific language comes out in the fact that we never use the word 'nuance' in the latter.

The second advantage of the new model is that it reminds us of the way in which different uses of words shade into each other, a point which is obscured by the labelling model since things labelled are distinct from each other in a way in which the jobs for which a tool is used are not.[1]

Consider the sentences 'What an abominable fellow he is!' and 'I think he is an abominable fellow'. The first has the grammatical form of an expletive, the second that of an indicative sentence. We are tempted to say that the first expresses the speaker's state of mind, while the second states what his state of mind is. The first could not be true or false while the second could. Yet it is clear that in some contexts the difference between them, if any, is very slight, far too slight to warrant a sharp logical division. A man who actually said the one might, we feel, just as well have said the other. But this is not to say that these sentences (always) mean the same thing or that they are (always) used in the same way as each other. For in other contexts there might be a considerable difference, especially if the speaker emphasized the words 'I think'.

Again: 'What a disgusting thing to do!'. A man might use this phrase simply to express his disgust, so that it would differ from a curl of the lip only in indicating more clearly what he was disgusted at. Yet in other contexts it might mean a lot more than this. 'Disgusting' might be at least an A-word, contextually implying that his disgust was not peculiar or

---

1. The use of mathematics as a model for logic makes the traditional terminology of logic singularly inappropriate for elucidating practical discourse. In mathematics each expression belongs to a distinct type; it must be a numeral or an equation or a function and so on. Mathematical uses of expressions do not shade into each other; and mathematics is primarily a written, not a spoken language. It uses symbols, while in ordinary language we use not symbols, but words. The inventor of printing must take the blame for quite a number of philosophical errors.

unusual, or a G-word, implying that his disgust was justified and that other people ought to be disgusted.

The fact that a given expression can be used to perform many different roles is by itself sufficient to undermine or at least to make us suspicious of all arguments in the form 'When we say . . . we mean . . '. And the fact that the same expression can do more than one job on one occasion is even more important.

The old model is not just misleading; it is wholly wrong. The words with which moral philosophers have especially to do, which are usually called 'value-words', play many different parts. They are used to express tastes and preferences, to express decisions and choices, to criticize, grade, and evaluate, to advise, admonish, warn, persuade and dissuade, to praise, encourage and reprove, to promulgate and draw attention to rules; and doubtless for other purposes also. These activities form the complex web of moral discourse and our problem is to trace the connexions between them and to come to understand how it is that the same word can be used in all these different ways. What a man is doing with a particular value-word at a particular time can only be discovered by examining what he says in its context, but it would be just as absurd to suppose that there is no connexion between these activities as to suppose that the same expression can only be used to do one job.

The connexion between the different uses is partly logical and partly a matter of fact; and it is for this reason that the analytic-synthetic dichotomy breaks down. It is possible and, in some circumstances, not unusual to prefer one thing and choose another, to praise a man without approving of him, to grade one thing as better than another without feeling any desire for, preference for, or interest in either, and so on. Since these things are so, we must, if we stick to the analytic-synthetic dichotomy, conclude that it is only a 'contingent fact' that people desire what they find pleasant, praise the good, reprove the wicked, vote for proposals they approve of, etc.

And so, in a way, it is. We could easily imagine a world in

which these connexions did not obtain, and this is the sort of thing that satirists like to do. But it would be a topsy-turvy world in which no one would survive for long. Things in our world are different; and when a number of logically distinct items such as desiring an end, thinking the means appropriate to it and voting for a proposal to adopt those means, normally go along together, the 'contingent' connexions between them become enshrined in the logic of the language. If a man says that a proposal is a good one and holds up his hand with the Noes he is making a logical mistake.

But this is not because there is an analytic connexion between calling something 'good' and voting for it. He is not contradicting himself if he can produce special reasons for his apparently inconsistent behaviour. He might, for example, believe that the proposal has no chance of passing or that it is sure to pass even without his vote and he may have special reasons for not coming out openly in its favour. But in default of such special reasons, his audience is entitled to infer that he would vote for and not against it.

The same sort of quasi-logical connexion holds between approval and exhortation. People do not normally exhort others to do or refrain from something unless they themselves approve or disapprove of the activity concerned. And, because this is so, the same set of words, bad, wicked, vicious, evil, etc., can be used both for expressing disapproval and for exhorting others to refrain. If a man discoursed for an hour on the evils of drinking and used a number of these pejorative adjectives, it would be odd for anyone to ask if he really disapproved of drinking, unless he were casting doubts on the preacher's sincerity. But to do this would be to suspect him of using words in a secondary way. It is not just that there is a high correlation between the things that a man disapproves of, the things he condemns, and the things he exhorts others not to do. This correlation is reflected in the logic of our language; but not so tightly that we could always convict a man of either insincerity or self-contradiction if he said "That is wrong, but I don't disapprove of it".

As Hume pointed out, there are some words which both describe the way in which a man behaves and also have a laudatory or pejorative force. If Jones tells Smith that Brown is courageous or honest or kindly, Smith knows that Brown can be expected to behave in certain more or less restricted ways in certain circumstances. Jones's remark is therefore partly predictive. But Smith is also entitled to infer that Jones thinks highly of Brown. It is because it is usual to commend and not disparage the types of behaviour described by these words that there is an air of self-contradiction about calling a man brave, honest, and kindly and refusing to praise him; for these words are terms of praise.

Since I shall make frequent use of the principle that a given word can not only do two or more jobs at once but also is often, in the absence of counter-evidence or express withdrawal, presumed to be doing two or more jobs at once, I shall give it the special name 'Janus-principle'.

[2]

Among the various performances for which value-words are used which shall be given pride of place ? To some extent this is, as in an axiomatic system, a matter of choice. But since I started by posing the fundamental question as 'What shall I do ?', it will be convenient to start with choosing, deciding, and preferring.

Choosing is something that we *do*. It can be done without using any words at all, as when a man chooses a card to play or an apple from a plate of fruit. It can be done with words, as when a man in a shop says "I'll have that one". This is not a prediction; for it would be odd if the shopkeeper replied "I don't expect you will", though he might without making a logical mistake reply: "No, you won't" or "That one is not for sale". Such formulae are not statements but expressions of choice; they are as much interventions in the world as a non-linguistic action is, and they differ from non-linguistic actions only in that they produce their effects in a conventional way.

Choosing, deciding, and doing. In some cases we choose without *doing* anything. For example a man can choose a place for his holiday next year. In this case we may equally say that he has decided or made up his mind where to go. The decision is, as it were, put into cold storage to be taken out and acted on when the appropriate time comes. Although it is quite proper to use 'choose' in this way, I shall limit my use of it to cases where choosing involves doing something at the time.

Since choosing involves doing something, a man cannot be said to have chosen until he has at least started on his chosen course. Merely to decide to play the ace of spades is not yet to choose it, and a decision does not therefore entail a choice. But the relation between the two is, nevertheless, not a contingent one. The fact that people choose to do what they have decided to do is not something that we discover by observation of human behaviour. The relation is one of quasi-implication. A man may decide, for example, to vote for Jones and be prevented from doing so by sickness or the cancellation of the election. But, in default of such explanations, there is no logical gap between deciding and doing.

If a man decides to do something in the future he may fail to do it because he has changed his mind; but it would be absurd to say in this case that he had not really decided. Decisions are none the less genuine for being revocable. A change of mind may be sudden and inexplicable. In this case *ex hypothesi* no reason can be given for it, and if a man decides to do X and suddenly changes his mind and does Y he acts irrationally. (There are other ways in which actions can be called 'irrational', for example if the agent has no good reasons for believing that they will produce the end which he desires; and in most uses 'irrational' is an opprobrious word. I do not wish to imply here that every action which deviates from a decision in an inexplicable way is irrational in any of the other senses or to imply that we ought never to act in this way.)

A change of mind can, on the other hand, be rational; the

old decision is scrapped and a new one made on the basis of new evidence. But 'choosing' and 'deciding' are used in such a way that it is analytic to say that if a man has decided to do something and does not do it then either he was prevented or he changed his mind. If neither of these explanations of the disparity between the decision and the choice can be given the man who in fact did X cannot be said to have decided to do Y.

Choosing and preferring. A man can choose without having any reason for his choice in sheer absence of mind or from sheer force of habit. These are minimal cases that hardly deserve the name of 'choice', and I shall consider only cases where a man has reasons for his choice.

The word 'good' can be used to express a preference and when so used is always a concealed comparative. Part of its function is to compare the thing called 'good' with others not so good, although the comparative element need not be prominent and no explicit comparison may be in mind. If challenged, however, the speaker must be prepared to make such a comparison. When used in the context of choice the comparative element is prominent, since choice is always between two or more alternatives. Preference begins with thinking this course better than that and ends with deciding that it is the best, and the sentences that we use to express preferences are tied to those used for expressing decisions in the same quasi-analytic way that the latter are tied to doing. There is no need therefore to try to bridge the gap between 'this is the best thing for me to do' and 'I shall do this'. In deciding that something is the best thing for him to do a man has already decided to do it.

The first sentence expresses a preference for one course of action over all others, the second a decision to take it. Choice would be an unfathomable mystery if these two sentences were interpreted as being only 'synthetically' connected with each other. A mysterious gap would always emerge; for it would make sense to say: "I prefer this course to any other (or this is the best course for me), but what shall I do?". These collocations of sentences are logically odd, but not self contradictory since, as we shall see, they could have a point in some circumstances. And recognizing the logical oddness of the question does not consist in having insight into a necessary connexion between preference and choice but in being puzzled to know what the question could possibly mean. In saying that he prefers A to B a man shows that he has already solved his problem of choice; yet in asking the question he appears still to have a problem. He can, of course, continue to ask himself "What shall I do?" even after he has decided that X is the best thing for him to do. But if he does so he is using words parrotwise or pretending to have a problem to solve when in fact he has not. The question cannot bear its usual sense; and this is a logical 'cannot'.

When I deal more fully with 'good', I shall examine the view that a man chooses to do something *because* he thinks it the best thing for him to do and try to show that 'thinking something is the best thing to do' is not a reason for doing it, because it is *too good* a reason.[1] We must now consider some cases in which it would not be logically odd for a man to prefer one thing and choose another.

(1) A man may prefer travelling by road to travelling by rail but in fact always choose to go by rail. But he can (logically) only do this if he is able to offer some explanation. For example he might be an employee of the railway company and get a free ticket, or his mother might think road travel very unsafe and he wants to humour her. As long as he can explain the discrepancy in some such way there is nothing logically odd about his saying that he prefers one thing when he always chooses the other. His preference entails only that he *would* travel by road if other things were equal. But in default of such explanations we should be entitled to infer that he did not really prefer going by road, whatever he may say. Our choices are better evidence of our preferences than our words.

(2) A man may prefer peaches to apples in general but choose an apple on a particular occasion, if, for example, there are not enough peaches to go round. What he prefers in this

1. P. 161, below.

case is not the apple to the peach but the total situation in which he has an apple and someone else has a peach to that in which he has a peach and someone else has an apple. But again, a man could not be said to prefer peaches to apples if he regularly chose apples without being able to advance any explanation. It makes sense to say: "I know you prefer peaches; why did you choose the apple?"; but it is logically odd to say: "I know you prefer peaches; but why did you choose the peach?".

CHAPTER 8

Reasons for Choosing

[1]

IN this and the following chapters we shall be concerned with the vocabulary used in deliberating, for expressing decisions, and for giving reasons for our decisions. The phrase 'good reason' is ambiguous. It may mean 'morally good reason', that is to say a reason which justifies an action and exempts the agent from moral censure; or it may mean 'logically good reason', that is to say a reason which leaves no further room either for the question 'What shall I do?' or for the question 'Why did you (he) do that?'. I shall use the phrase 'good reason' in the latter sense. In accordance with the principles laid down in the preceding chapters our task is not to discover propositions that entail a decision to act but propositions which are such that, once they are granted, it would be logically odd either to ask for further reasons for doing something or for a further explanation of why someone did it.

Precisely the same vocabulary is used both in deliberating *ante rem* and in explaining *post rem* why someone did what he did. If 'because . . .' is a logically good reason for doing something it also constitutes a logically good explanation of why someone chose to do it.

The questions involved are logical, not psychological, still less physiological ones. We are not at present concerned with questions about the general types of thing that people choose or choose to do. For example, Do people prefer oranges to lemons? Is fear a more powerful motive than greed? Still less are we concerned with physiologists' explanations correlating, for example, excess of adrenalin with anger or a craving for sugar with certain defects in metabolism. This point is important since philosophers have often written as if they were enunciating empirical laws of human behaviour, which they are not usually competent to do. They have said, for example, that men only desire pleasure, and they have put this in a way that leads one to suppose that, in their belief, men might (logically) desire all sorts of things but in fact never desire anything but pleasure. Since we all believe that we often desire food and drink and other things, the philosopher appears to be convicting the whole human race of a colossal mistake about its motives; he appears as a sort of Super-Freud, telling us that our motives are always quite other than what we thought they were.

But it is clear from their arguments that philosophers are really doing no such thing. What look like generalizations turn out to be logical observations; and these are either recommendations to adopt a certain set of concepts with certain logical relations between them or assertions to the effect that such a system already underlies, though unnoticed, our ordinary use of these concepts. In the latter case what the philosopher says can be verified or falsified, but it would be by an examination of linguistic usage, not by an examination of non-linguistic behaviour.

Are all the reasons that can be given for choosing to do something of the same logical type? Do they all enter into the logic of deliberation and explanation in the same way? Or do they play different roles, comparable to the different roles played by laws and facts in giving an explanation of a natural phenomenon? Perhaps the most celebrated attempt to explain all reasons for doing or refraining from something on a single model is that of Hobbes, according to whom all action is caused by desire or aversion.[1] It is worth while examining this theory at some length. I shall try to show later that the usual criticisms of it are misplaced; it is, however, open to a fatal objection.

The word 'desire' is commonly used in connexion with food, drink, and sex. We also talk of a desire to scratch, to

1. *Leviathan*, chapter 6. A desire is an 'endeavour toward' and an aversion is an 'endeavour fromward'.

smoke, or to be rid of some uncomfortable, irritating, or pain-ful sensation. Any of these desires, when very strong, would be called a 'craving', and this will turn out to be important, because it helps to explain our talk about 'being a slave to one's desires' and so explain why some philosophers have held the paradoxical theory that to act from desire is never to act freely.

One necessary element in the situations mentioned is that (a) there must be a bodily sensation or feeling of some sort. It is also necessary that the sensation should be (b) painful, distressing, uncomfortable, irritating, or unpleasant, and (c) that we should want to be rid of this sensation. And it is because we want to be rid of it that we take steps to remove it. This pattern of behaviour is so familiar that it needs no further description. If anyone says that he does not know what a 'desire' is, in this limited sense of the word, there is nothing that can be done for him. He knows well enough – I shall assume – what the facts are. The difficulties arise over the logic of the concepts used in discussing this type of situation.

The logical connexions between the unpleasant (etc.) sen-sation, the desire to be rid of it, and the taking of steps to be rid of it are so intimate that they make certain questions logically absurd. To ask someone who is in pain why he wants to alleviate his pain and to ask why someone who wants to alleviate his pain takes steps to do so are to ask logically odd questions; there is no room for them, unless they can be construed in an unusual way. But this is not to say that the connexions are analytic, that we could *define*, for example, a 'painful' sensation as one that a man wants to get rid of or 'wanting to get rid of' as a tendency to try to get rid of. The logical difficulties involved are, as usual, due to the fact that certain empirical connexions are so common and wide-spread that they have come to be enshrined as logical connexions in our talk. Almost all the words that I have used in this pre-liminary sketch are Janus-words.

We have no neutral language for talking about those sen-sations that, *as a matter of fact*, most people find painful. If asked to describe my sensation I must either use a periphrasis, such as 'as if someone was sticking pins into me' or 'as if someone were hitting me on the head with a hammer' or I must use a word such as 'ache', 'throb', 'tremor', 'palpitation', all of which, simply because most people find these painful on most occasions, already carry an overtone of painfulness.

These words can be used in a purely descriptive way to convey information about the sort of sensation that I am having: and, when so used, they carry no implication about my wanting to get rid of the sensation. Logically I could enjoy an ache or an itch and want it to go on; but the fact that most people usually do not tends to make us suppose that when someone says that he is itching or that a gnat bite irritates him he must want to remove the irritation. And this con-nexion then becomes a quasi-logical one, because the desire to get rid of the itch is contextually implied.

And this is especially true of the word 'pain' and its deriva-tives. If a man says that a sensation is painful we are entitled to infer that he wants to get rid of it. He may, of course, put up with it for the sake of something else. But as far as it goes the assertion that something is painful, irritating, unpleasant, or a source of discomfort implies that the speaker would rather be without it.

The phrase 'source of discomfort' is particularly dangerous; for it resembles 'cause of irritation' and thus tends to make us think of 'discomfort' as itself a kind of sensation. And this, as we shall see in the next chapter, is a fatal error. When a man 'feels discomfort' or 'is uncomfortable' he does not have two sensations, an itch (or whatever it might be) and a special sensation of discomfort; he has only one sensation which is an uncomfortable one. Similarly, when a man experiences a pain-ful sensation he has one sensation, not two. The painful sen-sation of having a pin stuck into you cannot be analysed into two sensations, a neutral pin-going-in sensation and a sensa-tion of pain. Indeed the philosophical phrases 'sensation of pain' and 'sensation of pleasure' are fatal corruptions of the ordinary phrases 'painful sensation' and 'pleasant sensation'.

And it is still more fatal to represent desires as sensations. The desires I am considering all involve sensations in so intimate a way that it is natural to try to identify the desire with the sensation involved. Thus we can say that hunger is 'a desire to eat'; but hunger is also the sensation that you feel in the pit of your stomach. So it follows, then, that a desire to eat is a sensation in the pit of the stomach? Not a bit of it. As is always the case with a complex of different sorts of elements, the same word or phrase can be used to refer to the whole complex situation or to any important element in it. 'I feel hungry' is a Janus-phrase that both refers to my sensations and also expresses a desire to eat. And it is used with this double force because it is an empirical fact that people who have the sensation referred to also want to eat.

Is fear a complex of sensations, for example trepidations, nausea, and a quickening pulse? Or is it a desire to run away? Or is it a tendency to run away? These are idle questions; for 'fear' can be used to refer to any of these things, and the logical fact that it is a Janus-word is due to the empirical fact that when people feel these sensations they usually want to run away and that, *ceteris paribus*, when they want to and can run away they usually do. So, if a man stands his ground with no counter-reasons for doing so in a situation that would make most people afraid, we say that he is not afraid; and this seems to entail that he did not have the sensations to which 'being afraid' refers. But in fact, of course, there is no such entailment. He may be having the sensations and be enjoying them. Now the fact that he enjoys the sensations concerned may be expressed either by saying that he enjoys these painful sensations (thus tying 'painful' logically to the sensations) or by saying that he does not find the sensations painful (thus tying 'painful' logically to non-enjoyment). And whichever way of putting it we choose we are inclined to suppose that a logical puzzle arises because what we say appears to be self-contradictory. But this is, of course, not so. We know that masochism occurs.

But we also talk of 'desires' in cases where there is not, at any rate not obviously, any painful, distressing, or unpleasant sensation that a man wants to get rid of. Hobbes' definition of 'Ambition', for example, as "desire of office or precedence" does not sound strained or unnatural. But in this case there is no sensation that the ambitious man wants to get rid of, at least so long as he is successful.

We certainly speak of ambition as 'gnawing' and this metaphor, which assimilates ambition to the itch-scratch pattern, must be explained. Thwarted ambition is commonly accompanied by feelings (not necessarily bodily sensations) of anger, regret, mortification, and spite. Indeed it must be so accompanied, since we should refuse to call a man 'really ambitious' if he had none of these painful feelings when he failed to achieve his aim. But although feelings are connected with ambition, they cannot be connected with it in the way that sensations are connected with hunger; for they arise only when the ambition is thwarted. Hunger might not unnaturally be called a desire to remove certain unpleasant sensations and might also be called a desire to eat; but no such double account could be given of ambition, since the feelings involved only arise when ambition is thwarted and ambition cannot therefore be construed as a desire to eliminate antecedent unpleasant sensations.

And there are many cases of wanting to do something from which antecedent sensations are even more conspicuously absent. A man who wants to smell a rose or to listen to a symphony is not disturbed by pains or discomforts of any kind, though, as in the case of the ambitious man, he may feel annoyance or regret if he fails to get what he wants. Moreover we have a number of expressions which are like 'desiring' and 'wanting' in that they provide logically impeccable explanations of choice but unlike them in that they do not obviously involve a reference to any feelings at all. These are 'being fond of', 'being interested in', 'having a passion for' (which, of course, does not involve being in a passion about anything), 'taking pleasure in', and 'approving of'.

These expressions are all used in such a way that it would

be logically odd to go on asking why a man was doing something once it was established that he was interested in it or fond of it, etc. This is the point they have in common with 'desiring'. But it would be a mistake to conclude from the fact that they explain an action in the same sort of way that a reference to desire explains an action that they are all desires. For to do this is to suppose that all these explanations must conform to the same pattern, and this tempts us to invent logical analogues in these cases for all the elements that must occur in cases of desiring. And it is just this mistake that Hobbes makes. By calling all motives 'desires' he invites us to believe that motive-explanations all conform to one pattern and specifically to the itch-scratch pattern; but to do this is to distort the logic of many of these explanations and to saddle our account of motives with fictitious elements.

[2]

Hobbes' treatment of all motives as desires is open to criticism; but it cannot be condemned merely on the ground that it conflicts with the ordinary English use of the word 'desire'. Ordinary language, being used by ordinary people on ordinary occasions, is not rich in highly abstract or generic nouns; we have, in fact, no very general word to cover desiring, liking, wanting, approving, enjoying, being fond of, interested in, and so on; and part of the reason for this is that these concepts are in many ways dissimilar. But it does not follow that Hobbes' general distinction between 'endeavour toward' and 'endeavour fromward' is altogether a mistake; and if there is, as I shall try to show, a good reason for making this general distinction, our only course is either to invent a new generic word or to adopt the more risky course that Hobbes adopts of selecting a word which normally has a narrow use and using it in a novel and wider way.

The only ordinary English word that is sufficiently vague to be made to cover (with a little terminological ingenuity) all the cases considered is 'wanting'; but this word, just by reason of its vagueness, is far too weak to cover the more violent passions or the most permanent and deep-seated desires. (It would be absurd to talk of a Christian 'wanting' to inherit the kingdom of heaven or of a near-hysterical bobby-soxer 'wanting' to see a crooner.)

With some hesitation I have chosen the expressions 'pro-' and 'con-attitude' to fulfil the required role; but it must first be shown that there is a need for any generic term whatsoever. Consider the following lists:

List A	*List B*
Like	Hate
Approve of	Dislike
Enjoy	Disapprove of
Love	Detest
Want	Reject
Accept	Decline
Pleasure	Shy away from
Comfort	Pain
Desire	Discomfort
Happiness	Aversion
Interested in	Try to avoid
Fond of	Try to prevent
Try to achieve	Try to get rid of
Try to acquire	Try to stop
Try to obtain	Try to avert
Try to prolong	

I have deliberately included in these lists concepts of different logical types in order to make clear that the use of the phrase 'having a pro-attitude towards' should not be restricted to any one pattern; and I am, for the same reason, unmoved by the criticism that many of the items on the list would not normally be said to have anything to do with 'attitudes' at all. The word 'attitude' has been selected just because it is vague. The important point that I wish to bring out lies in the words 'Pro' and 'Con'.

In spite of the heterogeneity of the lists, it can be shown

that there is a genuine basis for the distinction by remarking that the reader would have no difficulty in most cases in saying into which list, if either, some new concept ought to be put. I have also restricted the lists almost entirely to verbs; for, in most cases, to include nouns or adjectives would be to prejudice both logical and empirical issues. I might, for example, have included 'good' and 'bad' in the lists, for their places are obvious. But this would prejudge the issue whether to think something 'good' just *is* to have a pro-attitude towards it, in which case 'thinking good' should clearly be included, or whether thinking something good is not rather to suppose it to have some quality which is more remotely connected with having a pro-attitude.

To include nouns such as 'health' and 'disease', 'riches' and 'poverty', 'peace' and 'war' would be to prejudge an empirical issue and to suppose that men always have a pro-attitude to the first of these pairs and a con-attitude to the second.

PRO- AND CON-SENTENCES AS EXPLANATIONS OF CHOICE

Sentences containing pro- and con-words provide good – that is to say, logically complete – explanations of choice. If you ask a man why he is gardening or why he is going to turn on the wireless and he says that he enjoys gardening or wants to hear some music, he has given a reply that makes a repetition of the question logically odd. It must always be remembered that a repetition cannot be ruled out as senseless; the situation is that it could not have its ordinary meaning and would have to be interpreted in a special way which will depend on the context. For example, by repeating the question, the questioner might be trying to insinuate in a delicate way that the reason given was not the true one or that it was a morally reprehensible one. But in default of such special interpretations it seems senseless to ask anyone why he is doing something when he has told you he enjoys it, likes doing it, or wants to do it.

Pro-words differ from each other in many ways, but they all have this in common that they provide logically impeccable explanations of why someone chose to do something. They also provide logically impeccable reasons for deciding to do or not to do something. The 'reason for doing' which is expressed by such a phrase as 'because I want . . .' or 'because I enjoy . . .' may be counteracted by other and more weighty reasons for making the opposite choice; but each pro-sentence refers to *a* reason and, in the absence of counter-reasons, it would be logically odd not to choose.

Many philosophers have made the point that every action must have a motive, and that a motive can only be counteracted by another motive; and some have represented choice as simply the victory of the strongest motive or set of concurrent motives. These points have usually been put as if they were psychological laws; but they are really elucidations of the logic of concepts. To say, for example, that every action must have a motive is to state a tautology, since what a man 'did' without a motive would not count as an 'action'. The theory that a motive can only be counteracted by another motive is also a logical rather than a psychological theory. For it is the theory that we use the word 'motive' in such a way that anything which counteracts a motive is also called a motive. In the same way, my lists of pro- and con-attitudes must be so construed that anything which could be offered as a logically good reason for or against doing anything must be included in the lists. By a 'logically good reason' I do not mean a morally good reason; I mean anything which, when offered as an explanation of why someone chose to act as he did, has the force of making further questioning logically odd.

The proposition that any statement which gives a logically complete reason for choice must include a reference to a pro- or a con-attitude is thus a frank tautology. Its function is to draw attention to the existence of a class of words that have just this force. My purpose is not to prove an avowed tautology, but to show that many expressions which are normally used in giving reasons for choice do not give logically complete reasons. They are given and taken as complete explanations only because certain assumptions are involved when they are used. In particular I shall try to show that deontological words (right, obligation, duty, and their cognates) never give logically complete reasons for choice. To put the point in a paradox which I shall defend later, 'believing that something is the right thing to do' and 'believing that something is my duty' are *never* good reasons for doing it and such beliefs never explain why people do what they do.

It is important to notice that a reference to a pro- or con-attitude provides a good (logically complete) reason even in cases of morally reprehensible conduct. If a man says that he is fond of music he has fully explained why he listens to music in a way that makes it senseless to say "I know you are fond of music; but why do you listen to it?" And this is equally true if he says "because I enjoy it" when someone asks him why he is torturing the cat. The reply does not give a morally good reason; but logically it is impeccable.

To ask why people enjoy just those things that they do enjoy is to ask a psychologist's question which could be answered. (Hobbes, for example, propounds the psychological theory that we desire to do those things that help or fortify the "vital motions".) To ask whether people ought to enjoy what they enjoy is to ask a moral question; and this also can be answered. But to ask why people do the things they like and enjoy doing is not to ask a question but to raise a gratuitous philosopher's puzzle.

It is important to notice that there are no logical limits to the possible objects of pro- or con-attitudes, other than the logical limits of language itself. This is important since philosophers who have made pro-attitudes such as desire or approval the central concepts of their ethical system have often been accused of holding special (and very unplausible) theories about the sorts of things that people can desire or approve of. I shall try to show in later chapters that the tendency of some modern philosophers to accord a peculiar and prominent position among motives to the sense of duty is due to this mistake. The sense of duty is indeed peculiar and important; but its peculiarity and importance are not what they have been thought to be; and the current view of it leads to paradoxes and absurdities. But this interpretation can be avoided if we remember that to explain actions in terms of pro-attitudes entails no view whatsoever about the objects of these attitudes.

[3]

We must now consider certain apparent exceptions to the rule that every complete explanation of conduct must refer to a pro- or con-attitude.

1. *Means and Ends.* If a man does something, not for its own sake, but because he knows that unless he does it he will not be able to do something that he has a pro-attitude towards doing, it is not necessary that he should have a direct pro-attitude towards doing it as such. A man who buys concert tickets need neither like nor enjoy nor approve of buying concert tickets. He explains his action, not by saying that buying a ticket was just what he wanted to do, but by saying that without a ticket he could not go to the concert. But, in this case, it is clear that his action is not fully explained until he has stated the end towards which it is a means. It is only when he says "I like music" or "I wanted to hear the Emperor Concerto" that he has fully explained his action in a way which makes it senseless to say "But I still don't understand why you bought the tickets".

There is some point to the dictum that a man who wills the end must will the means. This is absurd if it is taken to mean that a man who wants something necessarily also wants to get it by hook or by crook. If, for example, the only way of getting tickets is to steal them, he may still want to go to the concert, but his *choice* is between getting-tickets-by-stealing and not-getting-tickets-by-stealing, and he may well choose the latter. But unless he has a con-attitude towards getting-X-by-doing-Y, it is irrational for him not to do Y. This use of 'irrational' is another example of the way in which the logic of language reflects obvious empirical facts. It is not, in Hume's sense, "contrary to reason" for him to refrain from Y; but it is silly. And the logic of the language we use in talking about human action is built up on the assumption that men choose to do what they have a reason for doing and choose means which they believe to be effective. This is why we use the logical words 'reasonable' and 'unreasonable' to characterize actions.

2. *Statements of fact.* In ordinary life it is often sufficient to point out the facts of the case or to single out some special fact in order to explain someone's action. Thus a proper answer to 'Why did Jones help that man across the road?' would be 'Because he is blind'. But such an answer is no more complete than 'because he is a philosopher' is a complete answer to 'Why is Socrates so inquisitive?' or 'because he's the Mayor' a complete answer to 'Why is that man wearing a chain?' In these cases the answers take the form of pointing out a fact which explains the thing concerned only *via* the generalizations 'All philosophers are inquisitive' and 'All mayors wear chains'. The very fact that the particular proposition is given as an explanation contextually implies that there is such a general rule; for only so could the particular fact alleged be an explanation. Equally we could have answered 'because all philosophers are' or 'because all mayors wear chains', and had we done so our offering a general rule in explanation would have entitled the hearer to conclude that Socrates is a philosopher or that the man was a mayor. In each case the explanation requires both a general rule and a particular proposition, and it is because this form of explanation is so common that we do not need to mention both. Which we choose to mention is determined in each case by our opinion as to which point is most likely to be unknown to the questioner.

In the same way, it is clear that 'because he is blind' is only a sufficient explanation in practice because a pro-attitude towards helping the blind is so common that it can be taken as understood. Indeed, by omitting to mention it, we show that it is so understood; for only so could 'because he is blind' serve to explain Jones' action at all.

It might be thought unnecessary to labour this point; and so it would be if some philosophers had not suggested that, because statements of fact are commonly given and taken as complete explanations, explanations can be given without reference to pro-attitudes. Hence they have dismissed as logically senseless in certain cases questions in the form 'I know that these are the facts, but why did he do it?' and, what is more important, 'I know that these are the facts, but why should I do it?'. But these questions are otiose in practice only because a pro-attitude of the agent towards doing his duty can, in practice, be assumed. They are not logically senseless in the way that it is senseless to drive a wedge between having a pro-attitude towards doing something and choosing to do it.

3. *A-sentences.* We often use A-sentences for the purpose of explaining someone's choosing to do what he did and also for making up our minds what to do. And they are more intimately tied to choosing than are ordinary statements of fact. Their explanatory function is, as we have seen, partly that of showing that the choice was not an unusual one and partly that of implying the presence of reasons for choosing and indicating of what general type they are without specifying them. I may choose a book because it is amusing and this is not a different reason from choosing it because it has a number of good stories or jokes in it.

In the context of choice the subjective-predictive force is usually prominent, because the question whether the book would amuse you or anyone else is irrelevant. But it is a mistake to suppose that the subjective-predicative force is essential. I may be choosing a book for a Christmas present; and in that case the question whether it would amuse me is irrelevant.

There is an air of tautology about 'I laughed because it was amusing', 'I ran away because it was terrifying' and 'I remonstrated because it was an objectionable proposal' which is absent from explanations in terms of statements of fact. But in spite of this A-sentences do not give complete explanations. This is partly because the explanatory force is inversely proportional to the obviousness of the tautology. 'I objected because it was objectionable' implies that I had some reasons for objecting but does not even begin to say what they were.

And even in the most tautological-seeming cases the A-sentence only shows that my choice was not unusual; it does not explain why I chose. One often refrains from objecting to things that are objectionable. In addition to believing that the A-word is applicable, I must have a pro-attitude towards the reaction; and, though the reaction may be anybody's, the pro-attitude must be mine. My belief that a book will amuse or enlighten me (or you) is not a sufficient explanation of my choice unless I also have a pro-attitude towards my (or your) being amused or enlightened.[1]

If a man were asked why he chose this car rather than that he might reply 'because it has more leg-room' or 'because it is more comfortable'. The second reply is nearer than the first to giving a full reason. 'Why do you choose a comfortable car?' has an odder ring than 'Why do you choose a car with more leg-room?'. But even so, it is not a full reply; and it is in some ways less adequate. The descriptive sentence gives more information about the car; while the A-sentence contextually implies that it has some of the attributes that make cars comfortable without specifying them. On the other hand, the A-sentence states what is only implied by the descriptive sentence, that the choice turned on the question of superior comfort. Neither gives a full explanation since it would not be logically odd to ask: 'Why did you want a comfortable car?'.

1. Failure to distinguish between the reaction concerned (which may be anybody's) and the pro-attitude towards it (which must be the agent's) is partly responsible for the philosophical muddle over 'egoism'. Your being hungry may, in one sense, be the reason for my sharing the last crust with you; but, in another sense, the reason is that I want to relieve your distress.

This point is obscured by the fact that A-words can acquire a pro- or con-force because people normally have only one of these attitudes to the reaction concerned. Thus because people, on the whole, like being amused and dislike being bored, 'because it is amusing (boring)' may be given and taken as a complete reason for reading (refusing to read) a book. But this only applies if and when the contextual background includes the relevant attitude. It would be excessively tedious if we had to give *full* explanations on all occasions.

4. *G-sentences, 'ought' and 'right'*. The role of G-sentences must be examined at length later; here it is only necessary to remark that 'because I thought it right (my duty)' is never, by itself, a complete explanation of why someone does something; nor is it a logically complete reason for choosing. If 'it was the right thing to do' and 'it was my duty' are taken to be statements of (non-natural) fact, they suffer from the same logical incompleteness as explanations of action as do all other statements of fact. Before they can be invoked as explanations they must at least be transformed into 'because I thought (or knew or believed) it was my duty'; and even this will not do. For a gerundive belief no more explains an action than any other belief unless 'and I had a pro-attitude towards doing my duty' is added.

In practice this addition is never made because it is contextually implied. For the phrase 'I thought it was my duty' is a Janus-phrase which we use not just to express a belief but to express a special pro-attitude towards doing something, namely the 'sense of duty'. It is logically odd to ask a man why he does something when he has said that he believes it to be his duty, because this phrase contextually implies that he has a pro-attitude towards doing his duty. Since there are no logical limits to the possible objects of pro-attitudes there is nothing absurd about having a pro-attitude towards doing one's duty as such.

The same applies to explanations of conduct in terms of fittingness or obedience to a moral rule. We often explain both why we did something and why we intend to do something by saying that it is fitting or appropriate to a situation or that it is in accordance with a moral rule. But these explanations are only logically complete if they contextually imply a pro-attitude to doing what is fitting or to obeying the rule; and this, in practice, they always do. But a part of an explanation that is so obvious that it can in practice be left out must not, on that account, be assumed to be unnecessary.

CHAPTER 9

Motives

[1]

IN the last chapter I mentioned a number of expressions that can be used in such a way that they block any further attempt to ask the question 'What shall I do?' or the question 'Why did you do that?'. And I tried to show that a number of possible candidates for this role fail to fulfil it and are only given and taken as full explanations in ordinary life because of their contextual implications.

In this chapter I shall examine a number of explanations that are altogether different in form. These are explanations which refer, not to the facts of the case, to the circumstances or characteristics of the circumstances, but to the regularity of the agent's behaviour, to what may be called broadly his 'disposition' to act in that way in those circumstances. And here again we shall find that some dispositional accounts fill the bill while others do not.

(1) *Explanation in terms of habit.* As usual the most lowly type of dispositional explanation is one that tells us little, if anything, more than that the action was only to be expected. It's what he always does in those circumstances. Such explanations differ from explanations in terms of physical laws or reflexes only in that habits are acquired and can sometimes be abandoned. The similarity between habits and behaviour as a natural object, behaviour that can be subsumed under laws which also apply to things, is marked by our calling habits 'second nature'; and the fact that such explanations can be complete – (so far as they go; for there is a sense in which no mere generalization *explains*) – without reference to a pro-attitude constitutes no exception to the rule. For a man whose action is explained in terms of a habit does not choose

122

to do what he does. He may have deliberately acquired the habit; but that is another matter. I may have a reason or motive for putting on my trousers in the morning by reference to which I could defend my action as a proper one, for example that I want to keep warm or do not wish to outrage the conventions of society; but these are not explanations of why I did it this morning. I did it from force of habit.

(2) *Explanations in terms of character.* These resemble explanations in terms of habit in that the because-clause asserts not a cause (antecedent event) but a uniformity; but the uniformity is not in this case of the single-track or relatively restricted type. In the case of reflex action both stimulus and response are relatively specific. In the case of habits they are wider; and when an action is explained in terms of character they are wider still. If we say that Jones helped the blind man across the road because he is a kindly person, we are committed to more than the assertion that he always helps blind men across the road or even that he always helps those in distress. Our hearer is entitled to expect to find Jones inquiring after the health of old ladies and giving lollipops to children. Though there is no definite range of things that he must do to count as kindly, he must not omit too many of them.

Character-explanations differ from habit-explanations in other ways also; but they have one important point in common. You could not explain a man's behaving as he does by saying that he is kindly, honest, or courageous unless he regularly does kindly, honest, or courageous things. The most important respect in which they differ from habit-explanations is that, while habit-explanations conflict with choice – a man does not choose to do what he does from force of habit – character-explanations do not. To say that a man did something because he is a kindly person is compatible with, but does not entail, his having chosen to do it. The names of virtues and vices are, as we shall see, character-words, and explanations of action in terms of these traits of character lie half-way between habit-explanations and the motive-explanations to be considered in the next section.

Character-explanations, therefore, do not constitute a distinct class. Their function is to explain an action without our committing ourselves either to asserting or denying that the action was one that the agent chose to do. A man may act from habitual honesty or because he decides to be honest, and to say that he told the truth on some occasion because he is an honest man is not to commit oneself to saying whether his truth-telling was chosen or habitual. The crucial contrast is between habit- and motive-explanations; and I shall now try to show that, while habit-explanations are logically complete since they do not require any reference to a pro-attitude, motive-explanations are only complete when such a reference is contextually implied. This is an important point since attempts have been made to construe motive-explanations in terms of a disposition or tendency to act in a certain way and thus to make them analogous to habit-explanations.

[2]

EXPLANATIONS IN TERMS OF MOTIVES

In ordinary life to ask what someone's motive in doing something was is usually to imply that the motive was a disreputable one; but this must not blind us to the fact that everything which a man chooses to do is susceptible of a motive-explanation. A motiveless action or 'acte gratuit' is logically impossible; for it is not something that a man could be said to 'decide' or 'choose' to do and so would not count as an 'action'. It is, of course, possible to do something apparently aimless, for example for the purpose of proving that a motiveless action is possible; but this is foolish, since the action in fact has a motive, namely to prove the possibility of motiveless action.

There is no special class of motive-words. Motives are often referred to by means of abstract nouns such as love, hatred, fear, greed, ambition, and jealousy; but the corresponding adjectives are often used to give habit-explanations and therefore not to impute a motive. Motive-explanations are usually given only in the case of characteristic and therefore regular conduct; but this is not necessarily so. A man cannot be called 'generous' unless he acts generously fairly often; but he can act once and once only on a generous impulse and we could then say that his motive was generosity, however uncharacteristic.

I shall now try to show that motive-explanations cannot be analysed wholly in terms of dispositions or habits or tendencies to act in a certain way; and to do this it is necessary to say something about the general distinction between explanations in terms of occurrences and explanations in terms of dispositions.[1]

If we wish to explain why a piece of glass broke we may either say that it was struck with a certain force or that it was brittle. The first explanation refers to an occurrence which was the antecedent cause of the breakage; but the second does not. To say that the glass is brittle is to assert what Professor Ryle calls a "law-like hypothetical proposition" to the effect that "the glass, *if* sharply struck or twisted etc., *would* not dissolve or stretch or evaporate but fly into fragments". Ryle then claims that motive-explanations are of this second, dispositional type. A motive is not an event or force inside you which functions as an antecedent cause; but is a disposition or tendency to behave in a certain way when certain events occur. There are, of course, many different types of disposition, for example habits, capacities, skills, and propensities; so that to call a motive a 'disposition' is not to confuse it with dispositions of other types. The cardinal points of the theory are that a motive-explanation can always be translated into a hypothetical or more or less complicated set of hypotheticals, and that the occurrences mentioned in the if-clauses of these hypotheticals must all be public, witnessable occurrences.

Now it is true that many of the words that we use to explain

1. This contrast is treated at length by Professor G. Ryle: *The Concept of Mind*, chapters 4 and 5.

conduct do operate in just this way, and some of the words that we use to give motive-explanations are also used to give purely dispositional explanations. But it does not follow that the two types of explanation are the same; for the same words can be used to give explanations of different types.

Consider, for example, the word 'patriotism'. Ryle is mainly concerned to refute the theory that a motive-explanation must necessarily refer to sensations (whether genuine or of the kind that philosophers sometimes postulate). In the case of patriotism he admits that there are sensations, swellings of the bosom, and sinkings of the heart, which might be called 'feelings of patriotism'; but he denies that an explanation in terms of patriotism must necessarily refer to these and, what is more important, that these feelings can be construed as internal prods which cause the patriotic man to behave as he does. Both these contentions seem to me to be correct. We decide whether a man is patriotic or not by what he does, not by what he feels; and even if he does feel his bosom swell this feeling is not an antecedent cause of his behaviour.

But what follows from this is not that patriotism is a disposition or that to explain someone's action as being due to his patriotism is to give a dispositional explanation. It may be to do this; but it may also be to do something else. For granted that he acts in these ways, it is still open to us to ask what is his motive for so acting. His actions are quite consistent with his wanting to gain kudos or his having his eye on the post-war political scene; and they are also consistent with his wanting to help his country. And it is only in this last case that we should call him 'truly patriotic', since patriotism consists in doing things for the sake of one's country. As Aristotle would have said, this 'for the sake of' clause is part of the essence of every motive, and it is just this clause that distinguishes a motive-explanation from a dispositional explanation.

The attempt to construe motives as dispositions fails also for another reason. It is an essential point in this theory that the protasis clause of the law-like hypothetical should refer, not to some internal event, but to something that happens to a man. Ryle adduces the example of politeness. "For example, a man passes his neighbour the salt from politeness; but his politeness is merely his inclination to pass the salt when it is wanted, as well as to perform a thousand other courtesies of the same general kind. So besides the question 'for what reason did he pass the salt?' there is the quite different question 'what made him pass the salt at that moment to that neighbour?'. This question is probably answered by 'he heard his neighbour ask for it' or 'he noticed his neighbour's eye wandering over the table', or something of the sort."[1]

Now 'politeness' can, but need not be, a motive word. A man can be polite from force of habit, and in this case Ryle's account is correct; the force of 'he acted from politeness' is merely that of relating what he did on this occasion to his ways of behaving on countless similar occasions. But 'politeness' is not a typical motive-word and is, indeed, not normally used as a motive-word at all. If we wish to add that he wanted to be of service to his neighbour (which would be necessary to make our explanation a motive one), we should tend to call it 'kindness', 'thoughtfulness', or 'considerateness'.[2]

[3]

But it would still be possible to construe motives as dispositions if a purely dispositional account could be given of enjoying, wanting, and the other pro-attitudes to one of which every

1. Op. cit., p. 113.
2. The same may be said of another of Ryle's examples, 'vanity' (op. cit., p. 86). On page 325 Ryle says: "We know quite well why the heroine took one of her morning letters to read in solitude, for the novelist gives us the required explanation. The heroine recognized her lover's handwriting on the envelope." But, although the novelist does not tell us so, it is logically necessary to add "and she wanted to read her lover's letter". This is necessary to complete the explanation; but novels would be excessively tedious if novelists did not take this point for granted.

motive-explanation must refer. I shall now try to show that pro- and con-words cannot be construed in a purely dispositional way, although they have dispositional uses and in some of them the dispositional element is more prominent than in others.

Ryle offers a dispositional account of enjoying which runs as follows. "To enjoy doing something, to want to do it and not to want to do anything else are different ways of phrasing the same thing. . . . To say that a person has been enjoying digging . . . is to say that he dug with his whole heart in his task, i.e. that he dug, wanting to dig and not wanting to do anything else (or nothing) instead. His digging was a propensity-fulfilment." "Delight, amusement, etc. are moods, and moods are not feelings." "In ascribing a specific motive to a person we are describing the sorts of things that he tends to try to do or bring about."[1]

Later Ryle distinguishes enjoying from other types of disposition, such as habits and professions, on the grounds that a person can only be said to 'enjoy' an activity if he tends to be wrapped up in daydreams and memories of it and to be absorbed in conversation and books about it. And the journalist who is keen on fishing "does not have to try to concentrate on fishing as he has to try to concentrate on speeches. He concentrates without trying. This is a large part of what 'keen on' means."[2]

This analysis of the differences between what we might call 'pro-dispositions' and other dispositions requires a reference to being 'wrapped up in', being 'absorbed in', and 'trying'. And all of these imply pro-attitudes; but it is not clear that they are all dispositional. Many pro-words, 'enjoy' for example, have dispositional uses. A man can be said to enjoy music even if he is not now listening to a concert. But this entails more than that he should frequently listen to music when he has no duties and be annoyed at interruptions while listening. He must enjoy it in the non-dispositional sense in which he can be said to be at this moment enjoying listening to Bach. A

1. Op. cit., pp. 108–12.　　　　2. Op. cit., p. 133.

man could not be said to enjoy or to be fond of music if he only once enjoyed a concert; but he could be said to have enjoyed the concert if he never enjoyed any other music before or after. Some pro-words are always used in a dispositional way, for example being 'fond of', 'keen on', or 'interested in'; but even these entail enjoying the activity concerned in the non-dispositional sense.

There seem to be two main reasons for trying to construe 'enjoying' in a purely dispositional way. (a) In the first place enjoyment is not an episode or occurrence. No one would call a man's enjoying a hot bath an 'episode in his career'; but the argument from the ordinary use of language is double-edged, and no one would call it a 'disposition' either. No doubt, if a man wallows long and frequently in hot baths when he is not compelled or obliged to do so, we are entitled to conclude that he enjoys them; but the conclusion goes beyond the evidence. And this is shown by the fact that unphilosophical people are more inclined to say that 'Only I can know whether I am really enjoying something' is more of a truism than an absurdity, a point to which I shall return later. The disposition-occurrence contrast is a piece of logical terminology tailor-made to elucidate the explanations that we give of non-human phenomena such as the brittleness of glass or the solubility of sugar. It is most valuable in these cases since it saves us from any temptation we might have to think of brittleness or solubility as antecedent causes. And it performs a similar service in connexion with many explanations of human conduct, for example habits, skills, and competences. But there is no reason to suppose that it will elucidate all our talk about men.

(b) The most important reason for the attempt is undoubtedly the belief that, if we cannot translate sentences about enjoyment into hypotheticals in which the if-clauses refer to publicly observable events and the then-clauses to publicly observable behaviour, we shall be committed to a belief in a Private World in which events occur that can only be witnessed by the man 'inside whom' they are going on.

It is impossible for me to go into the controversy about introspection here and I can only be dogmatic. There is point in such assertions as 'Only I can know that I am in pain, or listening to music, or enjoying the music'. Why else should doctors often ask us to attend to and make reports about our own pains? And how could we wonder whether a man is really interested or politely dissembling his boredom? A keen eye can often detect the stifled yawn; but there may have been no yawn to detect.

This concession to the Private World theory involves no dubious faculty of introspection. From Jones's posture and demeanour I cannot tell whether he is listening intently to Bach or so stricken with grief that he hasn't heard a note. To discover which is the case I have to ask him; and I trust what he says, not because I can correlate his statements with states of his mind inaccessible to me, but because I have found him to be trustworthy on occasions on which I am in a position to check what he says. But Jones's position is different; he can tell whether he is listening or not; but he does not need a special faculty to reveal this to him.

If a man claims to know that the dog caught the rabbit, it makes sense to ask him how he knows and he may reply "because I saw it"; and the notion of introspection as an internal faculty arises partly from supposing that the question "How do you know that you saw it?" requires to be answered in the same sort of way. But all that is necessary for him to be able to substantiate his claim is that he should have seen it and that he should know the English language. In the same way it makes sense to ask a man how he knows that the violins played sharp, but if he answers "because I heard them", it makes no sense to ask how he knows that he heard them. Nor does it make sense to ask a man how he knows that he is in pain. He feels the pain and knows that 'I am in pain' is the proper way to describe his feeling; he neither has nor requires a special faculty, over and above seeing, hearing, or feeling, by means of which he knows that he sees, hears, or feels. Perception verbs have a question-blocking role similar to that of pro-words. Just as the latter block the question 'Why did you do that?', so the former block the question 'How do you know?'. We can, however, change the question to 'Are you sure?'.

Nevertheless, although a man cannot see or hear or in any way 'witness' his own seeing or hearing, he can observe his own listening; for 'observe' here means 'attend to'. There are four comments that must be made on this situation. (a) This sort of observing is not analogous to seeing and is not infallible, and it therefore gives no support to the searchlight theory of introspection. (b) To attend to one's own listening, as opposed to attending to what one is listening to, is a rare and sophisticated thing to do. (c) A man who does this is almost certain to listen less well than a man who attends to what he is listening to, since it is notoriously difficult to do two things carefully at once. (d) It is logically impossible that all our observation should be self-observation of this kind. For a man could not pay attention to his own listening to music if he was not listening to music, and this entails that he is both hearing and paying some attention to the music. I shall return to this point in the next chapter since it has an important bearing on enjoyment.

'Enjoyment' is neither the name of a type of disposition nor the name of a type of occurrence. It is primarily a pro-word the function of which is to block the question 'Why did you do that?'. It is not the only pro-word and it would be a mistake to try to explain all pro-attitudes in terms of enjoyment, though not nearly such a grave mistake as to try to interpret them in terms of desire or pleasure. A more detailed discussion of the different types of pro- and con-attitude belongs to psychology; but one final caution is necessary. Just as there are really no A-words or G-words, so there are really no pro-words or con-words. A word has a pro- or con-force when it has the force of making any further explanation of conduct unnecessary. But almost any word can be used with this force if the context implies it; and any word that is normally used with a pro- or a con-force can, on occasion, be used with no such force or even with the force opposite to its usual one.

The logic of language reflects empirical truths that are so general and obvious that we can afford to ignore exceptions; and most people agree in their attitudes towards certain bodily sensations. This agreement is reflected in the logic of ordinary language in two ways. In the first place, words such as wounded, gored, mangled, bruised, out-of-joint, frost-bitten, pinched, scalded, and burned can be used to describe bodily conditions of which a man can be, and in severe cases often is, unconscious. They can also be used to describe one's own sensations. But, except in the driest of medical contexts, they are almost always used with a con-force. So that if we know that a man has frost-bite and is not unconscious it is needless to add that he is *suffering* from frost-bite. And 'because I have got cramp' is a complete answer to 'why did you move your foot?'.

Secondly words such as 'pain' and 'hurt' that are normally used with a con-force can also be used as generic expressions to refer to those sensations and bodily conditions towards which most people normally have a con-attitude. They then become descriptive, and as far as I can see there is no reason why 'enjoy', 'detest', 'like', and 'dislike' should not go the same way. It is sophisticated, but not logically impossible to enjoy a painful sensation and to want to prolong it; there are no logical limits to the possibilities of masochistic enjoyment. But this fact in no way weakens the logical thesis that, for a man to explain fully why he does something, he must at some point or other use a word with a pro- or a con-force, even though his case may be so complicated that he has to make use of a whole hierarchy of expressions.

CHAPTER 10

Egoism and Hedonism

[1]

ETHICAL theories are often divided into teleological theories, according to which the notions of duty, rightness, and obligation are supposed to be defined in terms of or in some other way dependent on the notions of goodness and purpose, and deontological theories, according to which the notion of obligation is incapable of being analysed or made dependent in this way. We saw in the first two chapters that, while the main ethical tradition from Plato onwards has been teleological, intuitionist theories are almost always deontological. The difference between the intuitionists and their predecessors (except Kant) is therefore more profound than might at first appear. It is not only that they make moral judgements theoretical or that they give a special account of how we come to know moral truths; these points would be interesting only to the professional philosopher. A point of more general interest is that they put an emphasis on the Sense of Duty as a unique motive which the older theories would not have put. Rightness and Obligation are, they say, the central concepts of ethics; goodness and purpose are of minor importance.

In the third part of this book I shall argue in favour of a modified teleological theory. I shall not try to *define* deontological words in teleological terms, but try to show that pro-words are logically prior to deontological words in a looser sense. They form part of the contextual background in which alone deontological words can be understood, while the reverse is not the case. In this chapter I shall examine one of the most important arguments for according such a pre-eminent place to the sense of duty. This argument is nowhere, so far as I know, clearly stated; it seems rather to be an assumption that certain writers do not question.

Kant was the first philosopher to make deontological concepts central in ethics in a clear and uncompromising way. As Professor Paton puts it: "Kant knew, of course, that he was trying to do something which no one had succeeded in doing before – namely, to set forth the first principles of morality *apart from all considerations of self-interest.*"[1]

The deontological argument starts by assuming that every action which is not done from the sense of duty is done from 'inclination' or from 'self-interest', and it further assumes that if an action is done 'from inclination' it is done *in order to satisfy this inclination.* Moreover an inclination is construed in the way that Hobbes construes desires and aversions, as a sort of itch or craving that I wish to satisfy. Eighteenth-century writers make frequent use of the word 'uneasiness' in this connexion, thus assimilating all voluntary action to that of a man who moves his limbs to remove some discomfort. Now from these premises it is easy to pass to the conclusion that all action, except that motivated by the Sense of Duty, is really *selfish.* Suppose, for example, that I do what everyone would call an 'altruistic action', such as giving money to a charity or helping a friend in need at great cost to myself and without hope of reward; and suppose that I do this, not because I think it my duty but because it is just what I want to do. Although the action is apparently altruistic, it is easy to make out that it is covertly egoistic. For, so the story goes, I do not do these things in order to help the recipients of the charity or in order to help my friend, but in order to satisfy my own desire, to allay my itch, to eliminate my uneasiness. Fundamentally I am indifferent to the welfare of others and concerned only to promote my own pleasure and minimize my

1. *The Categorical Imperative*, p. 15 (my italics). The assumption that Duty and Self-interest are the only two motives (or types of motive) comes out clearly in the same author's *The Moral Law*, pp. 14, 15, 19, 25, 31, 35, 46 and 52.

own pain; and surely to be concerned only with this is to be selfish?

Now, if it were true that all actions except those done from the sense of duty were really selfish, it would indeed be necessary to treat the sense of duty as a special, and as the only morally good motive. For two things are quite certain: (a) that men do in fact often act altruistically, and (b) that moral codes universally advocate altruism and condemn selfishness; and this they could hardly do if men were necessarily selfish. But in fact the premise on which this argument is based is a complete muddle.

[2]

Hedonism. I shall examine the accusation of egoism later; but since its plausibility depends largely on the view that all action which is not inspired by the sense of duty is aimed at getting pleasure for the agent or avoiding pain, it is necessary first to examine hedonism. This is the doctrine that all desire is for pleasure, and it has not been held nearly so often as its opponents suppose.[1]

For the hedonist is not propounding a psychologist's generalization about human nature, but a philosopher's paradox. He seems to be donning the mantle of a Rochefoucauld or a Freud and telling us (what we all know) that men mistake their own motives. They may think that they desire office or riches or the public good; but their real aim is something quite else. The only difference – and it is a difference that shows that the hedonist is a philosopher, not a psychologist – is that he seems to be telling us not that we *sometimes* mistake our aims, but that we *always* do. *Whenever*, he seems to say,

1. It was not, for example, held by Hobbes, who is always called a 'hedonist'. Hobbes takes the trouble to list a large number of desires, for office, riches, etc. Can it seriously be maintained that he is saying "Ambition is the desire for office; but don't bother to remember this. In fact no one desires office; men only desire pleasure."?

a man thinks he desires something other than pleasure, he is always mistaken.

But the hedonist is not really concerned to deny the obvious fact that people enjoy eating and drinking, playing golf and doing cross-word puzzles and even, on occasion, helping their neighbours. Rightly or wrongly, he is inviting us to construe 'pleasure' as an internal accusative after the verbs 'desire' and 'enjoy'. He is like a man who says (paradoxically) that we only see colours, when he means (truistically) that everything we see is coloured. This thesis is a paradox only because it seems to entail that we do not see men and trees and football matches. Similarly the truism that bomber pilots only aim at targets seems to be, though it in fact is not, incompatible with the statement that they aim at docks, factories, and marshalling yards. Except when 'target' means 'the round thing you shoot at on a practice range', it means 'whatever you aim at'. The word 'target' would not appear in the list of targets which a squadron-leader gives when he briefs his pilots, and it would be absurd for a pilot to say "I can't really aim at that factory, because, you know, people can only aim at targets".

The confusion between objective accusatives after the verbs 'desire' and 'enjoy' (e.g. enjoy food, climbing, a game of cricket, listening to Bach) and the internal accusative (desire pleasure, enjoy a good time) has led some philosophers to dismiss hedonism as a theory so obviously false that it must be a puzzle to know how it ever came to be held. Professor Vivas, for example, uses the well-known Paradox of Hedonism to refute it. The more you pursue pleasure, the less of it you get. "The glutton wolfs the food, the drunkard gulps the drink, and thus they put up with stuff of dubious quality. The result is ironic, even paradoxical; the man intent on pleasure is a poor sensualist and is likely to enjoy less of it than the man disinterested enough in pleasure to be able to discriminate the objective qualities of the objects of apprehension."[1]

This criticism altogether misses the mark; for the hedonist

1. *The Moral Life and the Ethical Life*, p. 67.

will reply – as Mill did – that Mr Vivas equates pleasure with gluttony and drunkenness and then contrasts these with the 'discrimination' that is the aim of the gourmet. But this, in the hedonist's terminology, is to dispute the rival claims of the pleasure of getting drunk and the pleasure of discrimination. Both the drunkard and the gourmet aim at pleasure; but what pleases each of them is a different thing. It may be an empirical truth that the gourmet gets more pleasure than the drunkard; but, if so, it is not because he is 'disinterested in pleasure' while the drunkard is not. A man may drink Chateau Laffitte because he enjoys it or because he wants to display his wealth or his ability to distinguish it from Chateau Latour or because he wants to get drunk. In the last three cases we might say that he drinks it as a means to something else or with an ulterior motive. But in the first case he does not; what pleases him is the drinking.

Suppose that a man were to say to himself: "The only thing in life worth going for is pleasure; let others waste their time reading books, drinking wine, doing cross-word puzzles, playing cricket. These are only means to pleasure. I, for my part, will have none of them. I shall go direct for the pleasure." Such a man would indeed make the mistake that Mr Vivas and many other critics attribute to hedonists and he would certainly fail to achieve his object; for it is a logical truth that you cannot enjoy the pleasure of playing cricket without playing cricket. But it is not a mistake that hedonists have either made themselves or supposed to be at all common.

What the hedonist really does is to treat pleasure as a common ingredient in all the various things that we find pleasant and to say that when a man does something he always does it either because he expects it to be pleasant or because he believes it to be a means to obtaining something pleasant. To desire something is to expect it to be pleasant and to enjoy something is to find it pleasant. 'Doing something for its own sake' means the same as 'doing something for the sake of pleasure'. But this is a mistake, not an empirical mistake about the sorts of things that people desire and enjoy, but a logical mistake about the use of pro-words. And we must now see why.

'Pleasure', like most of the abstract nouns in the philosopher's vocabulary, does all very well for a chapter heading or a short, summarizing phrase. In the body of the chapter we should be more concerned with 'pleasing', 'pleasant', 'being pleased with', and 'pleasures'. And, if he concerned himself with these, it would be immediately apparent that the philosopher was up to the well-known trick of using in a very general way a word or set of words that normally have a much more restricted use. These words are certainly pro-words; if a man says that he finds doing something pleasant, it is logically odd to go on asking why he does it. But 'pleasant' and its cognates are not the only pro-words and they do not enter into the more serious or important cases of choice.

There are many things that we do for their own sake, among them lying in the sun, doing Symbolic Logic, listening to music, and giving a helping hand to a neighbour. But only the first (and, in some cases, the third) of these would normally be said to be done 'for the sake of pleasure'. A man who says that he listens to Beethoven's *Grosse Fuge* or reads *Paradise Lost* because he finds it *pleasant* either has a lot to learn about music or literature or, more probably, is abusing the English language. The hedonist would have done better to express his theory, as Spinoza in fact does, in terms of 'enjoyment'; for this is a word that can be used of the most absorbing, profound, and noble pursuits as well as of the most trivial. Ordinary folk enjoy doing cross-word puzzles; but saints also enjoy the beatific vision.

The antipathy which is felt towards hedonism has its source partly in the choice of the word 'pleasure' as the key pro-attitude word. People have in fact advocated what we should ordinarily call 'a life of pleasure' as the best type of life; but the more reputable of the philosophers called 'hedonists' (for example, Epicurus, Spinoza, and Mill) have not done so. Nevertheless their choice of the word 'pleasure' is, as we have seen, unfortunate; and so is the choice of the word 'desire'.

For this word is most prominently used for the carnal desires and it is difficult altogether to free one's mind from the usual associations of a word.

Since carnal desires are desires for pleasant sensations, hedonists who represent all motives as 'desires' have misled their readers into supposing that, according to their theory, the goal of all action must be some delicious sensation. And, curiously enough, this has been accepted by many philosophers as an adequate account of all motives except the sense of duty. They have represented these motives as 'desires' or 'inclinations' and even called them all *sensuous*; and it is then but a short step to regarding them as disreputable or beneath the dignity of a rational man. But is the desire to help one's neighbour, to feed the poor, or to free slaves a sensuous desire? If so, the word 'sensuous' loses its sting.

And the hedonist's use of 'pleasure' has led to another unfortunate consequence. It has led philosophers to debate whether people enjoy an activity or the pleasure of the activity and to treat this question as one that might be settled by introspection. Now it makes sense to ask whether a mountain climber climbs for the sake of climbing or for the sake of getting a view from the top; but it makes no sense to ask whether he climbs for the sake of climbing or for the sake of the pleasure of climbing. 'Jones enjoys climbing' and 'Jones enjoys the pleasure of climbing' mean the same thing except that, since 'pleasure' is a narrower word than 'enjoy', the latter indicates the general type of enjoyment involved. ('Jones enjoys the pleasures of climbing' is, of course, quite different; for this implies that he enjoys such things as the view from the top, the long cool drink in the pub afterwards, or the plaudits of the press.)

A man who enjoys a bottle of wine, a game of cricket, or a symphony does not enjoy his own enjoyment any more than a man who observes the antics of a clown observes himself observing – though he might do so. But again this would be a highly sophisticated thing to do, and, since it is difficult to do two things well at the same time, he would almost certainly not enjoy the wine, the cricket, or the symphony as much as he would if he stuck to business. And again it is logically impossible that all our enjoyments should be of this type. For one cannot just 'enjoy'; one must enjoy *something*. And if a man enjoys his own enjoyment (where 'enjoyment' is not an internal accusative but the object that he enjoys), then his enjoyment must be enjoyment of something. A man cannot enjoy his enjoyment of a game of cricket without enjoying the game.

[3]

Egoism. Hedonism would not be an important philosophical theory if it did not seem to entail egoism, which is either the theory that men can only choose to do what is in their own interest or that it is only rational to do this. Genuinely altruistic action is either a logical impossibility or the prerogative of dupes and fools. Now, since it is obvious that moral codes commend altruism, we must, if the second version of egoism be true, either say that the notion of duty is one that sensible men will see through and discard or that doing one's duty is only long-term selfishness. And it is because each of these alternatives is so unplausible that philosophers have tried to show that there is a special motive called the 'Sense of Duty', which cannot be treated as a 'desire'. All other motives, it is assumed, are desires and the man who acts from them is selfish. Thus the protagonists of the sense of duty accept as an axiom what is really the most absurd point in their opponents' theory.

If we remember the confusion between an internal accusative and an object, it is not difficult to see how this absurdity has come to be accepted. Consider the following conversation.

A. Why are you buying those apples?
B. Because I want to give them to my sick aunt.
A. Why do you want to do that?
B. Because I *do*; that's all.

A's second question has point, since B's reply to the first does not necessarily imply a direct pro-attitude. He might have been currying favour, and in that case it would be quite proper to suggest that he is 'really' being selfish, because he was not really concerned for his aunt's welfare at all. But if he accepts B's second reply as the truth there is no further room for any questioning. But A is a philosopher and insists on probing a little deeper. "You want to", he says; "I suppose you mean that you like doing that sort of thing." B, not being a philosopher, falls straight into the first trap. "Why yes," he says, "I suppose I do like doing that sort of thing." Sure now of his victim, A continues: "You do it because you *like* it. So what you *really* wanted was not your aunt's happiness but your own pleasure." And B falls into the second trap; his selfishness is now revealed.

But A's argument not only reaches a conclusion that we can all see to be absurd; it is logically untenable. Paradoxically it is in cases where a man is really seeking his own pleasure that the absurdity of A's argument comes out most clearly. For, if he insists on translating 'I wanted to give happiness to my aunt' into 'I wanted the pleasure of giving happiness to my aunt', he must also translate the latter into 'I wanted the pleasure of the pleasure of giving happiness to my aunt', and so on for ever.

Benevolence, sympathy, and compassion are direct pro-attitudes towards the welfare and con-attitudes towards the suffering of others. And to explain someone's conduct in terms of a pro-attitude is not to lapse into covert egoism. For benevolence is not a desire to satisfy my own benevolent inclinations or desires, impulses, or itches; it is the desire to do good to another; and the accusation of covert egoism rests solely on the confusion between the object of desire (what the man wants), and the internal accusative after the pro-attitude verbs, 'want', 'desire', 'like', and 'enjoy'. This confusion is itself due to the philosophical habit of representing all pro-attitudes as 'desires'; since, of all these verbs, 'to desire' is the one that has the most obvious correlative, namely 'satisfaction'. But a man does not desire satisfaction in the same sense that he desires food or drink or the welfare of his neighbour.

If I want to relieve the distress of a beggar, I want to relieve the distress of a beggar; I do not want my own happiness, pleasure, or satisfaction. Likewise if I like giving pleasure to my sick aunt, what I like is giving pleasure to my sick aunt, not my own liking or even the glow of satisfaction that I might get from being benevolent. Indeed, if the latter were what I really liked, I should be doomed to eternal disappointment, because I could never get just that glow unless I had acted for the sake of giving pleasure and not for the sake of the glow.

A man may give sixpence to a beggar for any of the following reasons: to be seen and applauded by others for his generosity, to get the thanks of the beggar, in the hope that the bread he cast on the waters would one day return to him, to quiet his conscience, or to satisfy his generosity. In each of these cases except the last the relieving of the beggar's distress might plausibly be represented as a means to the agent's own happiness and he might well be accused of covert egoism, because in each case he was really indifferent to the beggar's welfare.

It is the last case that is important; for if we put it in this way, we are apt to suppose that a man who does something 'to satisfy his generosity' is concerned, not with the beggar's welfare, but with his own satisfaction. But this phrase is a misleading way of saying that his motive was generosity and this entails that he gave the beggar sixpence *in order to relieve the beggar's distress*. If this too is covert egoism, the accusation altogether loses its sting. It is a tautology that all my desires, inclinations, wantings, likings, and enjoyments are mine; but it is a plain falsehood that what I desire, like, want, or enjoy is necessarily my own pleasure or my own anything else; and it is also a plain falsehood that a man who does what he wants to do or 'acts from inclination' always acts selfishly.

To be selfish is not to do what one wants to do or enjoys

doing, but to be hostile or indifferent to the welfare of others. It comes out in two ways. (a) A man whose dominant desires were for his own pleasures (in the ordinary, not the philosopher's sense) and who seldom or never wanted to do good to others would be a selfish man. (b) A man who does what he wants to do or what he likes, *when he does it at the expense of others*, is a selfish man, even if what he does is not in itself selfish. To eat when one is hungry is certainly not altruistic; but it is not selfish either. What is selfish is to eat the last biscuit when others are hungry too. The man who *prefers* to give the last biscuit to his neighbour to eating it himself, whether or not he is morally better than the man who does it because he thinks it his duty, is certainly not a selfish man.

It is therefore quite unnecessary to invoke the Sense of Duty to account for the occurrence of altruistic action. Indeed the argument that is commonly used to show that altruism is disguised selfishness when it is not conscientious altruism can be turned against conscientiousness itself. If we are made to say that the man who purports to help others from a genuine desire for their welfare is really a covert egoist who only wants to satisfy his own benevolence, why should we not say that the man who purports to help others from a sense of duty is really a covert egoist who only wants to satisfy his sense of duty? The argument is as absurd in the one case as in the other.

Even if it were true that all non-conscientious actions were done in order to satisfy our own desires or inclinations, it would not follow that non-conscientious actions would all be selfish in any usual sense. For the line between 'selfish' and 'altruistic' could still be drawn in the place that we habitually draw it. The difference between the egoist and the altruist would now lie in the fact that the former is inclined or desires to do whatever benefits him at the cost of his neighbours, while the latter is inclined or desires to do what benefits his neighbour even when it is to his own disadvantage. And if both these types of action are called 'selfish' or 'egoistic' in some esoteric, philosophical sense, it is no longer *obvious* that we can only account for self-sacrifice by introducing the sense of duty as a special motive which alone is not 'selfish' in this strange sense. And, as we shall see, this device does not even do the job assigned to it; since the man who helps others because he thinks it his *duty* to do so is not an altruist. He may or may not be a morally better man than the altruist, but that is another matter.

CHAPTER 11

Advice and Exhortation

[1]

PRACTICAL language is not only used for making up our own minds what to do; it is also used for telling others what to do, and there are four main types of situation in which we do this.

(a) Cases of giving instructions about the best, simplest, most convenient, etc., way of doing what the recipient of the instructions has already decided to do or of achieving an end that he has already decided to aim at. These cases do not seem to give rise to any philosophical difficulties since, although such instructions cannot be identified with hypothetical statements in the form 'You will only succeed if you do . . .', their value as instructions depends mainly on the truth of the hypotheticals with which they are intimately connected; and this is an empirical matter.

(b) Cases in which Jones tries to help Smith to solve a problem of choice, which is not just a problem about means or methods. I shall call these cases of Advice.

(c) Cases in which Jones tries to persuade Smith to do something by using the language of advice without the proper contextual implications. I shall call these cases of Exhortation. The choice of the words 'advice' and 'exhortation' to distinguish the two types of case is somewhat arbitrary; but the distinction between the cases is real and important.

(d) Cases in which Jones commands or orders Smith to do something.

In this chapter I shall consider cases of advice and exhortation.

Advice. It is of the essence of 'advice', as here used, that if Smith accepts Jones's advice he chooses to accept it. Advice is addressed to a free, rational agent who can accept or reject it and who must, if he accepts it, have a pro-attitude towards carrying it out, since his acceptance is a decision on his part to do something. It is not, of course, necessary that he should have any pro-attitude prior to the advice being given; Jones may advise him to do something that it had never occurred to him to do. But it must be something towards which he has a pro-attitude now that he considers it.

Sentences which are not, on the face of them, hortatory but are normally used to state facts, can be used to give advice; but it is clear that they contextually imply more than they state. If Smith asks 'Shall I take an umbrella?', Jones may reply 'I don't think it's likely to rain'; but this only counts as *advice* if it carries certain contextual implications which I shall examine in connexion with A-sentences.

A-sentences in the context of advice. The situation is radically different from that of choosing, since there are now two people involved and we must consider each of their points of view. Since it must be presumed that men intend (and therefore wish for) the natural consequences of their actions, the giving of advice contextually implies a desire on the part of the giver that the advice should be accepted. It would be logically odd to say 'You had better do this, but I hope you won't'. We shall see that this does not imply that advice can never be given disinterestedly. Jones must hope that his advice will be taken, but he need not expect to gain by this.

Secondly, if Jones uses an A-sentence, part of its force will be predictive. The reaction predicted may be anyone's, but the pro-attitude towards this reaction must be Smith's, since it is Smith's problem that he is trying to solve and to this Smith's pro-attitudes are alone relevant.

Once again, it is clear that when an A-sentence is used to give advice it cannot function as an extra premise linking a statement of fact to the decision to accept the advice. Smith's problem is, for example, whether or not to go to the Super cinema this evening. As we have seen, his problem is solved

146

once he has been given a good reason for going, provided that there are no counter-reasons; and, if Jones's advice takes the form of an A-sentence, it must contextually imply that Smith has a pro-attitude towards the connected reaction. Thus if Jones says that there is an amusing or instructive film at the Super this can only count as advice if it is assumed in the context that Smith's problem is how to amuse or instruct himself. And the fact that other people have been amused by the film is not, by itself, a good reason for Smith's going to it. The only good reason is that he himself will be amused, and this is reached by an inductive step from 'many people have been amused'. If we try to construe 'amusingness' or 'instructiveness' as objective properties that do or do not reside in the film, Smith might well ask what reason there is for supposing that because the film has this property he will enjoy it, and that is what he wants to know.

It may sound absurd to say "I know it is enjoyable, but will I enjoy it?" and also absurd to say "I know most people have enjoyed it, but is it enjoyable?"; but these cannot be simultaneously absurd, for it is not absurd to say "I know most people have enjoyed this film, but I don't think I shall". The role of the A-sentence is not to refer to a property or to convert an inductive argument into a deductive one. The sentence is used in this context as a piece of advice and therefore constitutes a solution to Smith's problem, not something from which a solution could be deduced. But it differs from 'If I were you, I should go to the Super' and from 'Go to the Super' in that it contextually implies that Jones has good reasons for giving the advice, and this is but weakly implied or not implied at all in the other formulae.

Let us assume that Smith's problem is whether to go to the Super or not and that Jones knows this. Other assumptions are possible and they modify the analysis in various ways. But it is essential to consider a concrete case and in all cases of advice some assumptions must be gatherable from the background; otherwise Jones does not know what Smith's problem is and he is not competent to give advice. If Jones says there is an entertaining film on he contextually implies the following points:

(a) You are trying to decide whether to go to the Super or not and your decision turns wholly on whether you will be entertained by the film.

(b) I believe that you will be entertained.

(c) I believe this because I know you like thrillers and that the film is a thriller.

It is not suggested that Jones goes through any such train of thought or that this is what his reply 'really means'; still less that he states all this. He has obviously not, for example, stated the reasons on which he bases his advice. But all these points are contextually implied in that, if any of them is absent, Jones is not in a position to give definite advice and ought to reply more warily. If, for example, he does not know Smith's taste in films, he ought to reply "It's a thriller and was very well reviewed", thus giving conditional advice only. The implication would then be, not "Go to the film", but "Go, if you like thrillers". If he happens to know that Smith is bored by thrillers, he certainly ought not to say that the film is 'entertaining', even though he would quite properly say this to someone else; for it is Smith's problem that he is trying to solve and Smith would be justly indignant if the truth came out. The predictive force of 'entertaining' must be that Smith is likely to be entertained; for in this context it is the only thing worth predicting. Jones's reply is not a 'statement of fact' which can be extracted from its context and pronounced true or false; it is a piece of advice that depends for its interpretation on its context. If the right contextual elements are not present, it is deceptive, inappropriate, or irrelevant.

As in the case of choice, the reaction predicted need not be that of the recipient of the advice, but the pro-attitude towards it, the desire that it should occur, must be; for it is his problem that is being considered. If Smith asks whether or not *Charley's Aunt* is an amusing play it may be clear from the context that he is wondering whether it will amuse his children; his own reaction is irrelevant. But Jones's affirmative reply is improper unless he believes that Smith's children will be amused; and it is assumed that Smith has a pro-attitude towards his children's amusement.

This shows the futility of trying to give any general analysis of what is meant by 'X is amusing' divorced from its context. Does it mean that all or most people will be amused or that all people of a certain type will be amused? It means that the relevant person will be amused and this depends in each case on the context. This is obvious in the case of A-words; but we shall see that it also applies to G-words and deontological words, which is less obvious and more important.

It might be argued that the suggestion that an A-sentence combines a generalizing element (People like you have been amused) with a predictive element (You are likely to be amused) simply slurs over the gap which the consequential property theory tried to bridge. But this objection neglects the important distinction between logical and contextual implication. It is not impossible that the generalizing element should be true and the prediction false. And since this is so, we cannot say that the A-sentence either means or entails both of these. For, if it did, it could only be properly used in cases where there is a necessary connexion between the two elements. And since this never occurs, we should have no use for A-sentences at all. Such a demand would set the criteria for their use so high that they could (logically) never be fulfilled. The function of an A-sentence is not that of combining a prediction and a generalization, still less that of supplying some logical cement between the two. It is used to give advice; and its role must therefore be that of predicting the only thing worth predicting in the context, namely that which Smith is concerned to bring about or avoid. Jones could simply say "I bet you (your children) will enjoy it". The special role of the A-sentence is to indicate to Smith that the advice has some inductive backing. It is used to give advice based on reasons without saying what the reasons are, and we can only understand its role if we distinguish the purpose for which it is used from the conditions which limit its use.

The complexity of elements in an A-sentence used in the context of advice may be brought out by considering what would falsify it. Since it is not a statement but a piece of advice, we should not normally call it 'false' at all. We should say rather that it was bad advice or that Jones was not in a position to give advice. The advice might go wrong in any of the following ways.

(i) Jones may be deliberately deceiving Smith, knowing that the film is not to his taste. This is a form of lying.

(ii) He may have been mistaken in thinking that the film was a thriller. But since he did not say that it was he has not said anything false. He has misled Smith, but not culpably if he had good reasons for supposing it to be a thriller.

(iii) He may have been careless in supposing that Smith would enjoy what he enjoys himself. He said "It is enjoyable", when he should have said "I enjoyed it". In this case he has abused the conventions under which 'enjoyable' is used in the context of advice.

(iv) He may have given excellent advice; but Smith's enjoyment was spoilt by the lady in front who wore a large hat. The predictive element was falsified; but he did not give bad advice or advise improperly.

(v) He may not have known what Smith's problem was. In this case he was not in a position to give advice and gave it improperly, however good the advice may turn out. For his undertaking to give advice contextually implies that he believes himself to be in a position to give it, and this in turn implies that he knows what the problem to be solved is.

It is not suggested that this is an exhaustive list of the ways that advice can go wrong; the argument is designed to show that the notion of an objective property of 'entertainingness' which is either present in or absent from the film or present to a certain degree prevents our understanding the role of A-sentences. For, if there were such a property, Jones's reply would be true or false or true up to a point. But the concession to complexity involved in 'true up to a point' is not enough. Taken in its context the statement that something is entertaining or boring or frightening contextually implies a number of different elements the absence of which can nullify the remark in quite different ways. Advice can be misleading, inappropriate, unwarranted, disingenuous, improperly given, or bad.

[2]

G-sentences in the context of Advice. G-words are those that imply not merely that the relevant person is likely to have a certain reaction, but that he ought to have it. We have already seen that they cannot be sharply distinguished from A-words, partly because the same word (e.g. 'eligible') can have an A-force in some contexts and a G-force in others, and partly because there are some reactions that are so universally encouraged and others that are so universally condemned that it is impossible to use the A-word concerned without being taken to encourage or condemn the reaction. In default of an express withdrawal of the G-force, the A-word always carries it.

I have deliberately postponed all discussion of G-words until coming to advice, since their role here is more obvious than in cases of choice. This is not to say that we do not use G-words or 'ought' when making up our minds what to do, but that when we so use them we are, as it were, advising, exhorting, or commanding ourselves. If a man prefers one thing to another there is no temptation to represent the situation as one in which two people participate; but we do this quite naturally when a man tells himself that he ought to do something. It is an important fact that, while the personification of Desires is always strained and artificial, it has always seemed quite natural to represent Conscience as a little voice inside me that tells me what I ought to do. And there is, as we shall see, an excellent reason for this.

151

Just as it is useless to represent A-words as standing for objective properties, so it is equally useless to treat G-words in the same way. If, for example, there were such a property as 'rightness', it would be sense for a man to say "Yes, I know it would be the right thing to do; but shall I do it?". But this sentence is absurd unless 'shall' has a predictive rather than a decision-making role.[1] A man who says this is wondering whether, when the time comes, he will in fact carry out his decision (he might suspect himself of weakness of will); but he is not making up his mind or trying to solve a practical problem. He has solved that when he has decided that it would be the right thing to do.

In the example of the film Jones might have said, not that it is entertaining, but that it is *worth seeing*. The difference lies in the fact that, while the A-word is more specific – (it is the fact that Smith will be *entertained* that gives the remark its point as advice) – the G-word is less specific but indicates more clearly that it is advice which is being given. 'Worth seeing' bears on its face a hortatory, commending force that 'entertaining' does not. The film may be worth seeing either because it is entertaining or because it is instructive; and each of these implies that it has certain causal properties. But the gerundive phrase neither states what these properties are nor indicates whether they are such as to entertain or to instruct. Yet even so it is not a mere prediction; its use contextually implies (under Rule 2) that Jones believes it to have some of these properties and (under Rule 3) that he believes the properties to be relevant to Smith's problem of choice.

In the same way to say, as the Guide Books do, that a place is 'worth a detour' is not to say that it has a special, objective property of detour-worthiness. It is to advise the reader to visit it even at the cost of going out of his way. (Giving such advice is what guide books are for.) But a good guide book does not give advice irresponsibly. The conventions under which they are written, published, and read imply that there are reasons for making a detour and that there are a sufficient

1. See p. 268, below.

number of people for whom the reasons are good reasons. The place has a fine Cathedral, a good local wine, or is the birth-place of some celebrity. A long guide book will give the reasons; a short guide book will not, but their presence is implied.

When reasons are given they may themselves have a gerundive force without being overtly gerundive in form. Chartres has a *fine* Cathedral; Dijon supplies *Poulet à la Bresse*. (And this is not a mere statement of fact; its very mention in the guide book implies that it is a dish *worth eating*.) *Les Invalides* contains the tomb of Napoleon (and this makes it more *interesting* than a common graveyard). It is clear that the simple objective-subjective dichotomy is powerless to deal with the logic of such expressions. Is the author stating that he admires Chartres or expressing his admiration, as the subjectivists say? Nothing could be more absurd. He is probably by now profoundly bored by Cathedrals; and why should Mr Baedeker's tastes be relevant to my problems? Nothing could be more absurd – unless it be the suggestion that he is stating that the Cathedral has a property of visit-worthiness or admirability that is mysteriously connected both with the fact that others have admired it and that I am likely to.

The function of a guide book is to advise, warn, recommend, encourage, persuade, and dissuade; and the language it uses is tailor-made for just these purposes. Generalities drawn from the logic of mathematics or natural science or ordinary descriptive discourse are worse than useless for throwing light on the logic of these linguistic activities. But it does not follow that no generalizing is possible; these activities could only be carried on in a world in which certain facts obtain, and the logic of the language that we use in practical contexts naturally reflects our assumptions about these facts.

The first assumption is that there exists a known community of interests among a number of people. If you cannot tell *Poulet à la Bresse* from Spam or think that history is bunk, this guide book is not for you, because it has no answers to your problems. The second assumption is that you have a problem, that you are trying to make up your mind what to do. Advice must always be for one thing and against others, since it is the answer to the question 'What shall I do?' when this is addressed to someone else.

It would appear, then, that there is little to distinguish a G-word from an A-word and, in the contexts of choosing and advising, this is so; for, in these contexts, A-words are being used as G-words and differ from them in being for the most part more explicit as to the causal properties contextually implied. To say that a book is entertaining is not only to advise someone to read it but to begin to indicate the reasons for reading it. With G-words on the other hand, although reasons are always implied, they are in no way specified. A second distinction is that, while A-words are often used in non-practical contexts, G-words are only used in practical contexts. There is nothing odd about discussing the climbability of a mountain even when no one concerned is thinking about climbing and a man who says that it is climbable is not yet urging anyone to climb it. On the other hand the prime role of G-sentences is to urge, exhort, command, and advise and, while there is nothing odd about 'It's climbable, but I don't advise you to climb it' (1), there is something odd about 'It's worth climbing, but I don't advise you to climb it' (2), or 'You ought to climb it, but I don't advise you to' (3). It is worth examining the differences between (1), (2), and (3).

(3) is a contradiction-in-use not unlike 'It's a horse, but I don't believe it is'. The speaker is advising both for and against in the same breath or, if 'advising' is held to be too weak for 'you ought', he is commanding for and advising against in the same breath.

The logical oddness of (2) is less great; indeed it is not logically odd at all if the word 'you' is emphasized; for the speaker is, for some reason, expressly excluding you from the general injunction to climb. (1) on the other hand is not logically odd at all, for there is nothing unusual about telling people that something can be done and not advising them to do it.

This brings out one general difference between A- and G-sentences. Since the latter belong *par excellence* to the realm of choosing, advising, and exhorting and since the logic of these activities is such that sentences used to play a part in them must have a pro- or a con-force, G-sentences are always explicitly for or against something. A-sentences, on the other hand, are neutral unless the context shows which force they have. It may not be clear, for example, whether 'It's a dangerous (or onerous or responsible) post' constitutes advice for or against; but 'it's a post worth having' is not so ambiguous.

[3]

The redirection of attitudes. An important factor emerges in the context of advice that cannot be present in the context of choice. If Smith asks Jones what is the best thing for him to do the terms of the problem are set for him (Smith) by his actual pro- and con-attitudes towards the different situations that different choices would bring about. But the terms of the problem are not so set for Jones, since Jones may disapprove of Smith's pro- and con-attitudes in a way that Smith himself cannot, just because they are *his* attitudes. Jones's task, *qua* adviser, is to solve Smith's problem of choice, to which Smith's attitudes are alone relevant. The fact that Jones approves or disapproves is not, by itself, a good reason for Smith's doing anything any more than 'because he is blind' is.

But the terms of the problem are not set for Jones, since Jones has his own problem of whether to accept the role of adviser or not. If he disapproves of Smith's attitudes he may prefer not to solve Smith's problem but to alter it. Thus if Smith asks if the film at the Super is a good one in a context where it is clear that his problem is 'Shall I go to it this evening?', Jones may reply "You oughtn't to go to the cinema at all; you've got some work to do". If Smith asks him for the best way of evading income tax, Jones may prefer to redirect Smith's attitudes rather than answer the question. If Smith asks whether Higginbottom's *Introduction to the Calculus* is a good book (implying 'Shall I read it?') Jones may reply: "Are you sure it is worth while trying to learn the Calculus at your age?".

This point has certain important consequences; but it makes little difference to the logic of advice. For Jones is still advising Smith, only he has chosen to advise him on a different question and one that, perhaps, Smith had never faced. Though the discussion has shifted onto different ground, it remains true that nothing counts as advice unless it constitutes a solution to Smith's problem and that this problem is set by Smith's actual pro-attitudes.

If Jones chooses to re-direct Smith's attitudes he may do so in various ways, some of which take the form of drawing Smith's attention to other pre-existing attitudes of his.

(a) He may point out certain probable consequences of income tax evasion which Smith failed to consider. In this case he does not weaken Smith's desire to evade income tax but awakens strong counter-attitudes so that Smith no longer asks: 'How can I best evade income tax?'.

(b) He may point out that the object of Smith's pro-attitude is a special case of something towards which Smith has a general con-attitude, and thus weaken or destroy Smith's pro-attitude to this object. Thus he might point out that income tax evasion is a form of cheating, and Smith hates and despises cheating. When Smith sees the contemplated course in this new light he no longer wants to take it.

(c) He may exhibit his own con-attitude towards Smith's considering the original problem at all without, as in the last two cases, giving any reason. Now the mere fact that Jones has a con-attitude does not by itself constitute any reason for Smith's abandoning his original problem; but the very fact that Smith asks Jones (and not someone else) for advice shows that he has a general pro-attitude towards doing whatever Jones suggests, simply because Jones suggests it. Although we do not always have to accept advice, the asking of it implies some faith in the wisdom and morality of the chosen adviser. If Jones advises a course that Smith believes to be immoral, the effect may be that Smith's faith in Jones as an adviser is weakened or destroyed; but it may also be that Smith no longer regards the course as immoral; he is persuaded of its morality by the very fact that the wise and upright Jones approves of it. But it still remains true that, if Smith accepts the advice, he must have a pro-attitude towards carrying it out, even though this is only a pro-attitude towards doing what Jones tells him to do, as such.

It is sometimes said that the role of moral sentences is 'persuasive', that they are used to arouse emotions or attitudes or to get people to do things. But although, as we shall see, moral language can be used in this way, the theory confuses the job that moral sentences are used for with the ulterior purposes that we may have in using them. Influencing and persuading are things that we can do with or without words, and their importance for the logic of moral language has been seriously overestimated. A man may use advice, as he may use bribery, cajolery, or the thumb-screw to persuade someone to do something; but what he actually does with this bit of moral language is to advise, not to persuade; just as he may use a hammer for making boxes, but what he actually does with the hammer is not to make a box but to drive in nails.

The Persuasive Theory is an incorrect account of the use of moral language; but it enshrines an important truth. Advising is something that we choose to do and we must, therefore, have some reason for doing it. This reason may be a desire to persuade someone to do something and a man who gives advice (unless he gives it ironically) must, as we have seen, hope that it will be taken. This does not mean, however, that advice can never be disinterested. A man who advises another on the choice of a career may be concerned solely for the welfare of the recipient of his advice, and the father who gives death-bed advice to his son can hardly hope to gain by it. The Persuasive Theory, by implying that a man who gives advice must have an ulterior motive, makes an unfortunate and unnecessary concession to the doctrine that all human action is necessarily selfish.

[4]

Exhortation. Exhortation is the use of advising language without the contextual implication that the recipient has some pro-attitude towards adopting the suggested course. This might be called 'rhetoric', 'propaganda', or 'suggestion'. It is a technique much used by evangelical preachers on emotional congregations and by advertisers who instil desires into their victims by suggesting that they already have them. Statements of fact such as 'Spaghetti's, the only Restaurant for the real gourmet' or 'Splosh washes whiter' are often used in this way.

It is important to notice that this is a secondary use of language, parasitic on genuine advice; and this fact is fatal to the 'Persuasive' Theory of moral language. A man can only learn to seek, accept, and reject advice if, in the majority of cases, accepting the advice does in fact lead to the result he himself desires. No one would acquire a pro-attitude towards doing what Jones (or everybody) says, as such, if it was not on the whole the case that accepting the advice brought about what he wished to bring about. But once people have learned this, the language customarily used for giving advice can operate on them in a more direct way. If the words 'good', 'right', and 'you ought' had always been used by Jones for the purpose of getting Smith to do something which he (Smith) did not already want to do, it is inconceivable that Smith should ever be moved by Jones's exhortation. It is for this reason that the cynical theory that Virtue is the Offspring that

Flattery begot upon Pride cannot be wholly true.[1] Unless moral words had first been used in a way which connects them with our own interests — whether these be selfish or unselfish — we could never have come to be persuaded or dissuaded by their use and they could not act, as they sometimes do, as levers with which to manipulate the conduct of others.

1. B. de Mandeville: *Enquiry into the Origin of Moral Virtue*. Selby-Bigge: *British Moralists*, Vol. II, p. 353. For the criticism see Hutcheson: op. cit., Vol. I, p. 81.

CHAPTER 12

'Good'

[1]

'Good' in the context of choice. We have seen that when 'good' is used in the context of choice there can be no logical gap between deciding that something is the best or better than its rivals and choosing it. This does not imply that there can be no discrepancy between the decision which is, on the face of it, not a performance of any kind but a judgement, and the choice; but it does imply that if there is such a discrepancy a special reason must be given for it. And we must now consider the role of such expressions as 'because it is a good one' and 'because it is the best' when they are used to explain why a man chose the thing he did.

The answer to the question 'Why did you choose that car?' might be a statement of fact ('because it has more leg-room') or an A-sentence ('because it is more comfortable'); and I have already discussed the contextual background in which such answers can be given and taken as logically complete explanations. In each case the car must have some A-property and some ordinary, empirical properties on which its A-property depends. While the factual answer says what the empirical properties are and contextually implies an A-property without specifying what it is, the A-sentence does the reverse. And each answer implies a pro-attitude towards the A-property concerned; otherwise it would not be an answer to the question.

The answer 'because it is the best' functions in a similar way, but with certain important differences. In the first place it does not just imply a pro-attitude; it expresses it. But it does not only do this. If this were all I wanted to do I should have to say 'because I happen to like it more than the others'.

It contextually implies that I have reasons for my choice; but it does not say what they are and therefore does not explain my choice.

We are tempted to say that it gives the best possible reason. After all, what better reason could there be for choosing a car than the fact that it was the best available or the best that I could afford? What better reason could there be for doing anything than the belief that it is the best thing to do?

The trouble is that the reason is *too* good. It is like saying that I was frightened because it was a terrifying experience; and, as an explanation, it operates in much the same way. Just as 'because it was terrifying' shows that my fear was not an unusual one and contextually implies that the object had certain unspecified properties by which people are usually frightened, so 'because it was the best' shows that my choice was no passing whim, that it was considered more or less carefully, that the object had certain unspecified 'good-making' properties, and that my choice was not a peculiar one. Any of these contextual implications could be expressly withdrawn, especially, as we shall see, the last; but in default of such withdrawal my audience would be entitled to assume them. Just as a G-sentence showed more plainly than an A-sentence that advice was being given but was less explicit about the reasons, so 'because it was the best' shows more plainly that I was choosing but says even less about the reasons.

In fact it says nothing about them at all; it only implies that I have reasons. The goodness of something is not one of the properties for which I choose it. If it were, it would make sense to ask why its superior goodness was a reason for choosing it. To ask a man who chose a car because it was faster or more economical or had more leg-room why he chose it is to display ignorance of people's purchasing habits; to say to him "I know you thought it the best car; but why did you choose it?" is logically odd.

The same logical ties that bind goodness so closely to choosing bind it also to activities that are akin to choosing. A man who says that he voted for a certain proposal because he thought it good has not explained why he voted for it; he has merely guarded himself against accusations of flippancy, irresponsibility or indulging in complicated machinations. And it is logically odd to say "I think it is an excellent proposal, but I shan't vote for it". As we saw, reasons could be given for this discrepancy, and the logical nexus between thinking good and voting comes out in the fact that we should feel entitled to infer that there must be a special reason. To call something good is, in a way, already to vote for it, to side with it, to let others know where I stand. But it does more than this; it implies that I have reasons for casting my vote as I do.

'Good' in the context of advice. The considerations that apply to 'good' in the context of choice apply equally in the context of advice. And here again the subjectivist is right in connecting 'this is good' with the pro-attitude of the speaker. There is the same sort of absurdity in 'This is good, but I don't advise you to do it' as there is in 'This is the best course; but shall I take it?'. In the latter case the speaker both expresses a decision as to how he should act and in the same breath asks if he should; and in the former he gives advice and in the same breath retracts it. It would be equally odd if the hearer were to say "You have told me that it is the best course to take; but do you advise me to take it?".

The differences in the use of 'good' in advice and choice are due to the fact that the problem to be solved is now someone else's. The adviser is not making up his mind what to do, but helping someone else to make up his mind. And this difference brings with it another. The relevant pro-attitude is that of the audience. But in other respects the contextual implications are the same. To tell someone that something is the best thing for him to do is to advise him to do it, but not irresponsibly. The speaker implies that he has good reasons for his advice, that he knows what the problem is and that his advice is relevant. The same predictive and causal elements are present as in the case of A-sentences; and advice may, as before, be given disingenuously, improperly, mistakenly, or unfortunately if one or other of the contextual implications is absent.

[2]

Other uses of 'good'. I shall discuss the other uses of 'good' in the order in which they seem to diverge more and more from the fundamental use, which is to express or explain a preference.

(a) *Praising and Applauding*. Like choosing, these are performances, not statements; and, although in primary uses they do express the speaker's pro-attitude, they have other contextual implications which will be examined later. They can be done with or without words; but the gestures, handclapping and the like, which are used for praising have conventional, symbolic meanings. They mean what they do in the way that words mean, not in the way that clouds mean rain or cobras in the garden mean trouble. Virtue-words are words of praise; and relatively specific words like 'brave', 'honest', and 'generous' are also descriptive; for they describe a person's behaviour and predict the way in which he can be relied upon to behave in certain sorts of situation. They both praise and give the reason, what the praise is *for*. But 'good' does not do this. In cases where there are recognized standards that a man must reach to be worthy of praise they contextually imply that he has reached those standards; but they do not say what the standards are. 'Because it is a good one' does not explain why I praise something; but it does imply that the thing has certain unspecified properties for which I praise it. My praise was not casual or capricious.

(b) *Commending*. The verb 'to commend' is used in two ways. It may mean 'entrust to the care of'; but this sense is irrelevant, since 'good' is not used to commend in this sense. In the sense in which 'good' is used for commending it is akin to praising but has a more hortatory force. To commend something to someone is to advise him to choose it. The Oxford Dictionary, as we saw, calls 'good' "the most general adjective of commendation" in English; but it goes on to add "implying the existence in a high or at least satisfactory degree of characteristic qualities which are either admirable in themselves or useful for some purpose".

The form of this definition is interesting, since it brings out the difference between the job that the word is used for and the conditions limiting its use in a way that philosophers' definitions of 'good' never do. The writer of the dictionary sees clearly that the word is used to do a job which is not 'stating' but commending and that the elements of objective fact which some philosophers insist on treating as part of its meaning are really part of the contextual background of its use. In the uses which follow this contextual background looms larger and larger, so that in some uses the word 'good' almost comes to be a descriptive word, though, as we shall see, it never quite does this and in moral contexts it can never wholly lose its gerundive force or its pro-force.

(c) *Verdicts and Appraisals.* In chapter 1 we saw that moral language is not only used for choosing and advising, but also making moral judgements, which are not decisions to do something but verdicts or appraisals of something or somebody. Now appraisals are *judgements*, not just expressions of a man's own taste or preference; and it is this point that the Consequential Property Theory tries to bring out, but in a misleading way. When we judge something to be good we always judge it to be good in respect of some property, and it is a question of empirical fact whether it has this property or not. Thus to judge a wine to be good is not just to express a preference for it – and we shall see that it need not be to do this at all –; the judgement must be backed by my belief that it has a certain bouquet, body, and flavour, and these are objective qualities, since a man who found that he disagreed markedly from all the experts on these points would admit himself to be wrong. It is an essential feature of judgements that they are made by reference to standards or criteria; but it is necessary to be extremely careful in discussing the way in which the criteria are related to the verdict or appraisal.

Let us assume for the moment that the criteria used by experts at wine-tastings, horse-shows, beauty contests, and school examinations are agreed to be the proper criteria, though this will have to be questioned later. We might be tempted to say that if the criteria for being a good X are that the X must have properties a, b, and c in some specifiable degree, then 'good X' simply means 'X which has the properties a, b, and c in the requisite degree'. But this will not do. For it is possible to understand what 'good X' means without knowing what the criteria are. Thus, if I do not know the criteria used at Crufts I could not tell a good dog (in this sense of 'good') from a bad one or pick out the best dog from a group. But this does not mean that I cannot understand what 'good dog' means in the way that I could not understand what 'mangy dog' meant if I did not know what 'mangy' meant. For I do know that if it is a good dog it must have in a fairly high degree those properties which are mentioned in the list of criteria for judging dogs, although I do not know what these properties are or to what degree a dog must have them to rate as 'good'.

The next two uses are special cases of the appraising use.

(d) *Efficiency*. When 'good' is predicated of any object (natural or artificial, animate or inanimate) that is used for a purpose it implies the presence in a relatively high degree of those properties that the object must have to do its job. But again it would be a mistake to say that 'good knife' just *means* 'knife that is sharp, easily handled, durable, etc.'. The connexion between the properties which a knife must have to be efficient and its efficiency is an empirical one. We know from experience that a knife which has not got these properties at all just won't cut and that its relative efficiency at cutting depends on the degree to which it has these properties. Nor can we even say that 'good knife' means 'knife which cuts efficiently', because we could understand what 'good' means in the expression 'good knife' without knowing what knives were for. But 'good knife' (in this sense of 'good') does mean 'Knife which has those properties (whatever they are) which a knife must have if it is to do its job efficiently (whatever that is)'.

(e) *Skill.* When we call a man a good lawyer, scholar, cricketer or liar, the use is similar to the 'efficiency' use except for the fact that, since these are men, the purpose concerned is their purpose, not the purpose they are used for. Just as we could not use 'good' to imply efficiency unless we agreed about what the object concerned is for, so we could not use it to imply skill unless there was something that was agreed to constitute success at the activity concerned. But, just as we cannot say that 'good' means 'efficient' in the one sense, so we cannot say that it means 'successful' in the other. In activities involving skill there are rules for achieving success which are such that we know from experience that unless a man applies them he is unlikely to be successful. Thus, if we know the rules for success at bridge or cricket we can predict, in a very general way, what a good bridge-player or cricketer will do; and in calling a man 'good' we imply that he applies or follows the rules. This implication can, of course, be expressly withdrawn because we know that people sometimes achieve success in very unorthodox ways. But 'good' never quite loses its gerundive force and if we call a man a good cricketer without intending to imply that his methods ought to be imitated we mislead our audience.

(f) *The descriptive use.* Like most words, 'good' can be used to mean 'what most people would call good'. A man who uses it may not be choosing, advising, defending a choice or piece of advice, or appraising, but referring to an object which he or others would call good if they were doing one of these. Thus I may call a wine good even if I am not competent to apply the criteria, just because I have heard the experts praise it.

This use belongs to descriptive discourse because it is a question of historical fact whether people do or do not call the object good, and that is what is being asserted. It is necessarily a secondary use, since it would be impossible to use 'good' to mean 'what people call good' unless people called things good in primary ways. And 'good' is hardly ever used with this descriptive force alone. The speaker implies that he himself sides with those who call the thing good unless this implication is expressly withdrawn or obviously inadmissible in the context.

[3]

We must now consider the ways in which these uses of 'good' are connected with each other. It is clearly not an accident that the same word is used in all these different ways nor could this fact be explained in a purely historical or philological way. 'Good' is *the* Janus-word *par excellence*; it is often used to do more than one job on one occasion and the logical connexions between the various jobs are what they are because the facts are what they are. It is also most emphatically an ordinary, non-technical word and it is a consequence of this that the logic of its use reflects empirical truths that hold only for the most part and admit of exceptions. For ordinary language, unlike mathematics, is not deliberately constructed by men who have a keen eye for consistency and rigour; it is not deliberately constructed at all but grows and changes in an environment in which the exceptional case can be and must be ignored. The contextual implications of any use of 'good' are many and varied and, on occasion, any of them can be withdrawn, a point which should make us suspicious of counter-examples. It is impossible to understand the actual uses of 'good' by considering artificial and exceptional situations because the logic of ordinary language does not cater for such situations.[1]

But there is one element which seems to be common to all cases. Although a man need have no comparisons in mind when he calls something 'good', such comparisons are always implied. He must, if challenged, be able to produce examples of descriptively similar things that he would call not so good. For example, we always praise something with a certain

1. See pp. 239–44, below.

degree of warmth which lies somewhere on a scale between mild commendation and hysterical adulation. The word 'good' can be used to express almost any degree of warmth, but it must be less than that expressed in the same context by 'excellent' or 'superb' and greater than that expressed by 'fair' or 'tolerable'.

It is not difficult to understand the connexions between the more obviously performatory uses, praising, applauding, and commending; nor is it difficult to appreciate their intimate connexion with preference and choice. To praise is not to choose; but it is connected with choosing in that it would be odd for a man to choose the thing he was prepared to praise less highly or not at all. He must have special reasons for this, modesty for example, a sense of unworthiness to possess the 'better' thing or a desire that someone else should have it. Again, if a man habitually praises one pianist more highly than another we expect to find him attending the recitals of the former more regularly and to be more annoyed when he is prevented from going. But he might have been told that the second is really a better pianist and be trying to cultivate a taste for his performance. Explanations can be given of discrepancies between praising and choice; but in default of an explanation the connexion is contextually implied.

If, on a particular occasion, I call a man brave it would be logically odd to ask if I was in favour of what he did; for 'brave' is a praising word and by using it I show that I am in favour. Similarly, if I call courage a 'virtue' I show that I am, in a general way, in favour of courage, although I might not always want to praise a brave deed. It is an empirical fact that men are, for the most part, in favour of the modes of conduct that they call (descriptively) brave, honest, or generous. But this pro-attitude is so widespread that these words are not pure descriptive words; they are terms of praise and imply a pro-attitude unless this is expressly withdrawn.

Now praising and applauding are activities which are often performed with the special purpose of encouraging the person concerned to continue in the same style, and hissing and booing are used with the opposite intention. Although the words and gestures employed in praising owe their encouraging force to convention, they have, granted the convention, a natural effect on the people praised. For it is an empirical fact that, except in special circumstances – for example, if the praise is considered impertinent – people enjoy being praised and are therefore likely to go on doing what they are praised for. Praising is logically tied to approval; for if we heard a man praise something we could not wonder whether he approved of it or not unless we suspected him of being disingenuous or ironical; and it is logically tied in the same way to encouraging. But, although it is an empirical fact that men tend to encourage and try to promote that of which they approve, we must, as always, assume that men on the whole intend the natural consequences of their actions and therefore do not praise that which they would prefer to be otherwise. And this assumption is reflected in the fact that praising implies both approval and encouragement.

The same logical ties bind praising to advising; it would be logically odd to praise one candidate more highly than another and to go on to say that one was advising against his being given the job or the prize. Odd, but not impossible; for there might, as always, be special reasons for this.

The "characteristic qualities" which, according to the dictionary, are implied by the use of 'good' may be "either admirable in themselves or useful for some purpose". In contexts involving efficiency or skill it is the latter that we have in mind. In such contexts there need be no direct connexion between the performatory uses, which are all variations of 'preferring' or 'being on the side of', and the usefulness implied by 'good'. We may have no pro-attitude whatsoever towards the purpose for which something is used or the activity at which a man is skilful, as when we speak of a 'good cosh' or a 'good liar'. But there is still an indirect link with the pro-attitudes since 'good' in these contexts implies success, and 'success' is a pro-word. A man is not a good liar unless he fairly consistently achieves his aim.

Preference and Appraisal. But it is the connexions between the performatory uses and the verdict-giving, judging, or appraising use when the qualities on which the verdict is based are thought to be "admirable in themselves" that are the most important and the most difficult. I shall substitute 'preferable' for 'admirable', since admiration is itself a performance akin to praising and 'admirable' is therefore too narrow in scope to cover all appraisals other than those of efficiency or skill.

All the performatory uses contextually imply appraisal; for we have seen that it is improper to use 'good', at least in an impersonal formula, to express or defend a preference unless the preference is a considered one, based on reasons and not unusual. And to say that the preference is 'based on reasons' is to say that the speaker applied criteria or standards. It is not necessary that he should have done this deliberately; he may have done it automatically; but he must be able to defend his choice by an appeal to the standards which justify it.

But, although the performatory uses imply appraisal, it is not so clear that the converse is true. Indeed it is not true in any direct sense; appraisals often imply preference only in a roundabout way. For when 'good' is used to give a verdict it need neither express nor imply a pro-attitude on the part of the speaker. In such cases what a man is primarily doing with the word 'good' is *applying* those standards which are only contextually implied in the more subjective uses. Since 'good' is a Janus-word, he may, of course, be expressing his preferences or advising as well; but he need not be. The embittered schoolmaster may have no interest in the work of the examination candidates at all; he may even prefer stupidity to intelligence or have a private belief that the usual criteria for intelligence are quite wrong. Nevertheless he may still apply the grading words 'good', 'fair', 'poor', and so on in accordance with the accepted criteria either from conscientiousness or from habit or from fear of losing his job.

In the same way a professional taster of wine may dislike

all wine or prefer the less good to the better; his judgement is based solely on the presence of those "characteristic qualities" which, as an expert, he is able to detect and knows to be among the criteria for 'good wine'. But even in these cases there is an indirect reference to choosing and advising which comes out when we turn from the question "What are the criteria in fact used for grading Xs?" to the question "Why do we have the criteria that we do?". Professional wine-tasters are, after all, business men or the employees of business men and, though their job may be to taste wine, they only have this job because wine is to be bought and sold. It is no accident that the criteria for 'good Xs' are connected with the Xs that people prefer or approve of more highly. The professional wine-taster may not *like* Chateau Laffitte; but he uses criteria for judging wine under which it gets high marks because people are prepared to pay highly for wine which rates highly under these criteria, and they do this because they like it.

[4]

Nature and Convention. The dictionary's phrase "admirable in themselves" is unfortunately ambiguous. In its context it is clear that 'in themselves' is contrasted with 'for a purpose', and that what the author has in mind is the familiar contrast between good-as-means and good-as-an-end. But 'in itself' is often used in philosophy with at least three other meanings. (a) It is sometimes used as a synonym for 'really' or 'objectively' to imply independence of human opinion or judgement of value. But, in discussing Moore's 'two worlds' argument I have already suggested that it is doubtful whether any sense can be given to the idea of something being good if there was no one to judge it good.

(b) It is sometimes used with a gerundive force. What is admirable or preferable in itself is what people ought to admire or prefer. But to use it in this way is not to comment on the use of 'good' but to make a value-judgement and, if the author of the dictionary were thought to be using it in this way, he must be thought to subscribe himself to all the value-judgements he cites as examples of 'good'. (c) But 'good-in-itself' could also be used to mean 'naturally good', to imply that the criteria or standards used for judging the goodness of something are not, like the criteria for a good postage stamp, dependent on human convention. It is this contrast that I propose to discuss.

We call a taste (or any other pro-attitude) a 'natural' one if (a) it is pretty general even among people of very different societies and if (b) most people do not have to learn to acquire it. It is important to notice that both these criteria for what is 'natural' are extremely vague and that they both admit of exceptions. A taste for strawberries does not cease to be natural because Jones happens not to like them or because Smith did not like them at first. Benevolence and love of life are natural pro-attitudes, even though there are misanthropes and suicides.

The criteria used for appraising are partly natural and partly conventional. In music, for example, the criteria which critics apply to a composition or performance are conventional in that they vary in different cultures and it is necessary to learn what they are; and musical taste is also partly conventional in that it is not natural to like or admire a Bach fugue in the way that it is natural to like sweets or to love one's children. It may well be that no criteria or tastes are wholly conventional. Correlations can be found between the criteria employed and the physiological facts of hearing; for example we know that the musical intervals and key-relationships on which all western music is based and which enter into the criteria used for judging a musical composition are of a mathematically simple kind. And even in the case of the criteria used for judging dogs at Crufts, which are highly artificial, it is possible to trace historical connexions between the criteria now used and the criteria that were used when dogs were used for practical purposes; and these last were natural criteria in that the purposes, such as hunting and protection from wild animals, were based on natural pro-attitudes.

But in many cases the criteria now used are connected to natural criteria only through a long process of change and have become modified to such an extent that their original connexion with natural pro-attitudes has been entirely lost. And in such cases it often happens that we do not use the criteria we do because people have the pro-attitudes they have, but we have the pro-attitudes we have because the criteria are what they are. It may be that no one can now remember exactly why certain criteria were originally chosen to be the standards of judging something to be good or bad of its kind and that people are now prepared to admire, praise, and pay highly for objects because they conform to the accepted criteria, rather than accepting the criteria as 'proper' ones because, under them, the things that they admire rate highly. Taste is dictated by fashion, not fashion by taste.

But such cases must (logically) be secondary cases and it would therefore be a mistake to cite them in proof of the contention that criteria are logically prior to pro-attitudes. For unless there were primary cases in which we adopted criteria *because* we already had a pro-attitude towards the objects that in fact rate highly under them, it would be impossible to understand how the same set of words could be used both in applying criteria and for choosing, praising, and advising. It is only because 'good' is used in applying criteria in cases where we use the criteria we do because our desires, interests, and tastes are what they are that men can come to acquire a taste for what counts as 'good' under the accepted criteria even in cases where the original connexion between the criteria and the taste has been lost. Advertisers and pro-pagandists, arbiters of taste and leaders of fashion could not (logically) stimulate new tastes and attitudes by the reiterated use of criterion-applying language unless this language was also used for applying criteria in cases where there are pre-existing tastes and attitudes. Without genuine enthusiasts there could be no snobs.

In many cases, therefore, the answer to the question 'Why do we use the criteria for judging so-and-sos that we do?' may be of a purely historical kind; the criteria are traditional; they have been concocted and moulded by interested parties, and so on. But this sort of answer cannot be given in all cases; there must be some cases in which we use a set of criteria because, as an empirical fact, they give higher ratings to those objects which we prefer.

In discussing appraisals I assumed that there was no difficulty about saying what the proper criteria for judging Xs are or about selecting the experts, leaders of fashion, or arbiters of taste; and it might seem that these assumptions involve a vicious circularity in the attempt to construe the grading-scale of good, fair, poor, and bad in terms of the standards used by experts. But this is not so for two reasons. (a) In some cases there are tests of competence which are purely objective and empirical. Some men, for example, have perfect pitch, can detect minute musical intervals, can recognize and accurately reproduce long and complicated tunes and so on, while others cannot; and these are matters of fact. In judging their expertise we must, of course, rely on the ability of other experts to assess their competence; but the judgements of these experts is 'objective' because they fulfil the requirements for objective language discussed in chapter 4. It is possible that one man might have a finer ear than all other men, so that in a case in which he said that two notes were slightly different when everyone else said they were the same he would be right and they wrong. But if there were no indirect tests, such as the appeal to readings of scales and meters, for deciding whether he can really detect these differences or is only bluffing, and if those who honestly claimed to be able to make fine discriminations did not on the whole agree with each other, we could not call their judgements 'objective'.

Now from the fact that a man is able to make these fine discriminations or to perform better than others in these objectively testable ways, it does not, of course, follow that he is a good judge. For to say that he is a good judge is either to state that he is good at applying the accepted criteria for what is good (which is different from being good at passing the objective tests) or to express approval of his judgements, to praise him, to encourage others to accept his judgements, and so on; and in most cases it is to do all these things at once. But, once again, the reason why we allow that, in a general way, the most technically competent people are the best judges lies in the facts. A man who is tone-deaf is unlikely to be able even to distinguish one piece of music from another and his value-judgements (if he makes them), are not likely to be consistent with each other; so that his value-judgements would be useless as a guide to others. A man who knows little Greek could not be a good judge of a piece of Greek prose. Consistency and fine discrimination are not sufficient conditions of good taste or moral insight, but they are necessary conditions if criteria are to be used for the purposes for which they are used.

(b) Secondly, the person who rejects the criteria usually employed or the verdict of the acknowledged experts may do so in two ways. He may simply refuse to be guided by them on the grounds that he happens not to like what is usually called good. But, if he goes further and says that the usual criteria are not *good* criteria, he is not just rejecting them; he is himself using criterion-applying language and he implies that he has second-order criteria for judging (and condemning) the usual first-order criteria.

To the questioning of criteria there is no end; but if we ask whether the criteria for judging Xs are *good* criteria we must, at whatever level we have reached, use criteria for deciding whether they are good or not. It is logically absurd to ask a question without knowing how the answers to it are to be judged to be good or bad answers. The appeal to criteria accepted by experts is not circular, but regressive; and the regress is not a vicious one since, although we *can* always question the criteria, there is no practical or logical necessity to do so. The self-guaranteeing criteria so vainly sought by some moralists are neither possible nor necessary.

[5]

Non-practical appraisals. We often make appraisals in contexts where there is clearly no question of choosing or advising, for example moral judgements about historical or fictional characters. And this seems to involve a difficulty for theories which make appraisals logically dependent on pro-attitudes. Hutcheson and Hume, for example, tried to reduce moral judgements to expressions of feeling. They were not guilty of the Naturalistic Fallacy, since they were prepared to allow that moral approval and sympathy are special, moral feelings distinct from other types of feeling. But even this concession to the peculiarity of the moral use of language does not save them from an important objection that seems at first sight fatal to their case. Sentiments, as Hume noticed, seem to vary in rough proportion to the propinquity of their objects. We are not moved by the iniquity of remote historical characters as we are by those closer to us; and we feel more approval for and sympathy with those near to us than with those who are more remote. Yet our moral judgements do not vary in the same way. "We read Cicero now without emotion, yet we can still judge Verres to be a villain. According to Hume's theory our judgement must change as do our feelings. I do not feel indignation as strongly now about the German invasion of Czechoslovakia as I did at the time it happened; yet I do not judge the action to be less wrong than I did then, or the agents less criminal . . . . It is but a weak subterfuge to say we transport ourselves by the force of imagination into distant ages and countries, and consider the passions which we should have felt on contemplating these characters had we been contemporaries and had commerce with the persons. . . . I now feel completely indifferent to Verres, and know it. Yet, Hume tells me, when I judge Verres to have been a villain, I am so deceived by my imagination that I talk as if I felt a strong feeling of anger."[1]

Dr Raphael's criticism is fatal to the theory that a man

1. D. D. Raphael: *The Moral Sense*, pp. 88 and 91.

who makes a moral appraisal is always expressing a feeling; and a similar criticism could also be made of any theory which says that to appraise is always to praise, advise, commend, etc. On some occasions a man may be simply *applying* the criteria that he and others customarily use for these purposes. To call Verres a villain is to pass a verdict on him, to condemn him. Now the Moral Sense School were, I think, mistaken in construing moral approval and disapproval as *feelings*, since this suggests too strongly the analogy with itches, aches, and tickles. But they were right to connect moral appraisals and verdicts with approval and disapproval. For although a man who passes a verdict need not be expressing a pro- or con- attitude, we have seen that the criteria he uses are directly or indirectly linked with these attitudes; and in the case of moral judgements they must be linked in a special way that may be absent in other cases.

I said earlier that, although in other cases 'good' might lose its gerundive force, it cannot wholly do so when used to make moral appraisals. The reason is that, whatever may be the case with other types of appraisal, moral appraisals must be universal. Anyone who makes a moral appraisal even of a remote character must be willing to apply the same criteria universally. And it follows from this that he must be willing to apply them in practical contexts. If I am not prepared to condemn anyone whose behaviour is like that of Verres in all relevant respects, then, in calling Verres a villain, I am not making a genuine moral judgement; and the relevant respects are all of an empirical, objective kind. It would, of course, be trivial to include among them an objective property of villainy or moral turpitude; all that is necessary is that I should be prepared to condemn anyone who did the sort of thing that Verres is called a villain for having done, anyone who oppressed the poor, robbed the rich, took bribes, and cheated the treasury, and all for his own personal profit.

Moral appraisals are therefore connected with choosing and advising in a way that non-moral appraisals need not be. It is not logically odd to say "This is the better wine, but I prefer that"; but it is logically odd to say "This is the (morally) better course; but I shall do that".[1] And a man cannot be making a genuine moral judgement about Verres if he would himself be prepared to act on the same principles on which Verres acted and prepared to exhort others to do so. In condemning Verres he is not expressing any emotion; but he is affirming his own moral principles.

[6]

Objective-Subjective. In chapter 6 I said that the distinction between "For what job is the word '. . .' used?" and "Under what conditions is it proper to use that word for that job?" throws light on the objective-subjective dispute.

As we should expect, both parties are right. Just as the subjectivists are right in denying that A-words stand for special properties and explaining them in terms of people's reactions, so they are also right in connecting 'good' and 'bad' with people's desires, tastes, interests, approvals, and disapprovals. There is a logical absurdity about calling a play 'amusing' if the speaker believes that it never has amused anyone and never will; and there is the same logical absurdity in calling something 'good' without any direct or indirect reference to a pro-attitude. If the connexion between 'good' and the pro-attitude that is contextually relevant were not a logical one, a gap would emerge between calling something good on the one hand and deciding to choose it, choosing it or advising others to choose it on the other which would make these activities unintelligible. Moreover, the subjectivists are also right in connecting 'good' with the pro-attitudes of the speaker, at least in moral cases.

But the objectivists are also right. They are mistaken in denying the points made by the subjectivists above and in thinking that goodness must be a unique, non-natural

1. This may sound surprising. We all know what it is to take what we know to be the morally worse course. I shall try to remove the air of paradox in chapter 18.

property. It is sometimes argued that if there were no such property we could not account for the fact that we use the impersonal form 'this is good' rather than the personal form 'I approve of this', and those who use this argument are inclined to forget that we have an impersonal form 'this is nice' as well as the personal form 'I like it', so that niceness would have to be an objective property too.

It would indeed be puzzling to understand why we use these impersonal forms if we were just talking about or expressing our own approvals; but this argument does not show that we are talking about something else, still less that this must be a unique property. We can account for the objective formula, as we did in the case of 'nice', by saying (a) that 'X is good' is not only used in the context of choice and (b) that, when it is so used, it implies a great deal that is not implied by 'I approve of X' and is expressly denied by 'I happen to approve of X'. It implies that my approval is not an unusual one and that I could give reasons for it. It implies also – what is a matter of objective fact – that the object conforms to certain standards which are generally accepted.

It is sometimes argued that 'this is good' cannot just mean 'I approve of this' on the ground that we can say "I approve of this because it is good". Approval must therefore be an intellectual emotion which arises in us only when we recognize something to have the objective property 'goodness'. But it has never been clear what the connexion between the approval and the recognition of the property is supposed to be. Is it logically necessary that anyone who recognizes the property should feel approval or is it just an empirical fact that people who notice the property, and only they, have the feeling? Each of these answers involves insuperable difficulties; but if neither is correct we must find some other way of explaining the 'because' in 'I approve of X because it is good'.

The need for such an explanation vanishes when we see that this is not a reason-giving 'because' like that in 'I approve of Jones because he is kind to children' but more like

'I like Jones because he is likeable'. It rebuts the suggestion that I just 'happen to' approve of X and it implies that X has certain properties which make it worthy of my approval and that it conforms to the known standards for Xs.

The objectivist is right in drawing attention to the factual background which makes impersonal appraisals possible; but the facts which it contains are ordinary, empirical facts, not special, non-natural facts. Unlike the subjectivist (who tends to ignore the background altogether), he tries to include the background in the meaning of the word; and this, combined with the mistake of confusing practical and descriptive discourse, leads him into the vain pursuit of a single ingredient to which we always refer when we call something good.

[7]

The Naturalistic Fallacy. We are now in a position to see why the moral philosophers of the past subordinated the critical or appraising uses of moral language to the practical uses. Each presupposes the other, but in a different way. The practical uses presuppose the appraising use in that we could not use 'good' as we do for choosing, advising, and praising if we did not employ criteria or standards; since we only use 'good' for these purposes *when* we are employing standards. Nevertheless people who did not know what standards were could do things recognizably like what we, who have standards, call choosing, advising, and praising. They would be very rudimentary performances, hardly deserving the names of choice, advice, and praise; but they could occur. We draw a distinction between 'good' and 'happen to like' which people without standards could not draw; and we, who have the distinction, would describe their activities in terms of what they 'happen to like', because they could not do anything that we would call 'choosing the best'. In this way the practical uses of 'good' imply the appraising use.

But the practical uses are logically prior to the appraising use in a much more fundamental way. Unless men had pro-attitudes, there could not be even rudimentary analogues of what we know as appraising, judging, or passing a verdict. For these involve the use of standards; and without pro-attitudes we should neither have any use for standards nor even be able to understand what a 'standard' was. We can imagine a world in which there was choosing, but no appraising and also a world in which there was classifying, sorting, and ordering (for example by size) but no choosing; but, in a world in which there was no choosing, there could be no such thing as appraising or grading.

Ethical Naturalism is the attempt to trace logical connexions between moral appraisals and the actual pro- and con-attitudes of men, their desires and aversions, hopes and fears, joys and sorrows. One-track naturalistic theories always fail to do justice to the complexity both of the facts and of the logical connexions, since they suggest that there is only one thing towards which men have a pro-attitude, pleasure, or that all pro-attitudes are desires. And these theories are both psychologically and logically misleading.

Opponents of the Naturalistic Fallacy have pointed out the logical errors. It is true that gerundive and deontological words cannot be defined in terms of pleasure, desire, or even purpose; and I shall try to show how they are connected with these teleological concepts later. It is also true that gerundive judgements and value judgements do not follow logically from descriptive statements about what men like, enjoy, and approve of. But the reason for this is not that gerundive words and value words refer to special entities or qualities, but that a person who *uses* them is not, except in certain secondary cases, describing anything at all. He is not doing what psychologists do, which is to describe, explain, and comment on what people like, enjoy, and approve of; and he is not doing what moral philosophers do, which is to describe, explain, and comment on the way in which people use moral words; he is himself using moral language, expressing approval, praising, advising, exhorting, commending, or appraising.

181

The attack on the Naturalistic Fallacy is thus far justified. But the conclusion which is commonly drawn, that moral concepts are a special sort of concept which must be purged of all association with the 'merely empirical or phenomenal' concepts of enjoying, wanting, and approval is not justified. Psychology is not as irrelevant to ethics as some modern philosophers insist; for, although moral judgements do not follow from psychological statements, we cannot understand what the terms used in moral judgements mean unless we examine them in the context of their use; and they are used either directly to express a pro- or con-attitude or to perform some other task which beings who had no pro- or con-attitudes could not perform or even understand. The various ways in which 'good' is used are unintelligible unless they are directly or indirectly connected with choice; and I shall try to show later that the same applies to 'ought'.

Moral philosophy does not, therefore, "rest on a mistake". For the great philosophers were not primarily interested in the question whether deontological words could be analysed in terms of 'merely empirical' or 'natural' concepts. They believed that, human beings being what they are, there are certain types of activity that are in fact satisfactory to them and that it is possible empirically to discover what these are. No doubt they often made mistakes of fact, for example that of supposing that what is satisfactory to one man would be satisfactory to another; and they made mistakes of logic, for example that of supposing that 'good' could be extracted from its context and be said to mean the same as 'satisfactory'. But they do not seem to have been mistaken in their basic assumptions that the language of obligation is intelligible only in connexion with the language of purpose and choice, that men choose to do what they do because they are what they are, and that moral theories which attempt to exclude all consideration of human nature as it is do not even begin to be moral theories.

PART III

Duty and Purpose

CHAPTER 13

'Right' and 'Ought'

'DUTY' and 'Obligation' are chapter-heading words; I shall have more to say about them later; but it will be better to begin our discussion of deontological words with the words that we actually use when discussing duties in practice, of which the most important are 'right' and 'ought'.

The main purpose for which these words are used is to tell someone to do something, but they have subsidiary uses not unlike the subsidiary uses of 'good'. They can be used to express and to give reasons for verdicts in cases where there is no question of anyone's doing anything and even to imply no more than that something conforms to an accepted standard. But they only come to have these uses because verdicts are also made in practical contexts. The objective, fact-stating background of their use in practical contexts survives even when the context is not a practical one. Thus we can use them for passing judgement on a remote historical character or even a character in a novel. Henry Crawford ought not to have seduced Maria Rushworth. The Revocation of the Edict of Nantes was (morally) wrong. Novels and histories are not always written with a practical purpose and no one supposes that anyone who makes these judgements is advising, warning, or commanding. But it would still be wrong to say that he is just 'stating a fact'; for these are still moral judgements about which disputes could arise that could not be settled in the same sort of way that a dispute about a date could be settled. What he is doing is to condemn; and, although condemnation has in this case no practical point, it is difficult to imagine how we should ever have come to do such a thing unless we did it in practical contexts.

The difference between 'right' and 'ought' is, roughly, that while 'I ought' and 'You ought' are used to express decisions and injunctions, 'right' is mainly used to support these decisions and injunctions in a special way that must now be analysed.

[1]

Right. If someone is asked to explain why he did or intends to do something he may say "because it is the right thing to do"; but this explanation has the same near-tautological ring as "I was frightened because it was terrifying" or "I decided to do it because it seemed to me the best thing to do". It would be logically odd for a man to say "I know you thought it right, but why did you do it?"; but 'I thought it right' does not just express his decision. It indicates the type of reason which he had, though it does not give the reason any more than 'because I thought it best' does.

'I thought it right' is so near to 'I thought it best' that in many contexts there is little difference between them; but there often is a difference and sometimes a very great one. Since 'I thought it right' is tied so closely to the decision to act that it is absurd to insert a logical wedge between them, its use, as an explanation of choice, contextually implies a pro-attitude, which is overtly expressed and not just implied by the use of 'good' and 'best'. We have seen that 'good' is only used to express approval under certain conditions one of which must be that the action or object conforms to certain standards. There is a similar limitation in the case of 'right', only this time the implication is that the action is fitting or appropriate or that it conforms to certain rules. It thus indicates that the decision is of a different type from that which would be explained in terms of something's being good and one that is less directly linked to the agent's pro-attitude.

But, in practical contexts, it must be so linked. Philosophers have often attempted to define 'right' in terms of fittingness or obedience to a rule; but these attempts fail to do justice to the practical role of 'right'. For fittingness is not a two-term relation that we just 'see' to obtain between an action and a set of circumstances. At least one more term is required for a full analysis of 'fittingness', if the concept is to be used to elucidate 'right', namely the purpose of the person concerned. This reference to purpose is often so obvious that we can afford to suppress it in practice. No doubt the right key is simply the one that fits the lock in a straightforward spatial sense and the right peg to put in the square hole is the square peg. In the same way the right degree of deference to pay to a person is the degree which is fitting to his social status.

But this two-term fittingness is not enough. In the last example there is already a covert reference to a rule of propriety, a rule which determines what degree of deference befits each person; and in all the examples there is a covert reference to the purpose of the person for whom it would be right to do something. It is assumed that he wants to open the door or to fill the hole exactly. For a man who wants to fool the police into thinking that he cannot open the door the 'fitting' key to use is the wrong key.

The attempts of deontologists to explain 'right' without reference to purpose appear satisfactory only because, in some cases, a particular purpose is so much more common than any other that 'right' has acquired a purely descriptive force. Thus we could either say that the criminal ought to use the wrong key (thus tying 'right' analytically to 'fitting' and at the same time loosening its ties to 'ought'); or we could say that the right key for him to use is the one that does not fit (thus tying 'right' analytically to 'ought' and loosening its ties with 'fitting'). And we might even draw attention to the peculiarity of his purpose by saying paradoxically that the right key for him to use is the wrong key. But, however we choose to make the point, the fact remains that the key he ought to use is not the key that fits. We cannot at the same time tie 'right' analytically both to 'fitting' and to 'ought' and also construe the first of these as descriptive and the second as practical. If 'right' is used in such a way that it would be logically odd to question its connexion with 'ought' it cannot be synonymous with a word of which the function is to refer to an objective relation, even a non-natural one. Once more the objectivist confuses the job which a word is used to do, in this case to explain a decision, and the conditions that must obtain for this word to be used, in this case the existence of a relation of fittingness.

The analysis of 'right' in terms of 'in accordance with a rule' suffers from a similar defect. The word 'right' is often used in a context involving rules or laws and part of its meaning in such contexts is simply 'in accordance with the rule or law'. The rule may either be something that we could point to in a book of rules, a volume of Hansard, or a manual of etiquette, or it may be, more vaguely, one of the code of rules that ordinary, decent people observe. A similar element is often present in the meaning of such words as 'fair', 'honourable', 'equitable', 'merit', and 'deserve', and we shall see that in attempting to define deontological words in teleological terms, teleological writers have not always done justice to this element. But the mere existence of a rule is not a (logically) good reason for anyone's doing anything; and if the function of 'right' was simply to promulgate or draw attention to a rule without implying a pro-attitude towards obeying it, it could not be used to give logically impeccable reasons for choosing and advising.

The point is often obscured by the fact that, since there are no logical limits to the possible objects of pro-attitudes, a man may have a pro-attitude towards doing something which he would otherwise not want to do just because it would be in accordance with a rule. The desire to conform to the accepted code, to do what others do, to be an inconspicuous member of the herd, is an important though not always a decisive factor in conduct. And we expect others to be influenced by the same motive. If this were not so there could not be such a thing as an accepted moral code.

It is against this background of conformity that advice is given and taken. We have seen that it would be improper to use even so subjective a word as 'nice' in an impersonal sentence except against a background of general agreement; and the same applies, with even more force, to 'right'. Smith asks Jones for advice because he believes Jones to be wise and experienced in the ways of the world; and if Jones gives unequivocal advice, Smith is entitled to infer not only that Jones himself approves of the lines of conduct he calls 'right', but also that it is generally approved. If there is no such general agreement or if Jones knows that his moral view on this question is an unusual one, he ought to express it in a more guarded way which discloses its peculiarity. Suppose that Jones is, unknown to Smith, a conscientious objector, and Smith asks whether he ought to join the army. Jones certainly ought not to say 'yes', even though he knows that this is in accordance with the accepted rule; for this answer implies that he approves. On the other hand a plain negative would equally be an abuse of the conventions under which advice is given, since it would imply that the consensus of reputable opinion is on his side, which he knows to be false. He ought either to add 'that is my personal view; but many good people think otherwise' or to tell Smith to consult his own conscience, which is a refusal to give advice.

There is one peculiarity which 'right' shares with 'good' and 'ought' and with no other words. Except in ironical or other secondary uses it is always a pro-word. We saw that while A-words must always carry a pro-force when used in the contexts of choosing and advising, they do not always carry the same force, and we have to gather whether they are pro- or con-words from the context. This is never the case with 'right'. Some words that are akin to 'right', such as 'just', 'fair', and 'honourable', are almost always pro-words, but they admit of exceptions. They imply a code of rules but they could be used in cases where we want to advise a man to disobey the code. We might think, for example, that this was a case in which justice should give way to mercy and we should then say: "It would be the just thing to do; but in this case I don't think you ought to do it". But the word 'right' is seldom, if ever, used in this way. There is an air of self-contradiction about 'That is the right thing to do; but you ought not to do it' which is absent from 'that is the just (fair, honourable, gentlemanly, etc.) thing to do; but you ought not to do it'; for 'right', unlike these other words, is always used to give a verdict and not merely to draw attention to a reason for giving that verdict.

[2]

'*Ought*'. Sentences containing the word 'ought' have a complexity similar to that of A- and G-sentences. They are used for a variety of jobs and their contextual implications in each case include just those elements that must be implied if they are suited to the job they are doing. They cannot be construed in a purely subjective or performatory way because, although they are used for linguistic performances such as choosing, advising, exhorting, and commanding, they are only so used under certain fairly rigid conditions. If someone says "I happen to like doing X" it makes no sense to ask him why he likes it; for the phrase 'happen to' has just the role of indicating that he can give no reasons. But if he says "I ought to do X" he lays himself open to a request for reasons and he must be prepared with an answer. It is because we want to mark a contrast between a decision based on reasons and a decision not so based that we have these different forms of speech.

As in the case of 'because I thought it best', 'because I thought I ought to' does not give a reason for my choice; it gives too good a reason. But it indicates that the choice was a reasoned and not a casual one and, like 'because I thought it right', it indicates the type of reason, namely that it is a pro-attitude towards obeying a rule, whether the rule be a mere rule of procedure, a rule of etiquette or good manners, or a moral rule.

Similarly, 'You ought to do X' cannot be equated with

'please do X'; nor is it simply a stronger form of it which we use to give weight and authority to our requests. If this were the whole story it would be impossible to see how anyone could have come to believe that the 'you ought' formula is more weighty and authoritative. If someone says "Please shut the door" it makes sense to ask for a reason for his request. But by way of reply he can get away with "I would like it shut"; if he uses the 'you ought to' formula he must be prepared to support it in a very different way.

Commanding. It is sometimes said that G-sentences and 'you ought'-sentences are disguised imperatives and, since one of the most frequent uses of the imperative mood is to issue orders, that they are disguised commands. But this is an oversimplification, not unlike the theory that 'this is good' means 'I like this'. The truth contained in the theory is that both imperatives and ought-sentences are used for telling someone to do something; but they are used in different circumstances and the logic of their use reflects these differences.

A command can (logically) only be issued by someone who is competent to issue it, by a person in authority. In practice people who are not in a position to use the language of commanding often do so in order to give the impression that they have the necessary authority or simply to get something done, relying on the well-known docility and habits of obedience of their fellow-men. But these are secondary uses, parasitic on the proper use of commanding language. If someone issues an order it always makes sense to question his right to issue it, even if it is in practice impolitic sometimes to do so. But commands differ from ought-sentences in that a man who gives a command is not logically bound to give any reasons why it should be obeyed. On the other hand if a man says 'You ought . . .' or 'It's worth . . .' he must (logically) be able to give reasons. These G-sentences are to commands roughly what impersonal pro-sentences are to expressions of taste or approval.

Nor can ought-sentences be identified with commandments,

that is to say general commands issued to all and sundry and to be obeyed not once and for all, as commands are, but always. 'Soldiers will salute officers at all times' and 'Thou shalt not kill' are orders, edicts, or commandments issuable only by a competent authority who is not logically bound to give any reasons for issuing them or even to have any reasons beyond a desire to issue them. But we use 'you ought' sentences precisely when we are not in a position to issue orders; and this fact and the fact that these sentences must be backed by reasons provide an important clue to their logic. Although 'advice' is far too weak a word for many 'you ought' sentences, their logic in primary cases is always that of advising, never that of commanding. For they are addressed to a rational agent as solutions to his problem of choice and, in consequence, they imply a pro-attitude on the part of the recipient. The author of a command, on the other hand, is not logically bound to be concerned with the pro- and con-attitudes of his subordinates, though, of course, he may be.

It is for this reason also that it is a mistake to try to define moral 'oughts' in terms of God's commands or 'God's will'. For the mere fact that a command has been issued by a competent authority, even by God, is not a logically good reason for obeying it. Jones's 'thou shalt' does not entail Smith's 'I shall'; and neither does God's 'thou shalt'. We do in practice often appeal to the existence of a command in backing up an ought-sentence, in the same sort of way that we appeal to the existence of a rule; but this procedure contextually implies a general pro-attitude on the part of the recipient towards obeying the commands of that authority, as such. He might have no other reason for doing X, but decides to do it just because he has been told to by such an authority. For religious people the fact that God has commanded them to do something is a sufficient reason, perhaps the only reason, for thinking themselves obliged to do it. But this is because they have a general pro-attitude to doing whatever God commands. And if this were not so, the mere fact that God commands something is no more a reason for doing it than the fact that a cricket coach tells you to do something. No doubt, God, like the coach, will not tell you to do things that you ought not to do, but the fact that you ought to do it cannot be identified with nor is it entailed by the fact that God has commanded it.

The imperative theory of 'ought' fails for the same sort of reason that, as we saw in Chapter 3, the objective-property theory failed. Unlike the objective-property theory it recognizes the practical role of moral language; but it neglects to notice that except in secondary cases, such as exhortation and the aping of authority, practical sentences must constitute solutions to a problem of choice. This defect is partly due to the philosopher's habit of talking about 'obligation' instead of talking about 'I ought' and 'You ought'.

[3]

'I ought' and 'You ought'. Most of the verbs used in ordinary descriptive discourse are neutral in respect of pronouns. If Jones says truly to Smith "You are sitting on a chair", Smith's reply "Yes, I am" and Brown's comment "Yes, he is" must also be true. The office of the pronoun is to indicate the person to whom the verb applies and the truth-value of the statement is not altered by a change of pronoun appropriate to the person making the statement. But what is true of the logic of descriptive discourse is not necessarily true of the logic of practical discourse.

If Jones says to Smith "You ought to do X" and Smith replies "No, I ought not", are they contradicting each other? Must we say that one is necessarily correct and the other mistaken? We have seen that sentences used for registering decisions or giving advice contextually imply certain causal and predictive elements which are indeed true or false; so that if the dispute between Smith and Jones is found to be concerned with any of these elements, they are contradicting each other and one of them must be mistaken. Among these elements in the case of ought-sentences would be the existence of a rule recognized by both parties or a command issued by an authority whom they both recognize. These are objective questions of fact and there is no reason for saying that, if the dispute is about them, Smith and Jones are not contradicting each other.

But it is impossible that elements of this kind should be the sole elements in the use of ought-sentences. If they were it would be impossible to understand the rôle that these sentences play in deciding, advising, preaching, and exhorting. For the first of these activities it is necessary that Smith should have a pro-attitude towards doing what he thinks he ought to do; otherwise 'I ought' is irrelevant to his problem of choice. For the others it is necessary that Jones should have a pro-attitude towards Smith's doing what he tells him that he ought to do. Otherwise he is involved in the absurdity of urging Smith to do something that he (Jones) does not want him to do. Human conduct is only intelligible on the assumption that people intend the natural consequences of their actions; and to say 'you ought' is to act, to intervene in the world, not to describe it; so that, except in secondary cases – for example if Smith is known to be contumacious, counter-suggestible, or pig-headed – it is implied that Jones intends Smith to do what he tells him.

Now since Jones's and Smith's attitudes to the proposed course of action may differ, it is possible for them to agree on all the objective contextual implications and yet for Jones to say, rightly, "You ought", while Smith says, rightly, "No, I ought not". These remarks can both be logically right in the sense that each is the correct way of expressing what the speaker intends; whether they can both be morally right is another matter.

It might seem that this situation is still analogous to a dispute about an empirical matter. For if Jones says "It's a dog" and Smith says "No, it isn't", they can both be right in the sense that each has used the correct form of words to express what he intended to say, but they cannot both be right in the sense of saying what is true. But, as we have seen, there is in empirical matters a test of truth which is independent of the beliefs of a speaker, namely correspondence with the facts, so that in these cases there is a point to the distinction between the two senses of 'right'. But if the dispute is a moral one there is no test of this kind.

Now it is true that in ordinary life we should say that Smith and Jones were contradicting each other. But this only illustrates the danger of drawing philosophical conclusions from ordinary language. 'Contradicting', which literally means 'speaking against', can be used of almost any kind of verbal disagreement; but it also has a technical logician's use which was designed to elucidate empirical discourse. And if we speak of conflicting moral attitudes as 'contradictory' we run the risk of unconsciously assimilating moral disputes to empirical ones and of inventing in the logic of moral discourse elements analogous to those which are bound up with the notion of contradiction in empirical discourse. One of these is 'correspondence with the facts'. And this is to court disaster.

And disaster has followed. Philosophers have been led to talk in terms of a sentence in the form 'X ought to do Y' which is neutral in respect of pronouns and, if true when spoken by one man, must also be true when spoken by another. The temptation to do this is due to the fact that it does no harm when the moral dispute is in fact a disguised empirical dispute about the existence of a rule or command which both parties agree ought to be obeyed. But we have seen that the use of ought-sentences in moral disputes is not confined to such cases. And if, as I have suggested, 'Smith ought to do Y' when spoken by Smith expresses a decision, but when spoken by Jones expresses an injunction, it cannot be extracted from its context and pronounced true or false.

'He ought'. If Jones says "You ought" (giving advice) and Smith says "No, I ought not" (deciding to reject it), we should naturally say that one of them must be wrong or mistaken or even that what one of them says is false, thus once more assimilating the logic of moral discourse to that of empirical discourse. But the typical philosopher's phrase 'we

should naturally say' conceals an important ambiguity. It may mean (what it is intended to mean) that 'Smith is wrong' is in English a natural and proper formula for anyone to use if he wishes to express his moral disagreement with Smith and agreement with Jones. But the same phrase could also be used to make a moral comment, to express 'our' disagreement with Smith; for example in the sentence 'If Smith said that cruelty was right, we should naturally say that he was wrong'. The philosopher's point about the use of language must be sharply distinguished from the moralist's siding with Jones; for, while the former is true or false in a quite straightforward sense – it is a matter of historical fact how words are used – the latter is not.

There is this similarity between the moral and the empirical case that, since Jones's attitude conflicts with Smith's, Brown cannot side with both of them; and since his logical inability to do this is like his logical inability to agree with each of two people who contradict each other on a point of fact, we mark this similarity by using the same sort of language, correct, mistaken, true, false, etc., in the two cases. But this is as far as the similarity extends.

'True' and 'false' are used in moral discourse; and this is not an accident. Their use is identical with their use in other contexts, in that they are used to endorse what someone has said or to endorse its contradictory; and they are not used just to endorse, but contextually imply reasons for giving the endorsement. We must again distinguish between what a man does with a sentence and the conditions which make his use of that sentence for that job a proper use. When a man says of someone else's empirical statement 'that's true' he is not saying that it corresponds with the facts; he is endorsing it, siding with it or expressing his agreement with it. But, in empirical cases, one of the conditions which make the use of 'that's true' proper is that he should believe that the other man's statement corresponds with the facts. In other contexts there are different conditions; for example in mathematics there is no question of correspondence with facts; and in moral contexts there is no question of this either. In every case the conditions under which it is proper to say that what someone else said is true are the same as the conditions under which it is proper to say that thing. But the conditions are different in different types of case. In a moral context it is proper for Brown to say of Jones's advice 'that's true' if it would be proper for him to give the same advice, which is what he is, in effect, doing; but it is not necessary that he should believe that Jones's advice corresponds to the facts, because pieces of advice are not statements and neither correspond nor fail to correspond to facts.

Just as the logic of discourse about objective properties is intelligible only against a background of empirical agreement, so the logic of practical discourse is intelligible only against a background of agreement on moral principles. It is this similarity that leads us to use the same words 'true' and 'false' in both cases; but the background – what has to obtain to make the logic of our talk intelligible – is different in each case.

I shall return to the distinctions between 'I ought' and 'You ought' when I come to examine Conscience, the operations of which seem to combine the two.

CHAPTER 14

Duty and Obligation

[1]

WE have seen that the primary use of 'you ought' sentences is to tell someone to do something in cases where it is contextually implied that the speaker has reasons for what he says. And we have also seen that the logic of advising, exhorting, and commanding requires a pro-attitude on the part of the speaker to the advice being taken or the order being carried out. This need not, of course, be present on all occasions. Any use of language can become a mere habit; a corporal may pass on an order from a sergeant without caring a straw whether or not it is obeyed, and advice may be given in a similar way as a matter of routine. But such uses, however common they may be, are secondary uses, not unlike the use of 'good' when a man judges something in a professional capacity without himself having any interest in it.

Since this is so, and since we learn what our duties are by being told what we ought to do, it has always seemed natural to represent duties as the demands made on us by others. It is hardly necessary to say that any attempt to define 'duty' in terms of the demands of others is bound to fail, since any such definition cannot but fail to do justice to other contextual implications of the word; but there is an obvious element of truth in this view. Its crudest expression is to be found in the theory, which Plato ascribes to Thrasymachus, that my duty is what is advantageous to others and, by implication, disadvantageous to myself. Now it is clearly false that in all cases in which Jones tells Smith to do something, the thing that he tells him to do is advantageous to Jones and disadvantageous to Smith. I have already cited as examples the case of a man advising another on the choice of a career and the case of a father giving death-

198

bed instructions to his son. Plato – perhaps deliberately – confuses the fact that Jones must have a pro-attitude towards Smith's doing what he tells him with the question whether he (Jones) is going to reap any advantage from it, and thus gives a cynical and egoistic twist to an obvious platitude, namely that a man who says 'You ought . . .' has some pro-attitude towards the compliance of his audience. It would be logically odd if he were sorry to see his advice taken.

And there is a second contextual implication that is always present in cases where someone tells another to do something. Although we can and sometimes do use language without hope of success, this is a secondary use. In primary cases, Jones must believe that there is a considerable chance of his advice being taken or his instructions carried out. He must believe, that is to say, that Smith will make the required transition from 'You ought' to 'I ought'; and this implies that Smith has a pro-attitude towards the suggested course. This pro-attitude can be of various kinds. (a) In cases of advice, in the usual sense of the word and not the wider sense in which I have been using it, it was assumed that Jones is trying to help Smith solve his problem and that his advice merely takes the form of showing Smith how he can implement his existing aim. This is what happened in the conversation about the film in Chapter 11. (b) But we also saw in that chapter that Smith may have a pro-attitude towards doing whatever Jones tells him as such; if Jones tells him to do X, he may now want to and decide to do X, even though he was previously averse to it or had not contemplated it. And this situation is much more typical of moral advice; for we are there concerned not with advice about how to achieve an end but with advice about the propriety of pursuing the end.

We must now consider a third type of case. Jones may be in a position, not merely to give advice, but to oblige Smith to carry it out. Now 'obliging' does not, as we shall see, mean compelling. Jones does not have to use force, and if he does, then Smith does not choose to do what he is made to do, and the case is of no interest to the moral philosopher. But Jones may threaten Smith with consequences that he does not want or he may point out that, in the society in which Smith lives, such consequences are likely to occur. He may back up his 'You ought' with 'If you don't, I shall . . .' or 'If you don't, somebody will . . .'. In these cases Jones provides Smith with a motive for doing what he is told.

The reasons for which a man does his duty are many and various and cannot be profitably discussed at this stage. I am far from suggesting that fear of the consequences of disobedience is the only or even the commonest motive. But it is not for nothing that philosophers have spoken of a conflict between 'duty' and 'inclination', however absurd some of the conclusions they have drawn may be. The language of 'You ought' and particularly of 'duty' is frequently used in cases where the agent has no reason for doing what he is told other than the fact that it is his duty. He has no pro-attitude towards the course of action as such. And there is a reason for this.

[2]

The connexion between duties and the demands of others comes out clearly in the fact that we use the word 'obligation' as a synonym for 'duty'; and this word is derived from a root meaning 'tied', an obvious metaphor for coercion. My duties are what I am obliged to do and it is no accident that moral rules as well as the laws of the land are backed by sanctions. The language of moral obligation also contains many words, such as 'law', 'must', and 'necessary' which are also used both in connexion with logical entailment and causality. Philosophers have often drawn attention to the analogy between moral obligation and logical or causal necessity. Some have tried to identify it with one or the other of these; but others have seen that this will not do. If it were logically or causally necessary that I should do X, then it would be impossible for me not to do X and there could be no such thing as moral wrong-doing. So they have tried to represent moral obligation as a "third kind of necessity". After all, why should there be only two kinds?

Obligation by circumstances. When we talk about being obliged by circumstances to do something we seldom, if ever, mean literally 'forced'. We say 'the fact that the road was flooded obliged me to make a detour'; but we do not mean that we were bodily pushed round the longer route. Obligations of this sort prevent our carrying out our original plans rather than force us into doing something else. And they prevent us in two ways. There is the less interesting case in which I just can't continue along the road, because a landslide has washed it away, or because it is blocked by some object too heavy for me to move. And there is the more interesting case in which I could go forward, but the obstacle makes it undesirable to do so; for example the road is unsafe or would take, in its present condition, even longer to travel than the detour. (Compare: "I was obliged to stop because my car ran out of petrol" and "I was obliged to stay a night in Birmingham because I knew I shouldn't reach Oxford before two in the morning".)

The second type of case is the more interesting since in it I choose to do what I am 'obliged' to do, and if it is true that ethics is only concerned with what we do voluntarily it is here that the analogy with moral obligation must be found.

There is a sense of 'voluntarily' in which a man who chooses to do something acts voluntarily, even though he is 'obliged' to choose as he did. This is the sense in which doing something voluntarily and, *a fortiori*, deciding or choosing to do something are opposed to such phrases as 'I can't' or 'I couldn't help . . .', when this latter phrase is used to indicate physical impossibility. Thus the sailor who is obliged by a storm to make for the nearest port, nevertheless *decides* to make for the nearest port; his situation is unlike that of the sailor who is simply driven before the wind. Similarly the man who is obliged to make a detour because there is a flood or a lion in his path decides to go round by the longer way. But there is another and much commoner sense of 'freely' and 'voluntarily' in which a man who is obliged to do something does not act 'freely'. In the first type of case, if you asked him why he did not continue on his original route, he might reply: "I just couldn't; the path had been washed away". In the second type of case he would, if pressed, reply: "Well, I suppose I *could* have gone on; but the R.A.C. man told me that the road was very dangerous . . .". And he would add that, although he decided to take the longer road, he hadn't got a *free* choice. The notion of having a free choice or doing something as a result of a free choice is much narrower than that of choosing to do it. But it is not easy to pin down the difference and certain pseudo-problems have been raised by ignoring it.

The sense of 'free' which I shall now consider is one in which the word is opposed to 'obligatory' and its cognates. There are cases in which we are not free to choose, but are obliged to do something; and these two ways of putting it amount to the same thing. In addition to the cases I have mentioned the following cases may help to indicate the sort of choices that are not 'free' choices.

(a) I was obliged to move my rook to Q2 to protect my queen. (Otherwise my queen would have been taken.)

(b) I was obliged to raise my bid. (Otherwise someone else would have bought the house.)

(c) I was obliged to look it up. (Otherwise I should have probably got the answer wrong.)

There are three things which these cases seem to have in common. In the first place I *could* in any of the cases have omitted to do the thing I said I was obliged to do; but, secondly, the consequences of doing this would, in each case, to put it broadly, have been worse than the chosen course. Thirdly, in each case there is a stated or implied reference to some special factor that obliged me to take the course I did. The phrase 'I was obliged to do X' has in these cases, not the force of 'it was impossible for me to do anything else' but 'it would have been foolish or unreasonable for me to have done anything else'. This is a distinction which is easy enough to understand, but almost impossible to put in a general form that accurately reflects our use of language. And the reason is that, although the distinction is clear, it is in practice always blurred.

There is, so far as I know, no phrase used to indicate the physical impossibility of doing something that is not also used to indicate that doing it, though possible, would be unreasonable or foolish. Thus we even talk about its being 'impossible to get angry with Jones, because he is so kindhearted' or 'impossible not to smile'. And the same applies to all the quasi-synonyms such as 'I couldn't help . . .', 'it was out of the question . . .', 'I was forced to . . .', and, 'I had to . . .'. And there are two reasons for our peculiar habit of allowing phrases indicating physical impossibility to be extended to cover cases where it is possible, though unreasonable, to do something. In the first place we do not always know just what we could do if we tried. The man who says 'It was impossible not to smile' really does not know whether he could have re-frained from smiling if he had tried. Secondly, these phrases are often used in order to exculpate oneself from a possible criticism; and since the one cast-iron method of exculpation is to show that the suggested alternative was literally impossible, it is easy to see why people wish to represent cases which are really cases of great difficulty or cases where the alternative would have been unwise or unreasonable as cases of impossibility. They are trying to justify their conduct.

The contrast between doing something freely and being obliged to do something is made when the circumstance that 'obliges' is exceptional and not taken into consideration when the original action is planned. Everything that we do is done under conditions that are in some way set for us by natural circumstances; even in the most propitious circumstances the sailor must take on board enough fuel and set his course correctly. It is when the limits set by natural circumstances are narrower than usual or narrower than they were expected to be that we speak of them as 'obliging' us. For example we talk of being obliged to alter course, but not of being obliged to take the most direct route. If I wanted to visit a neighbour who lives a mile away, it would be odd to talk about being obliged to travel the intervening mile. I am obliged to protect my queen when my opponent makes an unexpected attack, but not to make a move that is part of my own planned attack.

Since everything that we do is done under limits set by natural circumstances, it is fatally easy to extend the concept of obligation by circumstances in such a way as to make it useless and to create pseudo-problems. If the brigands on the path oblige me to make a detour, might we not say that the fact that the normal road is twice as long as the route as the crow flies obliges me to do so? We might; but only if we wished to draw special attention to the fact that the normal road is more devious than most roads are hereabouts. If you live in very mountainous country, where all roads are circuitous, you expect such things and don't talk about being obliged to walk two miles to reach a place a mile from your starting point.

Before comparing cases of being obliged by circumstances with cases of moral obligation it is necessary to say a word about the ways in which one's own motives can be said to 'oblige' one, since the fatal tendency to generalize from the exceptional case to all cases has led to some curious philosophical theories in this connexion.

Each of the cases of the second type of obligation (but obviously not of the first or less interesting type) could have been put in terms of being obliged by a motive. Instead of saying that the brigands or the storm or an opponent's move obliged me, I could say that fear of the brigands, etc., obliged me. And just as everything that we do is done under some circumstances or other, so everything is done from some motive or other. If, then, we can say that fear of the brigands obliged me to make a detour, why should we not say that hope of gain or a desire to visit a friend obliged me to set out in the first place? There is something queer about talking in this way and we are clearly on the verge of a philosopher's paradox, that is to say of being forced by gradual steps from saying something usual to saying something very unusual.

Before attempting to deal with this paradox, let us examine the paradoxical conclusion. We shall be forced to say that everything which we choose to do, since it entails having a motive for doing it, entails that we are obliged to do it and so did not do it freely. This argument has been frequently used to show that there is no such thing as free choice at all; and some philosophers have accepted this conclusion. Others, accepting the premise that all ordinary motives 'oblige' and rejecting the conclusion, have tried to escape the conclusion by saying that the sense of duty is a very special motive which, unlike all other motives, does not oblige. We act freely, they say, only when we are not 'slaves to desire'. I shall try to show later that, while the sense of duty is indeed peculiar in many ways, its peculiarity does not lie in this and that this line of escape involves paradoxes of an even more startling kind.

The paradox we are here concerned with is startling enough. We must say that – leaving aside the sense of duty – whenever a man does what he wants to do he is 'obliged' to do it and so does not really act freely. If for example I decide to go to a concert rather than a cinema, because I like music more than films, I am 'really' a slave. To what am I a slave? Why, to my superior passion for music of course!

Now it may be true that philosophers who talk in this way about a man being a slave to his desires – not only in the case of drug-addicts, but *whenever* a man does what he wants to do – have a genuine point to make about human conduct. But the one thing that is certain is that they have chosen a most unfortunate way of putting their point. For we normally contrast 'doing something because I want to' with 'doing something because I've got to', 'doing what I like' with 'doing what I must', 'being free' with 'being a slave'. And it follows that anyone who says that what we normally call freedom is 'really' slavery, though he may intend to say something intelligible and even true, is using the word 'freedom' or the word 'slavery' or both in such unusual ways that he cannot be understood to mean what he says.

It is, however, easy to see that, though there may be some point to such remarks – for example to draw attention to the fact that people are often in the grip of some ruling passion to a greater extent than they imagine – the theory cannot be wholly true. It is logically impossible that all motives should oblige, since we talk of being obliged only when our desires are thwarted, that is to say when we are obliged to do something other than what we wanted or intended to do; and this implies that there was something which we wanted or intended to do. Obliging motives presuppose non-obliging motives; freedom is the ability to fulfil one's aims, not the state of being aimless.

In order to escape from the paradox that all motives 'oblige', we might for a start try distinguishing motives into two types, positive and negative. A negative motive will be one which is directed towards an object that the agent would prefer to be absent and which, if he were endowed with miraculous powers, he would simply wish away. For example the sailor prefers a calm sea to a storm and the chess player would have been happier if the opponent had not made the move which obliged him to protect his queen. (I shall ignore the complications introduced by the fact that people enjoy contending with difficulties; e.g. a chess player enjoys a game against a formidable opponent in spite of the fact that such an opponent 'obliges' him more often than a weaker one.)

The position is now that a person has some aim, something that he wants to do. If the doing of it involves a number of steps, which are simply means to the end and which he does not want to do for their own sake, it follows that he wants to reduce the number and difficulty of the steps; for every unnecessary step is a step towards which he has a con-attitude. If circumstances oblige him to take steps that he would not take under optimum circumstances, his motive for taking them

might be described as an obliging motive. This account enables us to do justice to the fact that we do talk about being
obliged to alter course by fear of the storm, etc., but not obliged to go to a concert by a desire to hear music. But unfortunately this line will not do. For the ingenious philosopher
who is trying to push us into the paradoxical position might
argue that people would in fact be better off if they had no
motives whatsoever, so that all motives would be 'obliging
motives'. Thus, instead of satisfying my desire to hear music
by going to a concert, would I not be better off if I had no
desire to hear music to be satisfied and was not, therefore,
'obliged' to go to concerts? In this way some philosophers
have actually recommended as the best life a life altogether
free from desire.

The flaw in this argument lies in the traditional equation
between 'pleasure' and 'satisfaction of desire' and in the traditional pattern of all voluntary action as consisting in the
attempt to remove pain or uneasiness. It is true that in cases
that do conform to this model it might be better for a man to
have neither the preceding desire nor the subsequent satisfaction, neither the hunger nor the food, neither the itch nor the
scratch. But we have already seen that not all motives conform
to this pattern. And it is primarily in cases which do not conform to this pattern that it is odd to speak of motives as
'obliging'.

Since there are pleasant smells and unpleasant smells a man
might be better off without a sense of smell; but if there were
no unpleasant smells, he would not be. The pleasure of smelling a rose cannot be thought of as a cancellation of the debit
balance of desire; it is a positive credit balance; so also is the
taste of good food and the conversation of one's friends; and
this enables us to modify our account and come closer to the
distinction between motives that oblige and motives that do
not oblige. When we do something for its own sake, i.e. because it is just what we want to do, our motive is one that does
not oblige us to do anything; we are not slaves to our own
desires or to anything else. On the contrary we are acting

freely because this is the model *par excellence* of what 'acting freely' means. And the circumstances involved in doing what we want do not oblige us either. It is when, in order to do what we want, we have to do other things that we do not want to do for their own sake that we talk of being obliged. And we do this most markedly when the circumstances are not only untoward but unusual.

So long as the necessary steps are not abnormally difficult, irksome, or roundabout we think of them as being the natural, inevitable way of bringing about our end and do not, therefore, think of them as obstacles to bringing it about. It is for this reason that it would be odd to talk about 'being obliged' to take the shortest and easiest route; for when we talk about being obliged to do something we always have in mind a less irksome or arduous or complicated alternative that might have been possible under other circumstances. If a man talks about being obliged to take the shortest and easiest route we are puzzled to know what he means. What is he contrasting it with? Of course he didn't want to take any route at all; he wanted to be at his destination; he would have been better off if he had miraculous powers of reaching his destination without traversing the intervening distance. The merchant would make more profit if New York were nearer to London than it is. But it isn't, and nothing that the merchant can do can alter this. Hence, in making his plans, he takes this into account. It is when we have to deviate from our plans because of circumstances which make our task more difficult, irksome, or complicated than it would be under the optimum *realizable* conditions that we speak of 'being obliged' by circumstances and of motives which 'oblige' us to revise our plans.

This discussion has been designed to bring out three points. (a) Obligation is not identical with but contrasted with 'free' choice. (b) Our own motives do not always oblige us; on the contrary there must (logically) be some motives that do not. (c) Circumstances which oblige us are untoward and unusual obstacles; or, rather, though they may be quite usual, they are only thought of as 'obliging' when contrasted with less obstacle-ridden courses which are within the bounds of possibility. We must now compare this analysis of being obliged by circumstances with other types of obligation.

[*3*]

Obligation by threats. Threats come into the picture in very much the same way that natural circumstances do. A man who does something because he is threatened does something that he would not, but for the threat, have done and something that he does not, apart from fear of the consequences, have a motive for doing. This need not always be the case; he may have been intending to do it anyway; and in that case the threat was otiose. But such a case is necessarily unusual. Threats would never be used unless the threatener believed that his victim would not adopt the suggested course but for the threat.

The other considerations also apply. A man who is threatened acts 'voluntarily' in the sense that he chooses to do what he does; but he does not act 'freely'; on the contrary the man with the gun obliges him. The threat is an untoward and unusual circumstance which interferes with his free choice.

Legal and Quasi-legal Obligation. By 'quasi-legal' I mean obligation to obey rules or laws of a fairly definite kind other than the law of the land and to execute orders other than those given by the officers appointed and authorized by the State to enforce the law of the land. Examples would be school rules or the rules of a club or society. These types of obligation are all associated with penalties for breaking the rules and this alone is sufficient to make them analogous in some ways (though not in others) to obligation by threats and hence to obligation by natural circumstances. If I do something because I am obliged to do it by a school rule, (a) I choose to do it, (b) my choice is not a free one; for I would not have done it but for the rule, (c) I have no motive for doing it apart from the rule, and (d) I must have some motive for doing it.

My motive may be fear of the consequences of disobedience;

but there is no need to be so cynical as to suggest that this is the only motive for obeying a rule. I may obey it because I have been trained to and obedience is now a matter of habit, and in this case I have no motive at all. But I may also obey it from a sense of duty; and this is a motive.

Moral Obligation. There are obvious connexions between legal and moral obligations; some moral laws are part of the law of the land though they are not made so by statute; some statute laws forbid behaviour that is morally wrong as well as criminal, though others do not; and disobeying the law of the land is thought to be morally wrong as such, even if the behaviour which the law makes criminal would not in itself be a breach of a moral rule. But, apart from these connexions, there are also similarities enshrined in the language that we use in common in the two cases. Both (moral) rules and (legal) laws enjoin and forbid; breaches of them are both wrong; and breaches are attended with penalties, though the penalties are different in the different cases.

Like other forms of obligation, moral obligation limits the range of free choice. I am not free to accept an invitation to dinner, because I am obliged by my duty as a member of the local Conservative Association to attend a meeting or because I am obliged by having made a promise to dine with someone else. I am not free to marry the girl of my choice, because I know that it would break my mother's heart and I am obliged by filial duty. A moral obligation is, like a natural obligation, something which obliges me to act in a way that, but for the obligation, I would not have acted. It is analogous to the second rather than to the first type of natural obligation, since, although I have not a free choice, I *could* always break the promise or my mother's heart. In fulfilling a moral obligation a man chooses to do what he does, but does not choose freely. The feature which distinguishes moral obligations from all others is that they are self-imposed; I shall discuss this point in a later chapter.

In moral, as in the other, cases the logic of obligation requires a conflict between the obligation to do something and the inclination not to do it. But it is important to notice that this conflict is part of the general background of the concept of obligation and need not occur in every case.

It is sometimes said that a man cannot have a duty to obtain pleasure for himself – and we must remember that philosophers use the word 'pleasure' in a very wide sense. But this is not quite true. If we thought that a man was ruining his life by excessive abstinence, we might well say that he ought to pursue pleasure more than he does. But there is, as usual, some truth underlying this view. It is paradoxical to tell someone that he ought to pursue pleasure more than he does; but this is only because most people do not need telling.

Codes of law and moral codes do not usually contain injunctions to do or to refrain from things that people would do or refrain from in any case. As we shall see the function of such codes is to provide people with motives for doing what they would otherwise not do. Thus, although a man may do his duty willingly or even gladly in a particular case, what he does would never have been incorporated in a code of duties if there were not a general presumption that the type of action concerned is one that people are, on the whole, disinclined to do.

If, for example, people were seldom or never disinclined to tell the truth we should never have come to regard telling the truth as a duty. In the same way people are, in general, not inclined to part with their money and if this were not so we should not think of paying a debt as a duty. We frequently promise to do things that we are otherwise inclined to do, for example to meet a friend. If all promises were of this kind, they would still be useful for the purpose of making arrangements for co-operative activities. But part of the point of making a promise is that a man who makes one binds himself to do something which, when the time comes, he may not want to do; and if we only promised to do things that we would do in any case because we enjoy doing them, promise-keeping would not be thought of as a *duty*. There is therefore a sense in which it must (logically) be the case that people who do their duty act unwillingly or against their inclination; but there is another sense in which they cannot be said to act unwillingly. How could they, when it is what they *choose* to do?

[4]

Learning the language of duty. We learn the language of duty at a very early age and, however different the child's use of this language may be from the adult's, there remains a connexion between the two. The latter grows gradually out of the former; and if this were not so it would be a mystery how adults come to use this language as they do. It is not necessary to be an expert child-psychologist to understand the main outline of the way in which children learn the language of duty. It is obvious that a child must learn to understand the use of a word by others before he can use it himself. This applies to all words; but it applies in a special way to such words as 'ought' and 'mustn't'. It is perhaps not logically necessary that it should be so, but there are obvious practical reasons for the fact that a child comes into contact with 'you mustn't' before he comes into contact with 'I mustn't' and that he learns the language of imperatives in the first instance from having them addressed to him by others. Telling himself to do things or not to do them is a relatively sophisticated performance. He learns to obey before he learns to command.

Now some desires are instinctive, in the proper sense of the word, even though a child may have to learn how to satisfy them; and in some cases babies can learn how to satisfy a desire without being told to try. A baby or young child tries to do what he wants to do and his wanting to do it does not seem to him to be commanded or even suggested by anyone else. On the other hand there are a host of things that others want him to do towards which he has no inclinations whatsoever. His conduct can be influenced in two radically different ways.

(a) We may attach penalties to a type of action that we wish to inhibit so that the child prefers not to do it, even when he wants to. And the child learns the language of duty in connexion with such penalties. The word 'mustn't' has no magic power and the child needs no special insight to learn to understand it. 'What I mustn't do' is, for him, simply 'What I get punished for' and it is through this connexion of 'mustn't' with punishment that the word acquires its practical force. No child is told that he must do, or obliged under penalty to do what he wants to do already; and for the same reason in each case, that he already has a motive for doing it and will do it 'of his own free will'. The fact that the commands and prohibitions are often issued in the child's own interest is quite irrelevant. Children have to be 'obliged' to do what is in their own interest because they are incapable of knowing that they already have a good reason for doing it.

(b) But it is not to be supposed that, in the twentieth century at least, children learn the use of moral words wholly or even mainly in connexion with a system of rewards and punishments. Most, if not all, small children enjoy the favour and affection of their parents, and fear more than anything else any signs of this favour being withdrawn. It would be wholly misleading to represent parental favour and disfavour as rewards and punishments. The child simply notices that his parents respond to some modes of behaviour in a way that he likes and to others in a way that he dislikes. He learns that what adults call 'being good' is identical with what makes Daddy smile and behave in a generally propitious way, while what they call 'being naughty' is identical with conduct that has the reverse effects. There is no other obvious common characteristic in all 'good' behaviour or in all 'naughty' behaviour.

These facts have an important bearing on what is meant by calling conscientiousness an *artificial* virtue. One of the most important and wide-spread of the natural pro-attitudes of human beings is the desire to conform to the habits of the group to which one belongs, to do 'the right thing'. Now, if the people around him habitually conform to a certain code of conduct, the child is likely to contract the same habits and hence to do many things towards which he has no natural inclination and which it would never occur to him to do if they were not habitually done by others. A child does not always have to learn to tell the truth either because he recognizes the intrinsic value of truth-telling or because lying is associated with punishment or parental disfavour. He does it because he lives in a society in which it is habitual; so that learning to tell the truth is almost synonymous with learning to talk. But to form a habit of doing something that is in fact part of the moral code is not the same as to form the habit of obeying the moral code. The imitative instinct or desire to conform will account for the former; but not for the latter.

Conscientiousness is an 'artificial' virtue in a sense in which altruism is not. In fact very young children are often selfish in that they display a complete indifference to the pleasures and pains of others. A child learns to seek its own pleasure and to avoid pain long before it comes to think of others as enjoying or suffering at all. But children do not have to be taught to be altruistic in the way that they have to be taught both to recognize and to do their duty. Affection for others, that is to say a desire for their welfare, comes naturally to most people as soon as they begin to think of others as 'people' at all. This natural benevolence can, of course, be inhibited by bad treatment; it is stronger in some children than in others, and it is absurd to ask if people in general are naturally altruistic or selfish. Since natural benevolence is, in most people, too weak to make them behave with that degree of altruism that we want them to acquire, most children have to be coerced into being more altruistic than they naturally are. But with 'conscientiousness' it is altogether different. There is no natural conscientiousness in the way that there is natural benevolence. Children learn to recognize and do their duty, not because they are endowed with a special faculty of recognizing it and a special, natural propensity to do it, but because they are artificially provided with natural reasons for doing those things that at the same time they learn to speak of in the language of duty. Undesired consequences – to use a conveniently vague phrase – are not only levers by means of which people are obliged to do their duty; they are an essential part of learning what 'ought' and other deontological words mean.

CHAPTER 15

Duty and Purpose

[1]

WE have seen that 'you ought'-sentences must be backed by reasons and that giving the reason often takes the form of appealing to a rule. This is not a peculiarity of moral oughts; we can appeal to a rule in support of any injunction or advice which is given in terms of 'you ought' or of 'right'. Moral rules are indeed a special class of rules and I shall discuss later the conditions under which we are prepared to call a rule a 'moral' one; but there do not seem to be any sharp logical differences between the way in which moral rules are connected with 'ought' and 'right' and the way in which non-moral rules are. If this were so it would be difficult to understand why we use the same words in the different cases, why we talk about the right train to catch, the right way to spell a word, the right way to address a duke, and the (morally) right thing to do. If moral right and wrong were, as some philosophers say, new entities, phenomena or qualities that we descry with a special faculty, it would be impossible to understand how people learn to use moral words and also to understand the way in which bad manners shade imperceptibly into social maladroitness on the one hand and immorality on the other. No one is going to postulate a special non-natural property of dukes in virtue of which we ought to call them Your Grace, though the obligation to address them in this way is 'non-natural' in the sense of artificial or depending on human convention.

The dispute between teleologists and deontologists turns largely on the status of moral rules and their connexion with 'ought' and 'right'. As we saw in Part I, intuitionists tend to adopt the deontological view while naturalistic philosophers tend to be teleologists. In this chapter I shall try to show that, as usual, both parties are right and to put forward a modified teleological interpretation which allows due weight to what is true in the deontological theory. On this occasion it is the deontologists who are, on the whole, right about the meaning of moral words but ignore the contextual backgrounds of their use, while the teleologists tend to treat this background as part of the meaning.

Rules and Ends. It is characteristic of teleologists to treat all 'oughts' as hypothetical and all rules as rules for attaining a given end. But this raises two difficulties about moral rules. Some of these are no doubt only binding because of the good consequences that they bring about. In these cases we need no direct apprehension of an obligation because we can justify the obligation by showing that it is only by fulfilling it that we can achieve something else that we ought to achieve. But what about this second 'ought'? It cannot be the case that all moral rules depend on other rules in this way; there must, it seems, be some rules – perhaps a very small number or only one – which cannot be justified by appeal to superior rules. Moreover moral rules differ from other rules in one very important way. They are supposed to be obligatory, not just on this or that occasion with this or that end in view, but *semper*, *ubique*, *et ab omnibus*. If there are occasions on which a particular moral rule ought to be disobeyed these can only be occasions when the rule comes into conflict with higher rules and the less stringent duty must give way to the more.

In order to do justice to these facts the deontologist must adopt one of two courses. He must either try to show that conflict between rules is, in the long run, only apparent and that there is either only one basic moral rule on which all others depend or that, however many basic rules there may be, they are all consistent with each other. This theory is known as Rationalism and represents a system of moral rules as analogous to a system of geometry or logic. The alternative is to adopt the intuitionist standpoint and to say that, while some generalization may be possible, in the last resort we discover what we ought to do by estimating the relative stringencies of moral claims on each occasion. What we know for certain is not that we ought to obey general rules but what our duty is in a particular case.

Teleologists cannot adopt either of these courses; but they still have to account for the universality, or at least the wide generality of moral rules and for the fact that not all rules can be shown to be dependent on other rules. From a laudable desire to be synoptic they have often tried to find some large general purpose which all men necessarily have and by reference to which hypothetical rules of a very general kind can be justified. Moral rules are to the achievement of happiness what the rules that you will find in a manual on How to play Cricket (but not in the Laws of Cricket) are to success at that game. They refuse to accept such a rule as 'Thou shalt not kill' as the fiat of God or Society or Conscience and claim that, however absurd it may be in practice, it always makes sense to ask 'Why shouldn't I?'. Moreover they have insisted that such sceptical questions can only be answered by showing that the course of action enjoined by the rule is, in the end, advantageous to the agent. This standpoint comes out clearly in Plato's way of making Glaucon and Adeimantus ask Socrates to prove that it is to the advantage of the agent to be 'just', i.e. to obey a certain moral code. The implication clearly is that if Socrates cannot prove this there is really no obligation to be just at all. Morality is moonshine; but not quite in the way that Thrasymachus thought. For Socrates is represented as agreeing with Thrasymachus on the fundamental point that the obligation to be just must be justified by reference to the good accruing to the agent; he differs only in thinking that Thrasymachus takes a narrow and short-sighted view of what that good is.

The same point comes out clearly in a famous passage of Butler. "Though virtue or moral rectitude does indeed consist in affection to and pursuit of *what is right* and good, as such; yet, when we sit down in a cool hour, we can neither *justify* to ourselves this or any other pursuit, till we are convinced that it will be for our *happiness*, or at least not contrary to it."[1]

This was the famous mistake of which Prichard accused almost all moral philosophers; and, if it is really a mistake, it is not difficult to understand the appeal of intuitionism. For, if it is a mistake even to try to justify obligation by reference to the purpose of the agent, there seems no alternative but to represent it as a unique entity or phenomenon of which we are immediately aware. I have already suggested in Chapter 10 that one of the main reasons for abandoning the teleological standpoint was that it appeared to entail the theory that all conduct, even the best, is ultimately selfish and that this criticism rests on a confusion; and I shall now examine some mistakes that teleological writers do in fact make.

The fundamental mistake is that of confusing three distinct sorts of questions, logical, factual, and moral. The logical questions are those about the meanings of the words used in moral discourse and about the relations between moral concepts. For example, "Can 'right' be defined in terms of 'good' or 'fulfilment of purpose' or is it an irreducible concept?". The factual questions are mainly historical, sociological, and psychological. For example, "What rules do we actually have?", "How did we come to adopt just this set of rules?", "What do men, in fact, desire, enjoy, find pleasant, etc.?". And the moral questions are "What ought I to do?","What rules is it best for me to adopt?". I shall examine the ways in which these different types of question are related in the next chapter; in this chapter I shall try to show how confusions between them have seriously distorted the answers which teleologists want to give to them and that these confusions have led to criticisms which are sometimes justified and also led to the belief that duties must be independent of purposes and directly apprehended.

1. *Sermon* XI (my italics).

[2]

(a) Teleologists, in their desire to construct a single all-embracing system of morality, have tried to represent all moral rules as dependent for their validity on their tendency to promote a single end which they call Pleasure, Happiness, The Good Life or, since it is obvious that virtue is not always rewarded in this world, Eternal Bliss. But, in so doing, they have distorted the logic of moral words and their conclusions either turn out to be disguised logical truisms or to be false or at least questionable. The more concrete and detailed the picture they paint of Happiness or Eternal Life the more obvious it becomes that no *obligation* to try to achieve this follows from the description. Primitive conceptions of Eternal Bliss are anything but vague; and just because they are fairly precise it makes sense to ask 'Ought I to try to achieve this state?'. And this gives the deontologist his strongest weapon. Paint the picture in as glowing colours as you can; it does not follow that you ought to try to bring it about.

(b) The same confusion has led some teleologists into representing empirical falsehoods as logical truisms. Thus Hobbes thought that to desire one's own death was a logical impossibility, although it is obvious that it occurs. There is no logical limit to the possible objects of pro-attitudes except the logical limit of descriptive discourse, which is self-contradiction; a point first clearly made by Hume.[1] So long as a man expresses the object of his desire or enjoyment in a way that is self-consistent, he cannot be convicted of any logical error. We are, of course, entitled to disbelieve him if he says that he would rather be roasted by the fire than warm himself at it; but this is only because we know that men are more apt to lie or to misrepresent their own desires than to desire any such thing.

(c) Again, Gay *defines* obligation as "the necessity of doing or omitting any action in order to be happy . . . and no greater

1. *Treatise*, Book II, Part 3, Section iii.

obligation can be supposed to be laid upon any free agent without an express contradiction."[1] But this is palpably false both as a theory of what people mean by 'obligation' and as a theory about the things that people in fact think themselves obliged to do. If Gay is right, the whole human race labours under a monstrous illusion. Did Regulus return to Carthage in order to be happy? And, if not, are we to say that he was foolish, irrational, or immoral? To meet this sort of objection teleologists sometimes say that Regulus must have supposed that he himself would be unhappier in Rome suffering the pangs of a bad conscience than he would be undergoing the physical tortures that he knew awaited him in Carthage.

But this will not do. In the first place it is difficult to see how the notion of 'conscience' could have arisen on this hypothesis or why anyone should have a bad conscience and suffer therefrom. And secondly, need we look further for Regulus's motive than to say that he may have acted from a sense of duty or that he may have acted in order to save his country? And the first of these motives cannot be represented either as a desire to spare himself the pangs of a bad conscience or as a means to this. For it is of the essence of 'pangs of conscience' that they can be allayed only by the knowledge that we have acted for the sake of doing our duty and they cannot, therefore, be allayed if we know that we have acted for the sake of allaying them, unless we deceive ourselves so grossly as to mistake the one motive for the other. And in the same way a desire to save one's country cannot be represented as a covert desire for one's own happiness or as a means to this. It is a contradiction to say that a desire to save one's country *is* a desire for one's own happiness (although the same course of action might satisfy both desires) and, since Regulus looked forward to certain death, he can hardly have desired the salvation of his country as a means to his own happiness.

Gay has, in fact, confused the truism that Regulus must have had a pro-attitude towards returning to Carthage with the empirical (and, in this case, obviously false) assertion that his

1. Selby-Bigge: *British Moralists*, Vol. II, p. 273.

motive was to reap some advantage for himself. The truth underlying the teleologist's theory is a logical truth, not an empirical assertion about the things that people in fact desire or enjoy. It is that Regulus must have had some pro-attitude towards returning to Carthage; otherwise he could not be said to have *chosen* to return. The theory that men can only aim at their own happiness is plausible only if 'happiness' is covertly used as a general word covering 'whatever men aim at'. Since this conflicts flagrantly with its normal use it is not surprising that some teleologists have slipped into covert egoism.

Gay is not the only or the best known philosopher to have made this mistake; Mill also seems, at times, to have supposed that 'right' *means* 'conducive to the greatest happiness of the greatest number' and Moore expressly says that "the assertion 'I am morally bound to perform this action' is identical with the assertion 'This action will produce the greatest possible amount of good in the Universe'.", although neither Mill nor Moore slips into egoism.[1]

To these attempts to discover a single purpose which justifies all moral rules or to define obligation in terms of purpose deontologists have rightly objected that the special role of sentences including the words 'ought', 'duty', 'obligation', and 'right' cannot be construed in this way. I have tried to show that the reason which they give for their objection, namely that deontological words stand for unique, indefinable, and immediately apprehended entities, is mistaken. And it is mistaken because the deontologists themselves represent the issue as one of fact, when it is really one of the logic of concepts; but on the logical point they are right.

[3]

Pro-words and G-words cannot be defined in terms of each other; but to admit this is not to say that there is no logical connexion between them or to require us to represent G-sen-

1. *Principia Ethica*, p. 147.

tences as statements of which the role is to describe a special world of 'values' or 'duties' altogether cut off from the pro- and con-attitudes of ordinary human beings, or connected to those attitudes by means of a string of necessary synthetic connexions.

Sentences containing pro-words are used to express and defend preferences, choices, and decisions. They vary considerably, as we have seen, among themselves, some having contextual implications which others lack. For example, some pro-words imply that the attitude is a relatively stable or a relatively widely-shared one, while others do not. But what is common to all pro-sentences is that they either express choices or give reasons for choice that are logically impeccable. Deontological sentences, on the other hand, are used primarily for advising, warning, commanding, exhorting, and admonishing and almost always contextually imply the presence of rules. Their use also implies the existence of certain pro-attitudes without which they could not be used for the purposes for which they are used. This is the truth underlying the teleologists' attempt to reduce G-words in one way or another to pro-words.

To be brief, pro-words belong primarily to the language of 'I shall', G-words to the language of 'You ought', and decisions never follow logically from imperatives. The logical gap between the two languages which Plato and Butler noticed and which led them and others to try to explain obligation in terms of purpose is often obscured by the Janus-character of all moral words. And this is due to the facts of the world in which we live. Since it can be assumed in a great many cases that a man has a pro-attitude towards doing what he is told and towards conforming to the customary code of his society, 'You ought' slides imperceptibly into 'I ought' and 'I ought' into 'I shall', and deontological words acquire a pro-force in addition to their deontological force. They can be used to defend or explain a choice or even to express a decision. One party makes much of the essentially practical role of deontological words and emphasizes their connexion with pro-attitudes, while the other party emphasizes their connexion with rules and standards, a connexion which is much more a matter of verifiable fact.

But in spite of the misleading way in which he sometimes puts his case, the teleologist has a valid point to make. And this is what we should expect when we consider the long and distinguished history of this type of theory; for it is difficult to believe that all theories of this type are altogether mistaken. His point might be put as follows: Deontological words cannot be defined in terms of or in any way reduced to prowords. The 'attitude' of the speaker – or of anyone else – that is to say his likings, enjoyings, desires, aims, and interests, may not enter at all into what he means by calling something 'right' or his 'duty' on a specific occasion; moreover there are many occasions when the only relevant attitude is his desire to do his duty as such. Nevertheless deontological words are logically posterior to teleological or pro- and con-words in a different way. The latter form part of the logical background without which deontological words would not be intelligible at all; but the reverse is not the case. We could imagine a world in which people used such words as good, desire, aim, purpose, choose, happiness, and enjoy, but in which they had no conception whatever of duty, obligation, right, and ought. In this strange world people's pro- and con-attitudes would be very different from what they are in our world; they would enjoy and desire very different things; but their use of pro- and con-language would be recognizably similar to our use.

We could also imagine a world in which people used prowords and also used the words 'right' and 'ought' in a purely hypothetical way; for they might discover that they could only achieve their ends by adopting certain courses which they would call 'the right course' or 'the course we ought to adopt'. But it is impossible to imagine a world in which people used the words obligation, duty, right, and ought but did not use any pro-words at all.

The reason for this is that all these words, both pro-, con-, and deontological, belong to *practical* discourse; and they could not be used in the way that we in fact use them in a world in which people did not know what it is to choose; and this they could not know if they were indifferent to everything in the universe. Deontological words belong to the language of advising, exhorting, and commanding rather than to that of choosing; but pro-words still form part of their logical background. For we should have no use for the language of advising, exhorting, and commanding if we were indifferent to everything that everybody (including ourselves) did. And we should have no use for this language because we should not know what it was to advise, exhort, or command. These are things that we *do* and unless we had motives we could not *do* anything.

This account of the relation between pro-words and deontological words has nothing whatever to say about what men's actual attitudes are, still less about what they ought to be. It is a logical thesis, not a psychological one, still less a recommendation to mankind to adopt certain aims or policies.

CHAPTER 16

The Purpose of Moral Rules

[1]

In the last chapter I suggested that teleological writers have sometimes confused logical, factual, and moral questions. In this chapter I shall consider three factual questions:

(a) Why does a man obey a rule on a particular occasion?
(b) Why do we have any moral rules?
(c) Why do we have the rules we do?

(a) *Why does a man obey a rule on a particular occasion?* There are two kinds of explanation which we can dismiss from the start. In the first place he may do something that is in fact in accordance with a moral rule from a motive that has nothing to do with the rules at all; for example it may be that it is what he wants to do. This does not count as 'obeying the rule' for our purposes. Secondly he may obey from force of habit; either he cannot break the habit or it does not occur to him not to obey the rule. This case can be dismissed on the grounds that he has no motive for obedience. When the explanation is given in terms of motives, the motive may be of any of the following kinds.

(i) He may treat the rule as a 'hypothetical imperative' laying down the best, simplest, most convenient, etc., way of achieving whatever it is that he wants to achieve. It is for this reason that people obey, follow, or apply the instructions in cookery books, manuals on how to play golf, and so on. It is clear that the value of such rules depends solely on the empirical question whether obedience to them tends to promote success; so that none of our three questions would be difficult to answer if all rules were of this type.

(ii) He may know that the rule has a sanction and be afraid

of the consequences of breaking it. This would give a complete explanation of why a man obeyed a rule on a particular occasion; but it cannot answer our second or third questions, unless we suppose that a direct desire to make others afraid is much more widespread than it would seem to be. Philosophers have said that the aim of the law is terror, but not terror for its own sake.

(iii) He may have a desire to conform to the code in use in his society, to do the done thing. This is an exceedingly common motive and accounts for a great part of our obedience to rules of good manners and minor moral rules when this is not habitual. But, again, it cannot answer our second question, since this motive presupposes a system of accepted rules.

(iv) He may obey the rule from a desire to obey the rule as such, and when the rule is a moral one this motive is called the Sense of Duty. This phrase does not refer to a special faculty by means of which we learn what our duties are; that we learn in the same way that we learn everything else; it refers to a special motive that is so important that I shall discuss it in full in the next chapter.

It should be noticed that these possible explanations are not mutually exclusive; they may be mixed, and, what is more important, the last motive may be mixed with a direct pro-attitude towards doing the action enjoined by the rule without regard to its being a rule. A man may give money to charity both because he wants to and also because he regards it as his duty and wants to do his duty.

(b) *Why do we have any rules at all?* To suggest a way of life in which there are no rules is to suggest something of which no one has ever had any experience and hence to indulge in speculations of a desert-island type.[1] There are indeed cases where we can contrast relatively arbitrary action – and by this is meant, not deciding by tossing a coin, but deciding each issue *ad hoc* without reference to general rules – with action which is bound by rules. Laws may be administered, for

1. Pp. 239, below.

example, either by an arbitrary despot who decides each case as he thinks fit, or by an administrator who is bound by rules to decide in a particular way. The rival merits of a society governed by an arbitrary ruler, who is assumed to be enlightened and benevolent, and one governed by a ruler who is not above the law have been debated for centuries; indeed this topic was one of the most important topics of political philosophy at least from Plato to Hobbes. All actual known systems involve a compromise between the two extremes. In our own legal system judges are bound by laws and precedents and by complicated, traditional rules of procedure which determine to a large extent how laws are to be interpreted and what constitutes a binding precedent.

It is hardly necessary to expatiate on the advantages of having some rules. Many of the things that we want to do involve large-scale operations extending over long periods of time. A man who wants to learn to play a Beethoven Sonata or to make a fortune or to convert a whole people to a new religion is hardly likely to be successful unless he co-ordinates his activities to suit his ends. This is an empirical fact, a feature of the world in which we happen to live; but it is such a prominent feature that it is difficult to imagine a world in which this is not the case, a world in which large-scale aims could be achieved in a haphazard way.

The harmonious life. Moral rules are necessary for two main reasons. In the first place every man has a great variety of aims which cannot all be fully achieved because they conflict with each other. If a man wants to be prime minister or a great pianist, for example, there are many other things that he also wants to do but cannot do if he is to achieve this particular aim. If this were the only reason for having moral rules we could treat all moral rules as rules of success, rules for co-ordinating a man's activities in such a way that he succeeds in living the type of life that he most wants to lead; for it is again an empirical fact that he is more likely to succeed if he sets about achieving this type of life in a regular rather than a haphazard way.

This reason for having moral rules is so obvious and so important that some philosophers have thought it possible to prove that we ought to follow what Butler calls 'cool self-love' rather than 'particular passions'. But this must be a mistake; for to say this is to make a *moral* judgement, to side with the 'calm' against the 'violent' passions and to recommend people to follow their long-term interests rather than do what they happen to want to do at the moment. And these decisions and injunctions cannot, as Hume noticed, follow from the empirical statement that *if* a man is to pursue his long-term interests satisfactorily he must curb his passions.

But, although Butler was wrong in thinking that he could prove the moral superiority of cool self-love, he was right in a way. The language of 'ought', in so far as it is necessarily and intimately connected with *rules*, is appropriate to the achievement of long-term interests and not to the satisfaction of desires. There are rules, sometimes only very rough rules or 'maxims', which must be observed by anyone who wants to achieve a long-term end, such as learning to play the piano; but there are no rules for acting on impulse. So that a man who asks himself what he *ought* to do has already decided against a general policy of acting on the spur of the moment.

Social Harmony. But the achievement of co-ordination between a man's own aims is clearly an unimportant reason for having moral rules when compared with the need for co-ordinating the aims of different people. Indeed, until we mention this, we hardly seem to have touched on *moral* rules at all; for, although we do sometimes talk about duties to ourselves, most of our duties are duties to others. There are two main reasons for having social rules. (a) To enable people to co-operate successfully in activities which, either logically or in practice, they could not carry on individually; for example commercial enterprises, amateur dramatics, games, and warfare. There must be honour even among thieves if robbery is to pay. (b) The aims of different people conflict, and if there were no rules for settling disputes the resulting anarchy would be such that no one would achieve his aims. Property-rules are rules which exist for this purpose, as is shown by the fact that in the case of goods which are so abundant that there is no competition for them we have no property-rules. There are rules for the distribution of water in the desert and where, as in cities, there are costs of distribution, but not elsewhere.

Now property-rules are not moral rules; but they are logically prior to many moral rules. There could be no moral obligation to pay debts if there were no property-rules, because there could be no debts. This is not to say that my obligation to pay a debt rests on the scarcity of the object concerned. The creditor may be in no need of it or easily able to obtain it elsewhere; and in neither case would my obligation be cancelled. But unless there was competition for goods in other cases we should never have come to include the obligation to pay debts in our moral code.

(c) *Why do we have the rules we do ?* We may divide the rules actually found in any society into two classes, superior rules and subordinate rules. Subordinate rules are those that nobody would think of calling absolute or ultimate rules of morality or categorical imperatives. The only reason for adopting such rules is that they are connected to some superior rule in one of two ways. Either they are special cases which follow logically from the superior rule in the way that the obligation not to make a false income-tax return follows from the general obligation to tell the truth; or they are supposed to tend to promote some very general object, such as the happiness of others, that we think we ought to try to promote. In the latter case the only good reason for adopting a new rule or adhering to an old one is the empirical fact that obeying it tends to promote the general object enjoined by the superior rule. To this class belong all the rules of etiquette and good manners and a great many moral rules, for example those governing sexual conduct.

Superior rules can be subdivided into two classes: (i) the general obligation to promote the welfare of others and (ii) rules of 'special obligation', as they have been called, the duty to pay debts, keep promises, tell the truth, and to distribute good and evil according to merit. I shall call the first class 'duties of beneficence' and the second 'duties of justice'; but it must be remembered that 'duty of beneficence' means an obligation to do good to others, not an obligation to feel benevolent or an obligation to act from the motive of benevolence. Acting from benevolence and acting from a sense of duty are quite distinct, even though the two motives may be present together.

(i) *Duties of beneficence.* There are two reasons why beneficence should be considered a duty. In the first place benevolence is one of our natural pro-attitudes. It is one that conflicts with other pro-attitudes and it is one that tends to be stronger in our calmer and more reflective moments. If to do good to others is one of a man's dominant aims he has a good reason for making this type of conduct a duty; for if he does so his desire to do good to others will now be backed up by his desire to do his duty, which is an exceedingly powerful motive. In this way he is more likely to try to do good to others even at moments when he does not much want to do so, and so come to fulfil his dominant aim more completely than he would if he did not adopt this rule.

But, even if the desire to do good to others were in fact much weaker in most men than it is, every man would always have a powerful indirect motive for it. He cannot fulfil any of his aims without the co-operation of others and people are unlikely to do what he wants if he does not do what they want. Security from interference and co-operation would be very unstable if we could rely on them only in cases where the parties have mutual interests; they can only be achieved among men as we know them if men can be brought to adopt and maintain a general system of doing good to others even when they do not particularly want to do so. If it be objected that this is to give a cynical account of the reasons for doing good to others, the answer is that I am not giving reasons for doing good to others but reasons for regarding this as a *duty*. In a world in which a regard for the welfare of others was more widespread and stronger than it is, beneficence would not be a duty.

(ii) *Duties of Justice*. It is notorious that utilitarian theories have great difficulty in explaining the duties of special obligation. For example, they have suggested that what we ought to do on a given occasion is the action which will bring about the greatest balance of good over evil that we can in the circumstances. Now, if this theory is put forward as representing the ordinary man's reasons for calling something right, just, or what he ought to do, it is patently false. Utilitarians have in fact tended to confuse five different, but connected questions:

(*a*) Why does a man in fact obey a moral rule?
(*b*) What sort of reasons do men usually give for obeying a rule? or: Why do they think they ought to obey a rule on a particular occasion?
(*c*) Why should a man obey a rule on a particular occasion?
(*d*) Why do men in fact have the moral rules they do?
(*e*) What moral rules ought we to have?

Considered as an answer to any of the first three questions the utilitarian theory is obviously false. We need distinguish the first from the second question only in order to allow for the fact that men's motives are not always what they think they are; and the first question is not of great interest to ethics. The second question can only be answered by examining the ways in which people do actually defend and justify their decision to obey a moral rule. Sir David Ross puts this admirably as follows:

"When a plain man fulfils a promise because he thinks he ought to do so, it seems clear that he does so with no thought of its total consequences, still less with any opinion that these are likely to be the best possible. He thinks in fact much more of the past than of the future. What makes him think it right to act in a certain way is the fact that he has promised to do so, – that and, usually, nothing more. That his act will produce the best consequences is not his reason for calling it right."[1]

Ross advances this argument to refute the theory that 'right' *means* 'productive of the greatest possible good'; but it is no less fatal to the theory that the belief that something will produce the greatest possible good is our only reason for believing that it is right. It is just untrue that most people think that they ought to give Christmas presents which are likely to cause a great deal of happiness rather than use the money to pay a debt to a rich creditor who does not need it, or to a drunken one who is likely to do harm with it. And it is also untrue that if a man is asked why he thinks he ought to do something he will always reply: "because it will produce the greatest possible amount of good".

Now the third question is not a question of fact, but a moral question, and cannot be so easily decided. An extreme utilitarian who says that the belief that an action will produce the greatest possible balance of good over evil is the only morally good reason for doing it is not necessarily trying to explain what 'right' means or telling us what most people think right; he may be advocating a special moral outlook. He is recommending people to consider only the good and evil consequences of alternative actions when making up their minds what to do. He may do this in one of two ways. (a) This may be the only moral principle that he espouses and is willing to recommend to others, or (b) he may admit the desirability of considering other points but say that it is desirable to consider these points only because we are more likely to achieve our ultimate purpose, which is to bring about the greatest balance of good over evil, if we do so. It is this last course that most utilitarians have in fact adopted; but they have confused justifying obedience to a rule in a particular case with justifying the rule, question (c) with question (e).

It is as an answer to questions (d) and (e) that utilitarianism can best be understood. As an answer to (d) it is, as it stands, untrue. For custom and tradition and the power of

1. *The Right and the Good*, p. 17.

interested persons account for a great many of the actual moral rules of all societies. We have the rules we do, not because we have deliberately adopted them as the best set of rules or because they were imposed on our ancestors by Philosopher-Kings, but because they are traditional. To understand the utilitarian theory we must distinguish between causes and reasons. Custom and tradition can explain why old rules are retained, and their force is made more powerful by the Janus-character of moral words. Since the words 'just', 'right', 'deserve', and 'ought' are used both to say what the rules are and also to defend adherence to them and recommend others to adhere to them, there is always an air of self-contradiction about any proposal to change the rules; for the conduct laid down in the new rule is necessarily unjust or wrong simply by virtue of the fact that it contravenes the old rule. Moral reformers have often found this a powerful obstacle.

But custom and tradition cannot account for changes in the rules and they do not even begin to answer the question 'For what *reasons* do we have the rules we do?'. To answer this question it is necessary to discover the pro-attitude which sufficiently explains why people adopt, adhere to, or change a rule. In many cases we need look no further than to the fact that a sufficiently powerful or influential set of people have a pro-attitude towards the inclusion of a particular rule in the moral code of their society. Their pro-attitude is a direct one; they want the rule adopted. And their power enables them to provide an indirect pro-attitude to their subjects in the form of penalties for disobedience. This is not to say that they make and enforce those rules which are in their own *interest*, but simply that they make and enforce those rules that they *wish* to enforce. Logically, the ruling class might be wholly altruistic and enforce only those rules which benefit its subjects. The rules which parents enforce on their children provide examples of rules which are enforced because a 'ruling class' wants to enforce them but which are adapted to the benefit of the subject class. But in practice it is to be feared that the cynical theory that laws are made in the interests of rulers is not far wrong.

Anthropologists are nowadays suspicious of attempts to explain moral rules in terms of their value to society. It is, for example, impossible to explain the ancient Hebrew taboo on the eating of pork as due to the unwholesomeness of the Palestinian pig. But the mistake of the older anthropologists was that of assuming that the ideas of all societies as to what constitutes the interest of society must have been the same as our own; they were not mistaken in thinking that rules are promulgated and enforced because they are believed to be in the interests of society, or of some class.

To illustrate this let us consider the various explanations that have been suggested for incest rules. Almost every known society has some incest rules, although the rules vary greatly between societies. Now it is often supposed that these rules are adopted because of their supposed biological utility. The offspring of incestuous unions will be insane or deficient in some other way. But it is impossible that all these rules should be biologically useful, since some of them contradict others; and a belief in biological utility could hardly account for the fact that in many societies a man is forbidden to marry his first cousin on one side and obliged to marry his first cousin on the other side. Moreover the question at issue is not whether the rules are biologically useful but whether they are adopted because they are believed to be. People who have not been influenced by our own tradition never in fact allege biological utility as their reason; without exception they explain and defend the rules either by reference to ancient tradition or by reference to the belief that social calamities, floods, crop-failures, and the barrenness of women will follow a breach of the rules.[1]

And these explanations are consistent with the utilitarian

1. The origins of and the justifications given for various incest rules have been examined by Lord Raglan in *Jocasta's Crime*. Lord Raglan shows conclusively that the explanations suggested by sophisticated people from Aristotle to Freud neither explain nor justify the rules and also that the belief that breaches cause social calamities is ancient and almost universal. His attempt to account for the origin of this strange belief is less satisfactory.

hypothesis. For the fact that the breach of a rule is not followed by the dire consequences supposed is not an argument against the theory that the rule was adopted because breaches were thought to entail these consequences. Dancing Sellenger's Round does not in fact help to keep the sun on its course; but it is almost certain that the practice originated because it was believed to do so. Why this strange mistake should have been made is another matter. If we allow for the part played by custom and tradition, the utilitarian theory is a plausible answer to the question 'For what reasons have men adopted the particular rules they have?'. It is at least a much more plausible answer to this question (*d*) than to the question (*b*) 'Why do men think that they ought to obey a rule on a particular occasion?'. We have the rules we do either because we have inherited them and stick to them uncritically or because we believe them to promote our ends.

[2]

The most important confusion and the one that has given rise to most of the misunderstandings of the utilitarian position is that between question (*c*) and question (*e*). To understand the utilitarian position it is necessary to distinguish between the judge's question and the legislator's question. Both the questions are moral questions, questions about what someone ought to do; but the logic of the answers is very different.

The duty of the judge is to pronounce verdict and sentence in accordance with the law; and the question 'What verdict and sentence ought he to pronounce?' turns solely on the question 'What verdict and sentence are laid down in the law for this crime?'. As judge, he is not concerned with the consequences, beneficial or harmful, of what he pronounces. Similarly, the question 'Was that a just sentence?' is one that cannot be settled by reference to its consequences, but solely by reference to the law. The logic of the phrases 'just verdict', 'just sentence', and 'just punishment' requires a reference to laws or rules at two points: (a) there must be a law forbidding the deed done, and (b) there must be a law attaching a certain penalty to breach of the first law.

In assessing the justice of a punishment in a particular case, therefore, we are concerned only with these two points. The punishment is just if and only if the accused committed the crime and the punishment is that laid down by the law for that crime. The question of the probable effects on the accused or on others (the reform and deterrence so greatly emphasized by utilitarians) is relevant only in so far as judges are allowed considerable latitude within which they may be guided by considerations other than what the law prescribes. In practice, both in civil and in criminal cases, judges often express regret at being in duty bound to give the verdicts they do and recommend the alteration of the law.

But the duty of the legislator is quite different. It is not to decide whether a particular application of the law is just or not, but to decide what laws ought to be adopted and what penalties are to be laid down for the breach of each law. And these questions cannot be decided in the way that the judge decides what verdict and sentence to pronounce. For if we interpret the legislator's question as one to be settled by asking 'What does the law lay down for such a case?' we shall either be involved in an infinite regress, a hierarchy of laws in which the justice is determined by reference to a higher law, or we shall be forced to claim intuitive insight into a system of axiomatic laws, themselves requiring no justification, but providing the justification of all lower laws.

This last course (which is the classical theory of Natural Law) is involved in all the difficulties raised earlier in connexion with intuitionist theories. It is equivalent to saying that we are quite certain that some laws ought to be adopted and others not, but cannot explain why. And it cannot explain the Janus-character of such words as 'just', 'deserve', 'blameworthy', etc. For these words have a gerundive force; to say that a law is 'just' is to recommend people to adopt or adhere to it; and if it were merely to state that it had a non-natural property, we should still have on our hands the question 'Why should we adopt this law?'.

Now since there are no logical limits to the possible objects of pro-attitudes it cannot be proved that men have not got a direct and natural pro-attitude towards certain forms of conduct such as paying debts, keeping promises, and punishing malefactors. I shall give reasons in the next chapter for supposing that, although the pro-attitude among people who have been brought up to obey certain rules is a direct one, it is not a natural one. The belief that it is natural seems to be due to the failure of the utilitarian account of what makes a particular action just or right. And this in turn is due to the utilitarian's confusion of the question 'Why should a man obey a rule on a particular occasion?' with the question 'What rules ought we to have?'.

It is worth noticing that Hobbes, who was a forerunner of the utilitarians, was alive to the distinction between the judge's duty and the legislator's duty, the difference between the way in which a verdict can be appraised as just or unjust and the way in which a law can be appraised. But he drew attention to the distinction in a misleading way which has led his critics to make his theory out to be far more shocking than it really is. Laws, he thought, could be good or bad, but not just or unjust; for, he said, 'just' means 'in accordance with the law'. His way of putting it illustrates the danger of monkeying with the usual meanings of words. We do in fact use 'just' and 'unjust' of both verdicts and laws; and although the logic of justification is different in the two cases, there is, as always, a good reason for our using the same word. We call decisions made in accordance with laws just and also call the laws themselves just. The reason for our doing this is not unlike our reason for calling empirical, mathematical, and moral propositions true. 'Just' is a pro-word which indicates our endorsement of the decision or of the law; but our reasons for endorsing it are different in each case. The tendency to confuse the two cases is partly due to the fact that we often want to do both at once. If a man calls a decision just without adding "but, mind you, I think the law is a very unjust one", he is always assumed to be in favour of the law as well as of the decision.

To understand utilitarianism we must, therefore, distinguish questions about the reasons for adopting, retaining, or discarding a rule from questions about our obligation to obey the rule. The obligation to obey a rule does not, in the opinion of most ordinary men, rest on the beneficial consequences of obeying it in a particular case in either the short or the long run, as utilitarians have almost always supposed. But the reasons for adopting a rule may well be of the kind that utilitarians suggest. It is, of course, impossible to prove that they are the only good reasons, since this would be a moral judgement. But it is a moral judgement that most men would be much more likely to endorse if it were not confused with the different moral judgement that we ought only to obey moral rules when the consequences of obedience are likely to be good.

It is only fair to the utilitarians to add that they were always more interested in the legislator's than in the judge's problem; and this explains their inadequate treatment of the latter. Their opponents, on the other hand, have tended to ignore the legislator's problem altogether. The fact that the moral rules adopted in a given society are believed to promote the ends of the members of that society and the fact that rules tend to fall into disuse when the beliefs are discarded are facts which ought to have puzzled deontologists more than they have.[1]

[3]

Desert Islands. I have suggested that it always makes sense to ask 'Why obey this rule?' even though it is often impolitic

1. As an example, when we discover that people who behave in a certain way are not in fact reformed by punishment, we tend to remove the type of conduct concerned from the list of crimes (although the law, for very good reasons, lags behind public opinion in this respect). But the question whether a certain type of conduct ought to be regarded as a crime is of a quite different sort from the question whether a man who has done what, as the law stands, is criminal ought to be punished for it. (cf. pp. 272, 306).

to do so. One of the commonest arguments against this view consists in inventing peculiar cases in which it is said to be *obvious* both that a rule ought to be obeyed and also that no advantage is going to accrue to anyone for obeying it. This is held to show that obedience to a rule neither can be nor requires to be justified by an appeal to consequences. Suppose, for example, that a man makes a promise to another man who is dying on a desert island to dispose of his goods in a certain way if he ever reaches home. Is he under any obligation to keep his promise if it is clear to him that some other distribution of goods is going to be more generally beneficial and if there is no chance of his breach of trust being detected?

We are invited to believe that the answer to this question is obviously 'yes'; and utilitarians have tried to reconcile this obvious answer with their theory in various ingenious ways. They point, for example, to the impossibility of being *quite* sure that the breach of trust will not be detected or that it will do more good than harm. They point also to the bad effects which such a breach is likely to have on the agent's own character. But it is clear that, as long as they admit the conclusion, these attempts at evasion are useless; for the relentless desert-islander will break them down one by one by adding stipulations to the terms of the original problem.

I shall adopt the more radical course of challenging the conclusion. It is always difficult to assess the force of these desert-island arguments that depend expressly on the improbability of the case supposed, precisely because the case *is* improbable and therefore not catered for in our ordinary language. Compare the question 'What would you say if half of the standard tests for deciding whether a piece of copper wire is electrified gave a positive answer and half a negative?'; or the question 'What would you say if you added a column of ten figures a hundred times and got one answer fifty times and another the other fifty times?'. The answers to these questions could only be either "I must see a doctor at once" or "I simply do not know what I should say; for the logic of my language for talking about electricity or adding does not allow for this sort of thing. If it occurred, I should have to treat some sentence which normally expresses an analytic proposition as expressing a synthetic one; but I certainly cannot say which."

In the same way I confess to being quite unable to decide *now* what I should say if a desert-island situation arose. Moral language is used against a background in which it is almost always true that a breach of trust will, either directly or in the more roundabout ways which utilitarians suggest, do more harm than good; and if this background is expressly removed my ordinary moral language breaks down. For it is the background which gives the air of *self-evidence* to the assertion that the rule ought to be obeyed. This self-evidence is due to the Janus-character of moral words, and the fact that they have this character is in its turn due to the normal background of their use.

Suppose it is said that to break the promise would be unjust, wrong, wicked, dishonest, or dishonourable. The minimum force of these expressions would be to point out the obvious fact that simply *qua* breaking a promise the action falls into a class of things to which these epithets are commonly applied. But this, though true, is not to the point. The objector clearly means to say more than this; he means to say at least that the customary moral code *forbids* breach of promise even in the circumstances alleged. And since customary moral codes are not designed to cover cases that are *ex hypothesi* unusual, this is at least doubtful. But the objector probably means more than this; he is suggesting that everyone would decide that he ought to follow the rule even in the peculiar case, whether or not customary morality enjoins it. But such a decision could never be self-evident unless it was in the trivial form 'I ought to do what I ought to do'. Now, since the very words 'just', 'right', 'honourable', and 'dishonourable' have a gerundive force as well as a fact-stating force, 'I ought to do the honourable thing' and 'To keep the promise is the honourable thing' both seem to be tautologous and the conclusion 'I ought to keep the promise' seems self-evident. But the trick is manifest.

The first premise is only tautological if 'honourable' is taken to be a G-word, the second only if it is taken as a fact-stating word about the customary code. Clearly I might decide that in this case I ought to do the 'dishonourable' thing.

The prototype of all desert-island arguments occurs in the second book of Plato's *Republic*, where Plato suggests that if a man had a magic ring which enabled him to escape detection and so evade punishment he would be under no obligation to be just. Now it is obvious that, in the world as we know it, the obligation to keep promises and pay debts is not dependent on the possibility of our being found out if we disobey the rules. But we are asked to say what would be the case in a world in which moral rules had no sanction apart from each man's conscience. The only possible reply to this question is that in such a world we should have no use for the concepts of rules or obligation at all. For, although it is not the case that people who obey rules always do so from a fear of the consequences of disobedience, the concepts of a rule and an obligation to obey it could never have arisen apart from that of a penalty for disobedience. The very word 'obligation' betrays this fact. In a moral Utopia men might always do the things that are in this world enjoined by our moral rules, but they would do them for some reason other than that of regarding them as obligatory. For, even if it is true that in our world a man's conscience is the only judge of his conduct, it is difficult to see how people could have arrived at the dualistic notion of 'me and my conscience' unless they were familiar with judges of a very different sort, a sort which could not have existed in the world depicted by Glaucon and Adeimantus since they could not have carried out their functions.

Part of the force of Plato's story lies in the fact that Glaucon and Adeimantus are made to assume that the lucky owner of the ring would indulge in a life of unbridled sensuality and selfishness. Once again, under the guise of an analysis of the logic of moral words, there is smuggled in a strange assumption about the sorts of things that people like doing and would do if the sense of duty did not restrain them.

But suppose that it is admitted that I should in fact recognize the obligation even in the desert-island case. What follows? Simply that my sense of duty is exceedingly powerful, more powerful than I thought it was and so powerful as to overcome any pro-attitude that I might have towards breaking the rule. I have, after all, been trained from my earliest youth to keep promises; and it is not unnatural that I should have acquired a strong repugnance to breaking them. "What makes him think it right to act in a certain way is the fact that he has promised to do so, that and usually nothing more." There is an irony in the word 'makes' that, I think, Ross did not intend.

The fact that a man has made a promise can no more explain why he keeps it than any other fact. He may keep it because he has been so thoroughly trained that it does not occur to him to break it; and in this case there is no need to ask for his motive, as he hasn't any. But if he chooses to keep the promise his choice requires to be explained in terms of a pro-attitude; and this may well be, not a pro-attitude towards the consequences, but a direct pro-attitude towards keeping a promise as such, a horror of or repugnance towards promise-breaking.

It is not easy to describe the peculiar feeling called moral repugnance that in fact restrains us from breaking a moral rule even in cases where we think it right to do so. But, although it is impossible to describe it to someone who has never felt it, it is unnecessary to describe it to someone who has. If the reader is puzzled to know what I mean, let him try, for example, stealing something under conditions in which it is highly improbable that he will be caught. He will, I think, find it exceedingly difficult, if not impossible, to bring himself to do it. Such is the force of moral training. And he will also find it exceedingly difficult to tell a lie, even in a case where he is convinced that he ought to do so. We might paradoxically, but not unfairly, say that in such a case it is difficult to resist the temptation to tell the truth. We are the slaves of our own consciences.

But what is the connexion between the *fact* that I feel this special moral repugnance towards breaking a moral rule which

I have been brought up to obey and the question whether I *ought* to break it? What, in Butler's terminology, is the connexion between the *power* and the *authority* of conscience? Butler thought that its authority was 'manifest', a contention I shall examine in the next chapter. What is manifest, at least in some people, is its actual power, that is to say the fact that people find it very difficult not to become slaves of their consciences. "Having read my Hume I should become a Thrasymachus."[1] I doubt if it is as easy as that to become a Thrasymachus even if it were true – which it is not – that a man who had no sense of duty would necessarily wish to become one. What the desert-island argument proves, if its conclusion be accepted, is not the fact that duties are intuited and independent of purposes, but that (a) the language of duty cannot be translated into the language of purpose, and (b) that moral habits die hard.

1. Raphael: op. cit., p. 94.

CHAPTER 17

Conscientiousness

[1]

IN defending the traditional, teleological approach to the understanding of moral language I may seem to have made so many concessions as to have abandoned the case. I have, for example, denied that deontological words can be defined in teleological terms and admitted that there are no logical limits to the possible objects of pro-attitudes other than the logical limits of language itself. It follows from this that a man might have a direct pro-attitude towards obeying a moral rule or towards doing what he thinks his duty, as such; he may have no desire whatever to do the action apart from its being his duty and no thought of the consequences, for himself or others, that the action is likely to produce. Now this motive is exactly what we mean by the Sense of Duty and the man who acts on it is called conscientious.

And is not to admit all this precisely to admit the truth of the deontologist's case? He would agree that it is a truism to say that every man must have a motive for what he does; since, if there were no motive, it would not count as 'doing' in any sense relevant to ethics. But he insists that the Sense of Duty is a very special motive; it is logically so different from other motives that it is a mistake to call it a pro-attitude at all; and it is morally peculiar in that, while a man can explain why he did what he did by reference to any motive, he can only justify his conduct when he acted from his sense of duty. Moral value, it is said, lies in conscientious action and in that alone. In this chapter I shall examine the claim of the sense of duty to be the only morally good, or at least the best, motive.

According to Kant an action has *moral* worth only if it is

done from the sense of duty. As Professor Paton puts it: "An action done solely out of natural sympathy may be right and praise-worthy, but nevertheless it has no *distinctively moral* worth."[1] How is this to be interpreted? It is allowed that an action done from sympathy may have some 'worth', but not 'moral worth'. It might, therefore, be suggested that Kant and his followers are deliberately using words in a special way of their own; but if this is so they meet with the usual fate of philosophers who recommend changes in ordinary usage. Questions which are either senseless or admit of an obvious answer when words are used in the ordinary way may become debatable when they are used in the new way. We might well agree that moral worth is superior to all other kinds of worth, for example that of talents and accomplishments and material goods. But this is because we normally think of moral worth as meaning the worth of any virtuous motive and we normally think of sympathy and benevolence as virtuous motives. But if moral worth is limited by definition to the worth of conscientiousness it is no longer so obvious that it is superior to all other kinds of worth.

But I do not think that this interpretation is correct. Kant claims to be elucidating the value-judgements of the ordinary man. And, while it is a tautology to say that only virtues have moral worth (for moral worth just is the worth of virtues), it is not a tautology that conscientiousness is the only virtue and hence the only bearer of moral worth. Nor is it even true that ordinary men regard conscientiousness as the only virtue; almost all men would include altruism in the list; and 'altruism' means, not 'doing good to others for duty's sake', but 'doing good to others for its own sake' or 'doing good to others for the sake of doing good to others'.

Kant in fact slides from an opening sentence in which he uses the phrase 'good will' to mean any virtuous motive to his full-blown theory that the sense of duty is the only virtuous motive. His first point is to prove that a good will is the

1. *The Moral Law*, p. 19. See also *The Categorical Imperative*, chapter III.

only thing that is good without qualification; and he tries to prove this by showing that other good things, talents, qualities of temperament, gifts of fortune, and even the classic 'virtues' of moderation and self-control, can sometimes be bad. "The very coolness of a scoundrel makes him, not merely more dangerous, but also immediately more abominable in our eyes than we should have taken him to be without it."[1]

All this may be true; but it is not to the point. For what Kant has to show is, not that non-moral assets and even some virtues are not good without qualification, but (a) that conscientiousness is good without qualification and (b) that no other virtue is.

The tacit equation between conscientiousness and moral virtue comes out well in Paton's treatment of the question whether moral virtue is the "highest" good.[2] He contrasts conscientiousness with non-moral goods, such as artistic activity and knowledge; but he does not even raise the question whether conscientiousness is 'higher than' other moral virtues. Nevertheless it seems that this is an open question.

And it is also an open question whether conscientiousness itself is good without qualification. Many of the worst crimes in history have been committed by men who had a strong sense of duty just because their sense of duty was so strong. I should myself have no hesitation in saying that Robespierre would have been a better man (quite apart from the question of the harm he did) if he had given his conscience a thorough rest and indulged his taste for roses and sentimental verse. There is a story of an Oxford don who disliked Common Room life and whose presence caused himself and others acute distress. Yet he attended Common Room assiduously because he thought it his duty to do so. He would have done better to stay at home.

In answer to this type of criticism Paton says: "It is certainly true that good men may do a great deal of harm; and this harm may spring, not from officiousness and vanity (which

1. Trans. Paton: *The Moral Law*, p. 62.
2. *The Categorical Imperative*, p. 42.

belong to moral badness) but from mere silliness and stupidity."[1] But may not the harm also spring from their very conscientiousness? We might adopt the moral principle that conscientiousness is so valuable that a man ought to be conscientious no matter what harm he does; but it is quite another thing to say that their conscientiousness is never the source of the harm that good men do.

Nor, I think, is the principle of the supreme value of conscientiousness one that we have any reason for accepting. Its claim seems to rest partly on a confusion to be examined in section (3) and partly on the assumption that non-conscientious action must be both impulsive and selfish.[2]

[2]

The Value of Moral Virtues. Virtues and vices are dispositions to behave in certain ways; but the names of virtues and vices do not merely designate those modes of behaviour. They are terms of praise and censure to such an extent that it would be logically odd to call a man 'brave' or 'honest' without intending to praise him. We must now examine the question why some modes of conduct are so universally praised and others so universally condemned that their very names always carry a praising or condemning force unless it is expressly or by implication withdrawn.

I shall try to show that the value of virtues is always an artificial value; but it does not follow that the modes of con-

1. Op. cit., p. 40.
2. It also rests on a confusion between acting on principle and acting for duty's sake. It is plausible to contrast acting on principle with acting on impulse and to suggest that every motive belongs to one or other of these types. But I think, with Paton, that Kant meant by acting for the sake of duty "acting out of reverence for the moral law"; and this, though compatible with, must not be identified with acting on principle. A man who acts on the principle of beneficence does not act out of reverence for any law, moral or otherwise; though, if the moral law enjoins beneficence, he does what the law enjoins.

duct that virtue-words designate are never natural. For we must distinguish between the question whether it is natural to behave in a certain way and the question whether it is natural to praise those who act in that way. The phrase 'natural virtue' is, in fact, ambiguous. It can either mean 'mode of conduct that is natural and also praised' or it can mean 'mode of conduct which is naturally praised'. I shall use the phrase in the latter sense and give reasons for supposing that there are no such modes of conduct.

A man may have a natural disposition to be beneficent, that is to say a natural pro-attitude towards the good of others, and he is called 'benevolent' if this is so strong that he regularly acts for the sake of doing good to others. No doubt this pro-attitude is naturally stronger in some men than in others, and it can be strengthened or weakened by education. But it does not follow that benevolence is a natural virtue. For to say this is to say, not that it is natural to be benevolent, but that it is natural to praise the benevolent man. Similarly to say that courage and honesty are natural virtues is to say, not that men are naturally brave or honest, but that it is natural to praise the brave and honest man.

Now it obviously cannot be proved that the value of moral virtues is always artificial. To prove this empirically we should have to examine the pro-attitudes of that well-known abstraction, the Natural Man without Society. Nor could it be proved *a priori*, since there are no logical limits to the possible objects of pro-attitudes. But it is a maxim in philosophy that we should never assume anything to be part of the original constitution of human nature if any cause can be assigned to it; and in this case a cause is not far to seek. There is an obvious connexion between the modes of conduct that men praise and the modes of conduct that they believe to bring about consequences towards which they already have a pro-attitude.

Since praising and condemning are things that we do, it is necessary that we should have some motive for doing them; and we should not conclude that a motive is a natural one if it is possible to account for it in some other way. Now it is tautological to say that every man has a pro-attitude towards other people doing good to him, since 'doing good to' means 'bringing about those things towards which he has a pro-attitude'. And, though not tautological, it is obviously true that most men have a natural pro-attitude towards other people's doing good to third parties, not perhaps to all other men, since such wide-spread sympathy is very rare, but at least their family, friends, and neighbours. Most men are not misanthropes, and in order to understand how artificial pro-attitudes arise it is essential to remember that we have to do with the majority, not with the exceptional case.

Now benevolence is the desire to do good to others, and it is fairly obvious that men are more likely to succeed in doing good to others if they try to do so than if they try to do harm. We could easily imagine a world in which this was not so, a world in which people were so stupid and inefficient that the more good they tried to do the more harm they did. And, if we lived in such a world, benevolence would be a vice and malevolence a virtue. That this sounds odd is due solely to the facts of the world in which we live. It does not sound so odd in the case of some other virtues.

Although some modes of conduct are universally praised, there are others which are regarded as virtues in some societies but not in others. And the reason in every case for regarding something as a virtue is that it is believed to be beneficial in the special social and economic conditions of the society concerned. Thrift, for example, is valuable in some economic conditions and harmful in others; consequently we find it sometimes praised as a virtue and sometimes condemned as a vice. As the world becomes more closely knit, so that the prosperity of one country comes to depend more and more on the prosperity of others, patriotism ceases to be a virtue; and we either cease to praise the patriotic man or change the descriptive content of the word 'patriotism'.

In saying that moral virtues are not natural objects of pro-attitudes I do not intend to say that these pro-attitudes are never direct. Men do not always praise benevolence or courage because they have a pro-attitude towards its consequences in a particular case. A man may admire and honour courage in an enemy though this virtue is greatly to the disadvantage of himself and his friends; indeed we often praise a good man without any thought of the good consequences of his virtue. But the pro-attitude which such praise implies is analogous to an acquired taste. Although it may now be direct and spontaneous, we have come to have it partly because we have been brought up to admire certain modes of conduct and partly because we recognize their instrumental value.

The Janus-character of virtue-words is a fruitful source of misunderstanding here. For it tempts us to confuse (a) the meaning of a virtue-word, (b) the causes of our treating something as a virtue, and (c) the motive for our so doing. (a) We use virtue-words as terms of praise, and a man who praises something need have no motive for praising other than a direct desire to praise it. (b) The cause of his praising a certain mode of conduct may well be that it is customary to do so or that he has been trained to do so. We learn what modes of conduct to praise and what to condemn partly by being told and partly by imitating others; and it is easy to see how it is that modes of conduct often continue to be praised even when they are no longer thought to produce good consequences. (c) But the original motive for treating any mode of conduct as praiseworthy must either have been that men had a direct pro-attitude towards it or the belief that it has, in general, consequences towards which we have a pro-attitude. For it is logically odd to encourage people to try to do things to which we are opposed.

[3]

Is conscientiousness necessarily the best motive? To say that conscientiousness is a good motive or a virtue is, among other things, to praise the conscientious man and to encourage people to be conscientious; and this is not to comment on the use of moral language but to make a moral judgement. It would therefore be very strange if it were logically necessary that conscientiousness should be the best motive. It is, however, worth while investigating this question, since so many philosophers have supposed that, while the value of other virtues is contingent, conscientiousness is necessarily good.

Sir David Ross uses the following argument to prove that we must regard a man who acts from a sense of duty as a better man than one who acts from any other motive. "Suppose that some one is drawn towards doing act A by a sense of duty and towards doing another, incompatible, act B by love for a particular person. *Ex hypothesi*, he thinks he will not be doing his duty in doing B. Can we possibly say that he will be acting better if he does what he thinks not his duty than if he does what he thinks *is* his duty? Evidently not. What those who hold this view mean by 'acting from the sense of duty' is obeying a traditional, conventional code rather than following the warm impulses of the heart. But what is properly meant by the sense of duty is the thought that one *ought* to act in a certain way. . . . And it seems clear that when a genuine sense of duty is in conflict with any other motive we must recognize its precedence. If you seriously think that you ought to do A, you are bound to think you will be acting morally worse in doing anything else instead."[1]

It should be noticed that Ross has loaded the scales in favour of the sense of duty by representing the only alternative motives as *impulses*, a word which suggests that they are sporadic, wayward, and capricious.[2] But sympathy, benevolence, patriotism, and ambition are not necessarily impulsive.

1. *The Right and the Good*, p. 164.
2. Ross in fact goes on to describe instinctive affection as 'wayward and capricious'. But, though affection may be instinctive it can be cultivated and need be neither wayward nor capricious. Ross's view seems to be another example of a mistake due to thinking of all motives other than the sense of duty as 'desires', 'inclinations', or 'impulses'.

A man can consistently adopt a policy of doing good to others, not because he regards it as his duty, but because that is what he most wants to do or enjoys doing. The word 'wants' is, of course, far too weak a word to cover the pro-attitude of the non-conscientious altruist. But his altruism is not necessarily less consistent or more easily shaken than that of the man who tries to do good because he thinks it his duty.

Secondly there is an ambiguity in the phrase 'acting better'. If this means that what he does is better in some non-moral sense, for example that it brings about better consequences, it is extremely doubtful whether a man who acts from a sense of duty in fact 'acts better' than one who does not. But if by 'acting better' Ross means that a critic would necessarily regard the man who acts from a sense of duty as a morally better man, the argument begs the question.

Indeed the passage I have quoted is mostly an appeal to the self-evidence of the proposition that a man who acts from a sense of duty is a better man than one who acts from any other motive. It is only in the last sentence that an argument is used to support this view; and the argument seems to depend on a confusion between what an agent necessarily thinks about his own action and what a critic or spectator necessarily thinks. Ross's object is to prove that Jones necessarily regards Smith as a better man if he does what he (Smith) thinks he ought to do; but the statement at the end of the quotation is only true if 'you' is taken to refer to the same person throughout. We must distinguish the following three statements:

(1) I think that I ought to do A but that I would be a better man if I did B.

(2) I think that you ought to do A but that you would be a better man if you did B.

(3) You think that you ought to do A, but you would be a better man if you did B.

Now there is an air of contradiction about (1) and (2), but not about (3). And the reason why (1) is logically odd is that 'I ought to do A' expresses a decision to act in a certain way and implies that the decision is of a certain type, namely one based on reasons which, in a moral case, may take the form of a belief that A would be fitting or in accordance with a certain moral rule. A man who said that he ought to do A but would be morally better if he did B is in the same breath deciding to act on a moral principle and condemning himself for making this decision. But to condemn himself is to abandon the moral principle in question.

And (2) is logically odd for a similar reason. To say "you ought (morally) to do A" is to advise a man to adopt a certain moral principle and the force of "But you would be a better man if you did B" is to retract this advice. It is as inconsistent to recommend and to condemn a moral principle in the same breath as it is to decide to adopt and to condemn a moral principle in the same breath.

But (3) is not logically odd at all; it is the natural way for Jones to express his moral disagreement with Smith. Now conscientiousness is an extremely valuable motive and it is so valuable that we often wish to encourage a man to be conscientious even in a case in which we think that the principle on which he thinks he ought to act is a bad one. In such a case we might well wish to encourage him to do what he thinks right without wishing to endorse the principle on which he proposes to act. We should then say "I think you ought to do B; but, if you are really convinced that you ought to do A, then you ought to do it. For what really matters is not that you should act on the right principle but that you should act on the principle that you believe to be right." But I do not think it is logically necessary that we should rate conscientiousness as highly as this nor that, as a matter of fact, we always do. Statement (3) is not logically odd except in the mouth of a man who has already accepted the very principle of the supreme value of conscientiousness which Ross is trying to establish.

[4]

The Value of Conscientiousness. The case of conscientiousness differs from that of other virtues in two ways. (a) The mode of conduct that the word designates is an artificial mode of conduct; and (b) the value of conscientiousness is artificial in a way in which that of other virtues is not.

(a) To be conscientious is to do what one believes to be right, not for the sake of bringing about a certain result nor for the sake of doing what is done, as such, but for duty's sake. And two different motives can lead a man to do the same thing. For example a man may be both altruistic and conscientious, and such a man will help a blind man across the road both because he wants to help him and also because he thinks it his duty to do so. But, in order to simplify the issue, I shall consider the case of a man who acts from the sense of duty alone and does something for no other reason than that he thinks he ought to do it and has a pro-attitude towards doing what he thinks he ought to do, as such. This certainly occurs; how has it come about?

I have incurred a debt and I pay it with no desire to part with my money, no thought of the welfare of the recipient, and no expectation of gain. My sole motive is the desire to conform to the moral rule 'Pay your debts'. It will hardly, I think, be argued that anyone has a direct, natural pro-attitude towards obeying this rule, or even the germ of such an attitude that could be fostered by education. It may be that men are naturally ritualistic, that they have an innate love of orderliness and doing things according to rule. Anthropologists are divided on this point; but in any case it is irrelevant, since conscientiousness is not the desire to conform to *any* rule, but the desire to conform to a rule which one regards as *right*. And it is therefore necessary to explain how I came to regard this particular rule, 'Pay your debts', as a right rule to adopt.

As usual custom and education can explain much but not everything. In the case of any given man it is no doubt true that he adopts those rules which are customary in his society and to which he has been trained to conform. But these causes are not reasons and they cannot explain how the customary rules which a man has been trained to adopt came to be accepted as the right rules. There must have been some motive for establishing the rule in the first place and, in so far as men are rational, there must be some reason for adhering to it. Now the motive for adopting a rule cannot have been the sense of duty, since the sense of duty is the desire to do whatever is laid down by the moral rules we have adopted. A man who acts from a sense of duty pays his debts because he thinks it right to do so; he must therefore have some reason for thinking it right *other than* the fact that his sense of duty bids him do it.

This argument is equally valid whether we think of the sense of duty as a desire to conform to 'objective' moral rules, to a customary code, or to those rules which a man adopts for himself. In each case, if he adopts the rule he must have some motive for adopting it, and this motive cannot be a desire to conform to it. It must be a direct or indirect pro-attitude towards doing what the rule lays down irrespective of the fact that the rule does lay it down.

(b) To say that conscientiousness is a natural virtue is to say that it is natural to praise (and therefore to have a pro-attitude towards) obedience to a moral rule. But this, although not logically impossible, seems very unlikely to be true. Here is a man who has incurred a debt and pays it for no other reason than that he thinks he ought to do so. Why should I praise and admire him rather than condemn and despise him? These questions sound odd only because 'conscientious' is already a term of praise. If we are careful to exclude the praising force and to think of it as meaning only 'acting from a sense of duty' it clearly makes sense to ask why we should praise the conscientious man.

And the reason cannot be found either in a regard for our own interest or in a regard for that of others. I may or may not have a pro-attitude towards the redistribution of wealth involved. This is immaterial, since the question is not 'Why do I approve of his paying the debt?', but 'Why do I approve of his doing this from a certain motive?'; moreover we approve of conscientious action even in cases in which we have no pro-attitude towards any element in the situation other than the motive of the agent.

Now the value of all good motives is, as we saw, artificial. We may come to have a direct pro-attitude towards the types of conduct designated 'virtuous' and praise the virtuous man without any thought of the consequences of his action in this particular case; but the type of conduct concerned would never have come to be called virtuous if it was not believed to have good consequences. But the value of conscientiousness is artificial in another way also. For conscientiousness is not the disposition to do certain sorts of things that are, in fact, valuable, but the disposition to obey certain rules; and its value therefore depends on the value of the rules, which are themselves artificial devices for ensuring certain states of affairs that we wish to ensure.

Now to be conscientious is not to conform to an accepted moral code, but to conform to rules to which the agent himself thinks he ought to conform. But, although it is possible for some individuals to adopt rules that conflict with the accepted code, it is logically necessary that such cases should be rare. There could be no such thing as an accepted code if most people did not accept it. It follows therefore that, although there may be exceptions, in the majority of cases a conscientious man will do those things that are laid down in the accepted code more often than a non-conscientious man will; and since the code consists of rules which are believed to promote the interests of society, it follows that a conscientious man must be more likely to do what is believed to be in the interests of society than a non-conscientious man. This belief may be false; but, even if it is false, it explains why people are praised for being, and encouraged to be conscientious even in cases in which we do not endorse the rule which they adopt and deplore the consequences of their actions.

The Unique Position of Conscientiousness. Apart from the bad reason provided by the dogma that all non-conscientious action is impulsive or selfish, there is a good reason for allowing conscientiousness a special place on the scale of moral virtues. A man who displays some other virtue, for example courage or honesty or generosity, can be relied on to do just those things that belong to his special virtuous disposition; and these virtues can only be exercised in comparatively narrow ranges of situations. But conscientiousness is a substitute for all other virtues, and its unique value lies in this fact. The so-called 'natural virtues' are dispositions to do certain sorts of things towards which we have, in general, a pro-attitude; and moral rules are rules enjoining these same things. Hence the conscientious man will do exactly the same thing that a man who has all the natural virtues will do. He does not do them for the same reason; and he is not brave or honest or kindly, since he acts for the sake of doing his duty, not for the sake of doing the brave, honest, or kindly thing. But he will do what the brave, honest, and kindly man does.

The value of conscientiousness is therefore not unlike that of money. Just as a pound note has no intrinsic value but is valuable because it can be used to buy any of a large range of goods, so the desire to do his duty, whatever it may be, will lead to a man's doing any of a large range of valuable actions. And the value of conscientiousness is like that of money in another way also. Just as a pound note is valueless except in a country where it is accepted in return for goods, so many of the duties of 'special obligation', for example promise-keeping and debt-paying, are only valuable in a society in which the rules enjoining them are generally obeyed. The ends which these rules are designed to promote would not be promoted by obedience to them unless there was a general system of obedience, so that people could be relied on to keep their promises and pay their debts. Without such a system the very notions of a 'promise' or a 'debt' would be unintelligible.

To ask whether conscientiousness is the highest virtue is not unlike asking the question whether money is more valuable than other goods. The answer depends on how much you have. Moreover this is a question the answer to which is a moral judgement and it cannot therefore be answered either by observation or analysis of moral language. Aristotle held that a man was not really good unless he enjoyed doing what is good, and I am inclined to agree. The sense of duty is a useful device for helping men to do what a really good man would do without a sense of duty; and, since none of us belongs to the class of 'really good men' in this sense, it is a motive that should be fostered in all of us. But it plays little part in the lives of the best men and could play none at all in the lives of saints. They act on good moral principles, but not from the sense of duty; for they do what they do for its own sake and not for the sake of duty.

CHAPTER 18

Conscience

[1]

At the end of chapter 16 I suggested that the actual power of conscience was more obvious than its authority and that a man might be a slave to his own conscience; and in chapter 12 I said that it was logically odd to say 'This is the morally better course; but I shall do that'. These paradoxes must now be explained.

It might seem to be tautologous to say that a man ought to do what his conscience tells him to do; for is not the Voice of Conscience precisely the voice that tells him what he ought to do? But this argument is plainly specious; for a decision to do something never follows logically from a command to do it. 'I ought' never follows from 'You ought', and if Conscience is described – as it is both in philosophical literature and common speech – as a voice that tells you what you ought to do, its function is that of advising, exhorting, or commanding, not of deciding or choosing. 'Everyone ought to obey his conscience' is a general moral commandment issued to everyone, including the speaker; it is not a logical truism.

Nor can this conclusion be evaded by saying that the voice of conscience is infallible, that 'you ought' entails 'I ought' in the special case in which it is conscience that issues the command. For if this were so we should have to say that men can mistake some other voice, perhaps that of the Freudian Father-Substitute, for that of conscience; and we should have no way of distinguishing the true conscience from the false except by saying that the 'you ought' is a genuine command of conscience only in cases in which it does entail 'I ought'. Nothing is more certain than the fact that the consciences of different men conflict; and, even if it were true that Jones necessarily thinks

Smith a better man if he follows his conscience (which I have given reasons for doubting), it is certainly untrue that Jones always thinks that Smith's conscience has given the right commands.

The philosophical tradition that treats conscience as an internal judge is partly responsible for the theory that conscience has "manifest authority"; for judges are notoriously people who have authority. If conscience is the court from which there is no appeal, it is tautological to say that it is right for a man to obey his conscience, since conscience is, by definition, the authority competent to judge what is right and what is wrong. But we must not confuse the office of the judge with that of the advocate. The role of the former is to pronounce a verdict, that of the latter to plead a cause.

The confusion is reached in the following way. 'I ought' is used to express a verdict or decision. It differs from 'I shall' in that, while 'I shall' can be used to express any decision, 'I ought' is only used to express decisions of a certain kind, namely those based on rules. It is for this reason that it is logically odd to say "I know I ought to do X, but shall I do it?". Unless 'shall I?' is being used in a predictive sense to be considered later, a man who says it has not yet reached a decision and cannot, in consequence, say 'I ought' in the judicial, verdict-giving sense.

But 'I ought' is also used, not to express a decision, but in the course of making up one's mind before a decision has been reached. A man may hesitate between two moral principles and say to himself at one time 'I ought to do X' and at another 'But on the other hand I ought to do Y' or he may contrast 'I ought' with 'I should like to'. In the first of these cases he is hesitating between two moral principles, in the second between acting on a moral principle and acting on some other motive. But in neither case has he arrived at a verdict. In the first case it is quite natural to represent the two 'oughts' as being spoken by internal moral authorities advising or telling him what to do; and in the second to represent the conflict as one between the Voice of Conscience and Desire. But these are the voices of advocates, not of judges; and what they say is, not 'I ought', but 'you ought'.

The difference between 'you ought' and 'I ought' is obscured by two facts, one empirical and one logical. In the first place moral struggles are comparatively rare; we have often only to recognize the 'you ought' of conscience to pass immediately to the 'I ought' of decision. (Whether we carry out the decision is another matter; we may lack self-control.) And secondly our talk *about* moral judgements, as opposed to the expressions we use in *making* moral judgements or decisions, is always put in indirect speech. And here both the verdict-giving 'I ought' and the self-hortatory 'you ought' become 'he ought'. In a description of a man making up his mind about a course of action "He thinks that he ought to do X" might mean "He is saying to himself 'You ought to do X' ", i.e. he is telling himself what to do. But it might also mean "He is saying to himself 'I ought to do X' ", i.e. he has arrived at a decision about what to do.

Duty and Inclination. This way of representing deliberation as a conflict between voices or forces is not wholly unnatural. But if either the metaphor of the council chamber or that of the conflict of mechanical forces is taken too seriously it leads to highly paradoxical results. According to some psychologists the Voice of Conscience in an adult is the ghost or memory of the father who told him what to do when he was a child and punished him for not doing it. Now so long as psychologists confine themselves to describing and explaining empirical phenomena and do not draw moral conclusions there is no reason why a philosopher should quarrel with them; and if he does, he ought to produce evidence that rebuts the psychologists' explanation. But philosophers often object to this account of the genesis of conscience on the grounds that it ignores the peculiar moral authority of conscience. They claim rightly that we are under no necessary obligation to do what the voice of conscience tells us if this voice is really what the psychologists say it is. But in their account of decision and obligation they tend to reproduce the very feature that makes the psychologist's account irrelevant to the question whether I ought to obey my conscience. Conscience, they say, is a special non-natural voice that speaks with authority; but they still represent it as a voice which issues orders. And if this is what it is it will always make sense for me to ask whether I ought to do what my conscience tells me to do. For a moral decision is a decision to act on a principle that one freely accepts, not a decision to act on a principle on which one is told to act. The 'voice' or 'force' to which conscience is likened in the council-chamber and mechanical metaphors is one of the participants in the contest and cannot be identified with the person who decides between the participants. To make a moral decision is neither to be ordered (though it may be a decision to obey an order) nor to be the prize of a victorious inner force (though it may be a decision to follow a certain inclination); it is to *decide*; and this is something that *I* do, not something that is done by voices or forces inside me.

Some philosophers will object to this account of the difference between the self-hortatory 'you ought' and the verdict-giving 'I ought' on the grounds that, in the special case of conscience, the two are identical. My conscience, they will say, *is* myself. While they are prepared to talk of desires or inclinations as internal forces which operate on 'me', the 'self' or 'self-acting-in-accordance-with-conscience' is, as it were, the billiard-ball on which these forces act. The only difference between the case of the billiard ball and that of the self is that, whereas the behaviour of the billiard ball is completely determined by the forces acting on it, the self is capable of spontaneous action. I choose freely only when I am not obliged by my desires or inclinations but do what my 'self' decides to do.

But this theory seriously distorts our account both of choosing and of responsibility. I shall consider its application to responsibility in the next chapter and confine myself here to the suggested analysis of choice. Moral conflict is now represented as a battle between 'me' (or my 'self' or 'my conscience') and 'my desires'; and if this is so it is nonsense to

263

ask whether or not I can choose to overcome a particular desire. For 'I' am now represented as one of the participants in the conflict. Either I win or I lose. If I win, I act freely because my action is that of the self-propelled conscience or conscience-propelled self; if I lose, I do not act freely, because the action is that of a desire which is not me at all. But in neither case can I choose between what I ought to do and what I want to do.

I have already suggested that it is paradoxical to represent all motives other than the sense of duty as 'forces' which oblige me to act as I do, since this entails that I do not act freely when I do what I want to do; and I suggested that a worse paradox was to follow. It is this. There can be no such thing as intentional or even voluntary wrong-doing, and therefore no such thing as just blame or punishment. In the mouth of a Socrates or a Spinoza there would be nothing strange about this conclusion; for Socrates thought that no wrong-doing could be voluntary and was puzzled to know how any man could deserve blame, and Spinoza was prepared to push the theory to its inevitable conclusion and say that blame is never justified. A wise man tries to understand why men behave as they do; only a fool blames them.

But the theory of the self-propelling conscience is often found in conjunction with the view that conscientiousness is the only virtue and acting against one's conscience the only vice. And it is this combination that is paradoxical, since on this theory a conscientious action is the only type of free action, all actions prompted by desire being unfree. If conscience wins the day I act freely and am good; if desire wins the day, I am bad but *I* do not choose to do what I do. Now all this may be true; but, if so, ordinary men have for centuries been labouring under a profound delusion. For nothing is more certain than that they believe that a man can choose to do what is wrong and that he chooses in exactly the same sense of 'choose' as he does when he chooses to do what is right or when he chooses to do something in a case in which morality is not involved. No doubt there are many differences between choosing the path of duty and choosing a place for a holiday; but it is paradoxical to suggest that we have to do with different senses of the word 'choose'.

[2]

Wickedness and Moral Weakness. We normally distinguish between two different types of wrong-doing; (a) cases in which a man adopts and adheres to bad moral principles, and (b) cases in which he has good moral principles but fails, on some occasion, to live up to them. The latter is moral weakness; for the former we have no unambiguous name and I shall call it 'wickedness', although this word is too strong for minor defects of this kind. The distinction is one of principle, not of the importance or gravity of the offence. What is common to both cases is that a man does something wrong, something, that is, that a spectator would condemn; the difference lies partly in the fact that the morally weak man condemns himself, while the wicked man does not.

We sometimes refer to what I have called wickedness as 'vice'; but we also use the word 'vicious' in respect of defects that, however much we may regret them and want to alter them, we do not regard as morally reprehensible. Addiction to opium is a vice, as is also any bad habit that a man cannot break however hard he tries. But these are not culpable states simply because, whatever may have been the case in the past, he cannot now avoid them. We shall see later that the concept of 'trying' is a difficult and important one and that it is difficult in practice to discover whether or not a man could have overcome his vicious habit or craving. But if he cannot, his vicious condition is one to be remedied by education, medical treatment, psycho-analysis or whatever means the wit of man can devise; it does not call for moral condemnation.

Now the theory considered at the end of the last section seems to me to make two profound mistakes. Since it treats all wrong-doing as succumbing to temptation, that is to say doing what a man knows that he ought not to do, it altogether ignores wickedness. And it distorts the nature of moral weakness by taking the case of the drug-addict as a model. The theory represents all motives other than the sense of duty as if they were cravings, that is to say 'external' forces which compel a man to act against his own moral principles; and drug-addiction is the model because this is indeed a case in which we do think of a desire or craving as an external force. 'External' is, of course, a metaphor; but the metaphor has point, since we use about the addict the same sort of language that we would use about a man who is physically compelled. 'He couldn't help it'; 'the craving was too strong for him'; 'he had no choice'.

But if the weak-willed man really deserves blame, drug-addiction is not a good model to use for understanding his condition; and if we represent desires as forces we shall have to find a criterion for deciding whether or not the craving was so strong that he could not have resisted it. In the next chapter I shall examine a theory that tries to do this. But the most paradoxical feature of the theory lies, not in the use of this inappropriate model, but in the complete neglect of cases in which it does not even begin to look appropriate. These are the cases of wickedness, cases in which a man, so far from struggling with temptation, neither tries nor thinks that he ought to try to do anything other than what he does. He may, of course, know that he ought not to do what he does in the sense that he knows that the practice is morally condemned by others. But he does not believe that he ought not to do it in the verdict-giving sense of 'ought'; on the contrary his action is an expression of the moral principles that he espouses. Now this is precisely the condition of the deliberately dishonest, cowardly, mean, or callous man, and to neglect these cases or to pretend that such men really know better but are continually giving in to temptation is to make nonsense of most of our moral judgements.

Can we really say that the poisoner who waits years for his

opportunity and plans every move with the greatest care does not act freely or that he has good moral principles but fails, through temptation, to live up to them? If a man consistently, over a long course of years, tries to get the better of his fellows in all the transactions of daily life or if he is never moved by the consequences of his actions for other people, we might say colloquially that 'he has no moral principles'. But this clearly means, not that he literally has *no* moral principles or that he has good ones and continually succumbs to temptation to act against them, but that he has *bad* moral principles. And it is surely absurd to say that, while it might be expedient to restrain him, it would be unjust to blame him. Yet this is precisely what we do say about drug-addicts. The drug-addict has to be dealt with, but he escapes moral censure just because he does not choose to do what he does.

[3]

'I ought' and 'I shall'. I have throughout treated 'What shall I do?' as the fundamental question of ethics and tried to show that moral concepts can only be understood by relating them, often in very indirect and complicated ways, to the concept of decision. But it might be objected that the fundamental question is not 'What shall I do?' but 'What ought I to do?' and the fundamental concept not decision but obligation. My reason for treating the 'shall' question as fundamental is that moral discourse is practical. The language of 'ought' is intelligible only in the context of practical questions, and we have not answered a practical question until we have reached a decision. 'I shall do this' is the general formula for expressing decisions.

Now 'I ought' can, as we have seen, also be used to express a decision, a solution to a practical problem; but when it is so used it is a special case of 'I shall'. For it is used, not to address a command or piece of advice to oneself, but to express a decision, and it differs from 'I shall' only in that it contextually implies that the decision is of a certain type, namely that it is based on reasons and, if it is a moral 'ought', that the decision is in accordance with my moral principles. If I say to myself 'I ought to pay that debt' in the verdict-giving sense of 'ought', I am not merely recognizing the existence of a moral rule; I am subscribing to that rule. Only so can we understand why there is no logical gap between 'ought' and 'shall'.

In such a case, therefore, 'I ought' entails 'I shall', of which it is a special case; and 'I ought, but I shall not' is a contradiction. But this contradictory character of 'I ought, but I shall not' is obscured by the fact that 'shall' also has another use in which it is not self-contradictory to say 'I ought, but I shall not' or logically odd to say 'I know I ought, but I wonder whether I shall'. This is the predictive use.

"I know that I ought not to get angry with Jones; he really means well; but I *expect I shall*, because I *always do find myself* getting angry with him." "I ought to take a firm line with Brown; but *I shall probably* give in to him in the end; his smile is so *irresistible*." "*I wonder whether I shall* have the courage to ask for the rise that I know I deserve."

In these cases the use of 'I shall' is not practical but predictive. As the phrases in italics show, we are adopting the standpoint of an observer, predicting our conduct in the future from a knowledge of our conduct in the past. We suspect ourselves of weakness of will or lack of self-control; for we know that, when the time comes, we do not always act on our own principles.

The very phrase 'self-control' shows that there is point in the traditional way of thinking of a man as consisting of two or more people, sometimes a better and a worse 'self'; and the phrases 'weakness of will', 'lack of self-control', and 'loss of self-control' are used to describe cases in which a man fails to do or predicts that he will fail to do what he has made up his mind to do, cases in which action runs counter to choice.

It is these cases that give some plausibility to the self-propelling conscience theory; for in these cases a man identifies 'himself' with his moral principles; but it is a mistake to treat such cases as typical of all moral wrong-doing; that is exactly what they are not. Ordinary moral language recognizes the distinction between having bad moral principles and being morally weak and ordinary moral practice reserves its severest condemnation for the former. But, as often, ordinary practice has no precise way of distinguishing these two cases or of distinguishing the wicked man, the weak-willed man, and the addict; and ordinary language has no precise way of formulating the criterion or explaining why we make the distinctions. It is the search for such a criterion that gives rise to the philosophical problem of freewill. Perhaps, in the last resort, the weak-willed man cannot be distinguished from the addict and perhaps even the man of bad moral principles cannot help being what he is? It would be strange if these things were so; but there are truths that we all accept that appear to entail them, and this is one of the main ways in which philosophical problems arise.

CHAPTER 19

Freedom and Responsibility (1)

[1]

WE have now to consider the logic of the language which we use to ascribe responsibility, to award praise and blame, and to justify our moral verdicts. I shall consider five types of moral judgement.

He broke a law or moral rule.	(1)
He could have acted otherwise.	(2)
He deserves censure (or punishment).	(3)
It would be just to censure (or punish) him.	(4)
He is a bad (cruel, mean, dishonest, etc.) man.	(5)

It is clear that all these are logically connected. It is not just a fact about the world that we learn from experience that only bad men deserve blame or that it is only just to blame those who could have acted otherwise. Yet the items cannot all be treated as analytically connected; for we should then find that it was senseless to ask certain questions that obviously do make sense.

For example, the character-words used in (5) are partly descriptive; and it makes sense to ask whether a person who is consistently mean or dishonest deserves blame. To give, as most of us would, an affirmative answer would be to use, not to analyse moral language. It would also be a mistake to say that it must (logically) be unjust to blame someone who could not have acted otherwise, on the ground that this is part of what 'unjust' means. For (2) is a theoretical statement, while 'unjust' is a G-word contextually implying that no one ought to blame him. Nor does it help to say that we have insight into necessary synthetic connexions between the items on the list; for this is simply to say that we know them to be connected but cannot understand how. The connexions are of the quasi-logical kind that can only be understood by examining the conditions under which the various expressions are used and the purposes of using them.

I shall start by considering the connexions between (1), (3), and (4). The connexion between (3) and (4) seems to be analytic. If a man deserves blame, someone would be justified in blaming him. Not necessarily you; for you may be in no position to cast the first stone or to cast any stone at all.

Now 'punishment' is a legal term and, in the case of punishment at least, (3) and (4) logically imply (1). A man can be justly punished only if he has broken a law, and the same applies, although naturally in a looser way, to moral censure. To deserve censure a man must have done something wrong, that is to say broken a moral rule. Now why should this be so? This question has already been partly answered in chapter 16. 'Punishment' is a complex idea consisting of the ideas of inflicting pain, on someone who has broken a law, in accordance with a rule laying down the correct punishment. But we have still to ask why we make use of this complex idea at all. Remembering that 'just' is a G-word, it is necessary to suppose that anyone who says that Jones deserves punishment must have a pro-attitude towards his being punished. But why should we wish to encourage the infliction of pain on those who have broken a law? The classical utilitarian answer is that it will either reform the criminal or deter potential criminals or both. Now, since laws and moral rules are devices for bringing about ends, we must have a pro-attitude towards reforming those who break them and deterring others. So, if it is a fact that punishment has these effects, this will explain the connexion between the infliction of pain and the breach of a rule.

But this simple theory will not do, if only because potential criminals would be as efficiently deterred by the punishment of an innocent scape-goat who was believed to be guilty as by that of a guilty man; and, whatever the effects might be, this would not be just. And we have also seen in chapter 16 how this simple theory can be amended. For we there saw that, although we might have a system of dealing with each situation as it arose, there were great advantages in having legal and moral codes. And it is because we have these codes that neither the punishment of Jones nor an adverse moral verdict on him could (logically) be called 'just' unless he has broken a law. Without the code we could still recommend people to inflict pain on Jones to stop him doing what he does, but the peculiar force of 'just' could not be carried by any word. And, granted that we have rules, it is clear that the *purpose* of punishment and blame is relevant, not to the question 'Should Jones be punished or blamed?', but to the questions 'Should the sort of thing that Jones did be prohibited by a rule to which a penalty is attached?'.

The question 'What justifies punishment?' in fact conceals an ambiguity which is largely responsible for the dispute between those who answer it in terms of retribution for crime and those who answer it in terms of deterrence and reform. If we have in mind the judge's problem, the utilitarian answer is clearly inadequate; but if we are thinking about the legislator's problem, it seems very plausible. Each party has tried to extend their answer to cover both cases. But even if we are thinking about the legislator's problem, it would be an oversimplification to say that legislators either do or should decide what laws to have solely by reference to the purpose of having laws. There are two reasons why they do not do so, one bad and one good. The bad reason is that they are still to some extent in the thrall of the philosophical theory of Natural Law, which itself confuses the judge's problem with the legislator's. But there is also a good reason. It is desirable (on grounds of utility) that the law should be consistent and stable and that the penalty laid down for one offence should not be wildly out of line with those laid down for others. Consequently, unless we are to revise the whole legal code every time we make a new law, it is expedient not to consider the proposed law in isolation but to consider it as part of a system that we do not, on this occasion, wish to disturb.

Just as we might, but do not, live in a world in which every case was decided by an omnicompetent judge without reference to any general principle other than that of utility, so we might live in a world in which legislators decided what laws to pass solely by reference to this standard. But there are as good reasons for rejecting this system as there are for rejecting the system of judges not bound by laws. We know too little about the probable effects of any particular penalty and about the repercussions which a new law-cum-penalty is likely to have on other parts of the system. Hence even legislators do well to criticize proposed laws not only by reference to the purpose of having laws but by reference to the current system of laws, that is to say 'Justice'. The connexions between the justice of a punishment and its utility are thus exceedingly complex; but the fact that utilitarians have oversimplified them is a reason, not for abandoning their theory or retreating into the asylum of intuition, but for revising the theory. It cannot be an accident that the punishments we call 'just' on the whole tend to reform and deter. And if in a particular case we find that they do not serve these ends, we tend to amend the law. On the Natural Law theory it would only be right to amend a law if we discovered that it conflicted with natural law. How we discover this is in any case a mystery, and it would be most remarkable if the discovery always went hand in hand with the discovery that the law fails to fulfil its purpose.

[2]

The most difficult and important of the items on our list of moral judgements is 'He could have acted otherwise' (2). The facts about its logical connexions with the others are tolerably clear. It is a necessary condition of all except (1) and it is also a necessary condition of (1) if 'He broke a law' is taken to imply that he broke it voluntarily. What is not so clear is what (2) means or why it should be a necessary condition of the other items.

A man is not considered blameworthy if he could not have acted otherwise; and, although it is often easy to decide in practice whether he could have acted otherwise or not, it is not clear how we do this or why we should think it necessary to do it. Let us first examine the use of 'could have' in some non-moral cases.

'Could have' is a modal phrase, and modal phrases are not normally used to make straight-forward, categorical statements. 'It might have rained last Thursday' tells you something about the weather, but not in the way that 'It rained last Thursday' does. It is sometimes said that it is used to express the speaker's ignorance of the weather; but what it expresses is not just this but his ignorance of any facts that would strongly tend to rule out the truth of 'It rained'. It would be a natural thing to say in the middle of an English, but not of a Californian summer. But, whatever it does express, what it does *not* express is a belief in a third alternative alongside 'it rained' and 'it did not rain'. Either it rained or it did not; and 'it might have rained' does not represent a third alternative which excludes the other two in the way that these exclude each other.

But these modal phrases are also sometimes used in cases in which they cannot express ignorance since they imply a belief that the event concerned did not occur. It would be disingenuous for a rich man to say 'I might have been a rich man'; but he could well say 'I might have been a poor man' while knowing himself to be rich. The puzzle here arises from the fact that, if he is rich, he cannot be poor. His actual riches preclude his possible poverty in a way that would seem to imply that we could have no use for 'he might have been poor'. But this is only puzzling so long as we try to treat these modal expressions in a categorical way.

'Would have' and 'might have' are clearly suppressed hypotheticals, incomplete without an 'if . . .' or an 'if . . . not . . .'. Nobody would say 'Jones would have won the championship' unless (a) he believed that Jones did not win and (b) he was prepared to add 'if he had entered' or 'if he had not sprained his ankle' or some such clause.

It is not so obvious that 'could have' sentences also express hypotheticals; indeed in some cases they obviously do not. If a man says 'It could have been a Morris, but actually it was an Austin', it would be absurd to ask him under what conditions it could or would have been a Morris. 'Could have' is here used to concede that, although I happen to know it was an Austin, your guess that it was a Morris was not a bad one. But 'could have' also has a use which is more important for our purpose and in which, as I shall try to show, it is equivalent to 'would have . . . if . . .'. It refers to a tendency or capacity. Consider the following examples:

(1) He could have read *Emma* in bed last night, though he actually read *Persuasion*; but he could not have read *Werther* because he does not know German.

(2) He could have played the *Appassionata*, though he actually played the *Moonlight*; but he could not have played the *Hammerklavier*, because it is too difficult for him.

These are both statements, since they could be true or false; and to understand their logic we must see how they would be established or rebutted. Neither could be established or rebutted in the way that 'He read *Persuasion*' could, by observing what he actually did; and it is partly for this reason that we do not call them categorical. But, although they could not be directly verified or falsified by observation of what he did, this might be relevant evidence. It would be almost conclusive evidence in the first case, since it would be very odd if a man who actually read *Persuasion* was incapable of reading *Emma*. On the other hand, his having played the *Moonlight* is only weak evidence that he could have played the *Appassionata*, since the latter is more difficult and also because he might never have learnt it.

In each of these cases, in order to establish the 'could have' statement we should have to show (a) that he has performed tasks of similar difficulty sufficiently often to preclude the possibility of a fluke, and (b) that nothing prevented him on this occasion. For example we should have to establish that there was a copy of *Emma* in the house.

Statements about capacities, whether of the 'can' or of the 'could have' kind, contextually imply unspecified conditions under which alone the person might succeed; and 'could have' statements can be refuted either by showing that some necessary condition was absent (there was no copy of *Emma*) or by showing that the capacity was absent. The first point could be established directly. How could the second be established? In practice we do this either by appealing to past performances or failures or by asking him to try to do it now. It is clear that neither of these methods could be applied directly to the occasion in question. We know that he did not read *Emma*, and it is nonsense to ask him to try to have read *Emma* last night. And the very fact that evidence for or against 'could have' statements must be drawn from occasions other than that to which they refer is enough to show that 'he could have acted otherwise' is not a straightforward categorical statement, at least in the type of case we have been considering. Whether it is possible or necessary to interpret it categorically in moral cases is a point which I shall examine in the next section.

It might be argued that the sort of evidence by which 'could have' statements are supported or rebutted is never conclusive; and this is true. The argument used is an inductive one, with a special type of conclusion. We might use an ordinary inductive argument to predict his future performance from known past performances or in support of a statement about an unknown past performance. But in this special case we know that he did not do the thing in question, because we know that he did something else; so we put our conclusion in the form 'he could have done X'.

Whatever the evidence, it is always open to a sceptic to say "I know he has always succeeded (failed) in the past; but he *might* have failed (succeeded) on this occasion". Now this sort of scepticism is not peculiar to 'could have' statements; it is one variety of general scepticism about induction. It is *possible* that if I had tried to add 15 and 16 last night (which I did not) I should have failed; but it is also possible that if I tried now I should fail. Our use of 'could have' statements, like our use of predictions and generalizations, always ignores such refined scepticism; and it would be absurd to try to base either freedom or responsibility on the logical possibility of such contingencies. In practice we ignore the sceptic unless he can produce reasons for his doubt, unless he can say why he believes that a man who has always succeeded might have failed on just that occasion. If no such reason is forthcoming we always allow inductive evidence which establishes the existence of a general capacity to do something to establish also the statement that the man could have done it on a particular occasion. Nor is this practice due to the fact that (the world being what it is) we are unfortunately unable to find better evidence and must fall back on probabilities. Our practice lies at the heart of the logic of 'can' and 'could have'. For the sceptic is, here as elsewhere, asking for the logically impossible; he is asking us to adopt a criterion for deciding whether a man could have done something on a particular occasion which would make the words 'can' and 'could have' useless. What would be the result of accepting this suggestion? We should have to say that the only conclusive evidence that a man can do (could have done) X at time t is his actually doing (having done) X at time t. Thus the evidence that entitles us to say 'He could have done X at time t' would also entitle us to say 'He did X at time t', and the 'could have' form would be otiose.

Capacities are a sub-class of dispositions. To say that a man 'can' do something is not to say that he ever has or will; there may be special reasons why the capacity is never exercised, for example that the occasion for exercising it has never arisen. A man might go through his whole life without ever adding 15 and 16; and we should not have to say that he couldn't do this. Yet a man cannot be said to be able to do something if all the necessary conditions are fulfilled and he has a motive for doing it. It is logically odd to say "Smith can run a mile, has had several opportunities, is passionately fond of running, has no medical or other reasons for not doing so, but never has in fact done so". And, if it is true that this is logically odd, it follows that 'can' is equivalent to 'will . . . if . . .' and 'could have' to 'would have . . . if . . .'. To say that Smith could have read *Emma* last night is to say that he would have read it, if there had been a copy, if he had not been struck blind, etc., etc., and if he had wanted to read it more than he wanted to read anything else. Both the 'etc.' and the last clause are important; we cannot specify all the necessary conditions; and, granted that the conditions were present and that he could have read it, he might still not have read it because he did not want to. But if he did not want to do anything else more than he wanted to read *Emma*, he could not in these conditions be said to have *chosen* to do something else. He might have *done* something else, but not in the important sense of 'done' which implies choosing.

[3]

Libertarianism. Before considering why 'he could have acted otherwise', interpreted in this hypothetical way, is regarded as relevant to ascriptions of responsibility, it is necessary to examine the theory that, although the hypothetical interpretation is correct in most cases, in the special case of moral choice the phrase must be interpreted in a categorical way. It would indeed be remarkable if modal forms which are normally used in a hypothetical way were used categorically in one type of case alone; and I have already suggested that their logic is partly determined by the method that would be used to support or rebut statements which employ them. The thesis that 'he could have acted otherwise' is categorical is equivalent to the thesis that it could be verified or falsified by direct observation of the situation to which it refers.

It is essential to notice that the categorical interpretation is supposed to be necessary only in a very small, but very important part of the whole range of human choice. And this too is remarkable; for it implies that the words 'free' and 'choose' are logically different in moral and in non-moral cases. There is a sense of 'free' to which I have already alluded in which it is contrasted with 'under compulsion'; and in this sense actions are still free when they are completely determined by the agent's tastes and character. For to say that they are determined in this way is not to say that he is a Pawn in the hands of Fate or a Prisoner in the iron grip of Necessity. It is only to say that anyone who knew his tastes and character well enough could predict what he will do. The fact that we can predict with a high degree of probability how Sir Winston Churchill will vote at the next election does not imply that he does not cast his vote freely. To be 'free' in this sense is to be free to do what one wants to do, not to be able to act in spite of one's desires.

According to the theory to be examined most of our voluntary actions are 'free' only in this sense which implies no breach in causal continuity. I choose what I choose because my desires are what they are; and they have been moulded by countless influences from my birth or earlier. But, it is said, *moral* choices are free in a quite different sense, and one that is incompatible with their being predictable. This unpredictability is an essential feature in the categorical interpretation of 'he could have acted otherwise'; for, if anyone could predict what I am going to do, I should not really be choosing between genuinely open alternatives, although I might think I was.

Professor Campbell puts the contrast in the following way: "Freewill does not operate in those practical situations in which no conflict arises in the agent's mind between what he conceives to be his 'duty' and what he feels to be his 'strongest desire'. It does not operate here because there is just no occasion for it to operate. There is no reason whatever why the agent should here even contemplate choosing any course other than that prescribed by his strongest desire. In all such situations, therefore, he naturally wills in accordance with his strongest desire. But his 'strongest desire' is simply the specific expression of that system of conative and emotive dispositions which we call his 'character'. In all such situations, therefore, whatever may be the case elsewhere, his will is in effect determined by his character as so far formed. . . ."

. . . (On the other hand) "in the situation of moral conflict, I, as agent, have before my mind a course of action, X, which I believe to be my duty; and also a course of action, Y, incompatible with X, which I feel to be that which I most strongly desire. Y is, as it is sometimes expressed, 'in the line of least resistance' for me – the course which I am aware that I should take, if I let my purely desiring nature operate without hindrance. It is the course towards which I am aware that my *character*, as so far formed, naturally inclines me. Now, as actually engaged in this situation, I find that I cannot help believing that I *can* rise to duty and choose X; the 'rising to duty' being affected by what is commonly called 'effort of will'. And I further find, if I ask myself just what it is I am believing when I believe that I 'can' rise to duty, that I cannot help believing that it lies with me, here and now, quite absolutely, which of two genuinely open possibilities I adopt; whether, that is, I make the effort of will and choose X or, on the other hand, let my desiring nature, my character as so far formed, 'have its way', and choose Y, the course in the line of least resistance."[1]

Now it is certainly true that many determinists have paid too little attention to the concept of 'trying' or 'making an effort'; but I think that there are certain difficulties in Professor Campbell's account of moral conflict and, in particular, in his attempt to construe 'I could have acted otherwise' in a categorical way. The first point to which I wish to draw attention is the question of method.

(1) Campbell insists that the question whether choice is 'free' in a contra-causal sense must be settled by introspection.[2] But is this so? To doubt the findings of his self-examina-

1. *Mind*, 1951, pp. 460-3.   2. *Scepticism and Construction*, p. 131.

tion may seem impertinent; but the doubt is concerned, not with what he finds, but with the propriety of the language he uses to describe what he finds. The universal negative form of statement ('Nothing caused my decision', 'No one could have predicted my decision') does not seem to be a proper vehicle for anything that one could be said to *observe* in self-examination. That I know introspectively what it is like to choose may be true; but I cannot be said to know introspectively that my choice was contra-causal or unpredictable; and this is the point at issue. He represents 'I can rise to duty' as a report of a mental event or, perhaps, a state of mind, not as a statement about a capacity, and 'I could have . . .' as a statement about a past state of mind or mental event. But, if this is really so, it is at least surprising that, in this one context alone, we use the modal words 'can' and 'could have' for making categorical reports. The issue between determinists and libertarians is an issue about the way in which expressions such as 'choose', 'can', and 'alternative possibilities' are to be construed; and this is surely an issue which is to be settled not by self-observation but by logical analysis.

There are many other phrases in Campbell's account which give rise to the same doubts about the propriety of the introspective method. The phrase 'conative disposition' is embedded in a large and complex mass of psychological theory and its use implies the acceptance of this theory; so that one could hardly be said to know by introspection that one has a conative tendency to do something. And phrases such as 'determined', 'contra-causal', and even 'desiring nature' take us beyond psychology into metaphysics. To say this is not to condemn the phrases; perhaps metaphysics is just what is needed here. But a metaphysician is not a reporter; he is an interpreter of what he 'sees'; and it is over the interpretation that the disputes arise.

(2) A more obvious difficulty – and it is one of which libertarians are well aware – is that of distinguishing a 'free' action from a random event. The essence of Campbell's account is that the action should not be predictable from a

knowledge of the agent's character. But, if this is so, can what he does be called *his* action at all? Is it not rather a *lusus naturae*, an Act of God or a miracle? If a hardened criminal, bent on robbing the poor-box, suddenly and *inexplicably* fails to do so, we should not say that he *chose* to resist or deserves *credit* for resisting the temptation; we should say, if we were religious, that he was the recipient of a sudden outpouring of Divine Grace or, if we were irreligious, that his 'action' was due to chance, which is another way of saying that it was inexplicable. In either case we should refuse to use the active voice.

The reply to this criticism is that we must distinguish *In*-determinism from *Self*-determinism. Choice is a creative act of the 'self' and is not only unconstrained by external forces but also unconstrained by desire or character. But the difficulty here is to construe 'self-determinism' in such a way that the 'self' can be distinguished from the 'character' without lapsing into indeterminism.

If we could construe 'self-determined' by analogy with other 'self'-compounds, such as self-adjusting, self-regulating, self-propelled, self-centred, self-controlled, and self-governing, there would be no difficulty. Some of these words apply to non-human objects, and they never imply that there is a part of the object called the 'self' which adjusts, regulates, or controls the rest, though the object does have a special part without which it would not be self-adjusting, etc. I can point to the self-starter of a car, but not to the self that starts the car; to say that a heating system is 'self-regulating' is to say that it maintains a constant temperature without anyone watching the dials and turning the knobs. Coming to the human scene, to say that a state is 'self-governing' is to say that its inhabitants make their own laws without foreign intervention; and to say that a man is 'self-centred' is to say, not that he is always thinking and talking about something called his 'self', but that he is always thinking and talking about *his* dinner, *his* golf-handicap, the virtues of *his* wife, and the prowess of *his* children. In each case there is a subject and an object; but the 'self' is neither subject nor object.

But if we construe 'self-determined' in this way, it is clear that being self-determined implies only that a man acts freely in the ordinary sense of 'freely' which the libertarian rejects as inadequate in the special case of moral choice. There would be no incompatibility between an action's being 'self-determined' and its being predictable or characteristic of the agent; for 'self-determined' would mean 'determined by *his* motives and character', as opposed to 'forced on him by circumstances or other people'. But the libertarian regards explanation in terms of character as incompatible with genuine freedom and must therefore draw a contrast between 'the self' and 'the character'. But if 'self-determined' is to mean 'determined by the self', it is necessary to give some account of what the 'self' is. And if the question whether an action was determined by the 'self' or not is to be relevant to the ascription of responsibility and the justice of adverse verdicts, we must be able to provide some criterion for deciding whether the self which determined the action is the same self that we are proposing to hold responsible or condemn.

Now the problem of Personal Identity is admittedly a difficult one and the danger of desert-island argument is particularly acute here, since Jekyll-and-Hyde cases that a layman would dismiss as flights of fancy have been known to occur. In fact we decide whether the man I met yesterday is the same that I met last year partly by seeing whether he looks the same, partly by observing an identity of characteristic behaviour, and partly by discovering what he can remember. And if we are to avoid the rather crude course of defining 'same self' in terms of the spatio-temporal continuity of bodily cells, it seems that we must define it in terms of character and memory. But the libertarian's 'self' is neither an empirical object nor displayed in characteristic action.

(3) If it is necessary to decide whether or not a man could have acted otherwise before ascribing responsibility, it is necessary that we should have some criterion for deciding this; and on the libertarian theory such a criterion is quite impossible. For, let us suppose that we know a great deal about his

character and also that the temptation which he faced seems to be a fairly easy one for such a man to overcome. On the libertarian hypothesis this information will not be sufficient to enable us to conclude that he could have acted otherwise. If he in fact does the wrong thing, there are three alternative conclusions that we might draw. (a) The action was not against his moral principles at all, so that no conflict between 'duty' and 'inclination' arose. This is what I have called 'wickedness'; (b) he knew it was wrong and could have resisted the temptation but did not (moral weakness); (c) he knew it was wrong but the temptation was *too* strong for him; he *could* not overcome it (addiction). Now it is essential to be able to distinguish case (b) from case (c), since (b) is a culpable state while (c) is not. By treating 'he could have acted otherwise' in a hypothetical way, the determinist thesis does provide us with a criterion for distinguishing between these cases; but the categorical interpretation cannot provide one, since no one, not even the man himself, could know whether he could have overcome the temptation or not.

(4) The libertarian theory involves putting a very special construction on the principle that 'ought' implies 'can', which it is very doubtful whether it can bear. If we take this principle in a common-sense way it is undoubtedly true. It is no longer my duty to keep a promise, if I literally *cannot* do so. But when we say this we have in mind such possibilities as my being detained by the police or having a railway accident or the death of the promisee; and it is possible to discover empirically whether any of these exonerating conditions obtained. But if 'cannot' is construed in such a way that it covers my being too dishonest a person or not making the necessary effort, it is no longer obvious that 'ought' implies 'can'. These reasons for failure, so far from exonerating, are just what make a man culpable.

(5) Even if it were possible to discover whether or not a man could have acted otherwise by attending to the actual occasion, as the categorical interpretation insists, why should this be held relevant to the question whether or not he is to

blame? I shall try to explain this connexion in the next chapter; but on the libertarian hypothesis it will, I think, be necessary to fall back on insight into a relation of fittingness between freedom and culpability.

[4]

The Concept of 'Trying'. It might be thought that the libertarian could discover a criterion for distinguishing culpable weakness of will from non-culpable addiction in the concept of 'trying'. For the addict fails, try as he may, while the weak-willed man fails because he does not try hard enough. The concept of 'trying' is an important one for ethics since, whatever may be the case in a court of law, the question of moral blameworthiness often turns, not on what the agent did, but on what he tried or did not try to do. Morally we blame people, not for failing to live up to a certain standard, but for not trying hard enough to do so; and this is because, while we do not believe that they could always succeed, we do believe that they could always try. We must now see whether the introduction of this concept helps to save the categorical analysis.

We all know what it *feels* like to make an effort. These feelings are phenomena or occurrences that we experience in the same sort of way that we experience aches, pains, qualms, and twinges. And, if we take the introspective language of the libertarian seriously, it would seem that the question 'Did he try?' can be answered only by the man himself and that he answers it by observing whether or not one of these feelings occurred. The logical status of this question will be like that of 'Did it hurt?'. But on this view an effort is not something that a man *makes*; it is something that *happens* to (or inside) him; and it would be highly unplausible to make the question of his responsibility turn on the occurrence or non-occurrence of such a feeling. If 'making an effort' is to be relevant to responsibility, it must be thought of as something which a man can choose to do or not to do. The substitution of the active for the passive voice is an important advance; unfortunately it is fatal to the categorical interpretation of 'he could have acted otherwise'.

For 'trying' is now thought of as something that a man can choose to do or not to do, and the difficulties encountered in construing 'he could have acted otherwise' will emerge again in construing 'he could have tried to act otherwise'. On the libertarian analysis, if a man fails to act rightly, we must say either that his failure is inexplicable or that it was due to circumstances beyond his control – in which cases he is blameless – or that it was due to his not having tried as hard as he could have tried. For what exonerates is not 'I tried', but 'I tried as hard as I could'; and, in order to distinguish the blameworthy man from the addict who literally couldn't help it because he tried as hard as he could, we must be in a position to answer the question 'Could he have tried harder than he did?'. But how can we answer this question? *Ex hypothesi* he did not try harder than he did; so that we must say either that his failure to try harder is inexplicable or that it was due to circumstances beyond his control – in which cases he is blameless – or that it was due to his not having tried to try as hard as he could have tried to try.

But this is absurd. In the first place 'try to try' is meaningless; and, if this be doubted, we must push the analysis one stage further. In fact he did not try to try harder than he did. But can he be justly blamed for this? Only if he could have tried to try harder. We must say either that his not having tried to try harder is inexplicable or that it was due to circumstances beyond his control – in which cases he is blameless – or that he failed to try to try harder because he did not try to try to try harder . . . and so on.

Libertarians sometimes speak in terms of our failure to make the best use of our stock of "will-energy"; but this usage gives rise to the same infinite regress. If using will-energy is thought of as something that we do not choose to do, but which just happens to us, it would appear to be irrelevant to responsibility; but if it is something that we can choose to do or not to do, we must be able to distinguish the man whose failure to use sufficient will-energy was due to circumstances beyond his control from the man who failed (culpably) to use it because he did not try hard enough to use it. And this involves answering the question 'Had he sufficient second-order will-energy to enable him to make more use of his first-order will-energy?'.

On these lines there is clearly no way out of the wood. The attempt to discover one is, I think, due to two mistakes. (a) It is noticeable that, on Campbell's analysis, a man's desires and even his character are continually referred to as 'it'; desires are thought of as forces which, sometimes successfully and sometimes unsuccessfully, prod a man into doing what he ought not, and his "character as so far formed" is the sum of these forces. Thus I am said to be able to choose whether or not to "let my desiring nature, my character as so far formed, have *its* way". And this is to treat all cases of 'doing what I want to do' on the model of the opium-addict, as the actions of a man who is a slave to his desires.

And since Campbell uses 'desire' for every motive except the sense of duty, his treatment presupposes that I can choose whether to act from a certain motive or not; and this is not so. If I am both hungry and thirsty I can choose whether to have a meal or a drink; but I cannot choose whether to act from hunger or thirst, unless this strange phrase is used simply as a (very misleading) synonym for 'choosing whether to eat or to drink'. In the same way, if I have a certain sum of money, I can choose whether to pay a debt or give my aunt a Christmas present. If I choose the former, my motive is conscientiousness; if the latter, it is generosity. And we might, therefore, say that I can choose whether to do the conscientious or the generous thing. But I cannot choose whether to act from conscientiousness or from generosity. What I do will depend on my character; and this 'cannot choose' is not a lamentable restriction on my freedom of action. For to say that my choice depends on my character is not to say that my character compels me to do what I do, but to say that the choice was characteristic of me. The creative 'self' that sits above the battle of motives and chooses between them seems to be a legacy of the theory that a man is not free when he does what he wants to do, since he is then the victim or slave of his desires; and it is postulated to avoid the unplausible doctrine that all action is involuntary.

(b) Campbell takes as a typical and, by implication, the only case of moral choice to which appraisals are relevant, that of a man who knows what he ought to do but is tempted to do something else. Now this, so far from being the only case, is not even the commonest or most important. For in the great majority of cases of moral difficulty what is difficult is not to decide to do what one knows he ought to do, but to decide what one ought to do. This sort of difficulty arises in three main types of case. (i) A humble and unimaginative person who accepts a customary code of morals without much question may find that two rules conflict; the voice of conscience is in this case ambiguous. (ii) A more self-confident, imaginative, and reflective person may wonder whether he ought, in the case before him, to do what the customary rule enjoins. He knows very well what the rule enjoins; but what prompts him to depart from it is not "part of his desiring nature", but a suspicion that the rule is one that, in this particular case, he ought not to follow. (iii) A man of fixed moral principles (whether or not they are those customarily adopted) may find himself in a radically new situation that is not catered for in his code. What is he to do? It is here, if anywhere, that the idea of an unpredictable 'creative' choice seems to make sense. He takes a leap in the dark, but just because it is a leap in the dark I doubt if we should be inclined to blame him if he leapt in what turned out to be the wrong direction.

Men who belong to a generation for whom the questioning of accepted principles has been no mere academic exercise and who have found themselves faced with momentous choices in situations not covered by their traditional rules will be less likely than their fathers perhaps were to suppose that the only sort of moral difficulty is that of resisting temptation.

If, in the first two of these three cases, a man decided that he ought to do something and did it, he might still be held to blame. For reasons given in chapter 17 conscientiousness is so valuable a motive that we should be chary of blaming a man who did what he honestly thought he ought to do, however misguided we thought him. But we should not necessarily excuse him, which we should have to do if all wrong-doing were failure to resist temptation. Integrity is not the only moral virtue, any more than it is the only virtue in an artist; and the belief that it is is one of the more regrettable consequences of the Romantic Movement. We blame people, not only for failing to live up to their moral principles, but also for having bad moral principles; and I shall examine the logic of this type of blame in the next chapter.

Perhaps the most crucial objection to the libertarian thesis lies in the sharp discontinuity which it presupposes between moral and non-moral choice and between moral and non-moral appraisal. It is not enough to admit that we can, within broad limits, predict what a man of known habits, tastes, and interests will do and to insist that our powers of prediction only break down in the small, but important area of moral choice. For it is not the extent of the area open to prediction that is at issue.

It is true that we can, within broad limits, predict what a man will choose from a menu, whether he will make a century to-day, or finish his cross-word puzzle; but we can also predict, again within broad limits only, whether or not he will resist the temptation to run away or to cheat at cards. Our reliance on the integrity of a bank clerk is not different from our reliance on his accuracy. In neither case do we believe that he 'must' or 'is compelled to' be honest or accurate; and what is paradoxical is not so much the libertarian's defence of moral freedom as his willingness to accept mechanical determinism as an explanation of non-moral action. For the rigid distinction between 'formed character' (where determinism reigns) and 'creative choice' (which is in principle unpredictable) it would be better to substitute a conception of continual modification of character in both its moral and its non-moral aspects. This not only does justice to the fact that we use both choosing and appraising language in the same way in moral and non-moral contexts, but it is closer to the facts. A man can grow more or less conscientious as time goes on, just as he can become better at tennis or more fond of Mozart.

CHAPTER 20

Freedom and Responsibility (2)

[1]

In the last chapter I tried to show that 'could have' sentences in non-moral contexts can be analysed in terms of 'would have . . . if . . .'; and we must now see whether the application of this analysis to moral cases is consistent with our ordinary use of moral language.

The first question to be considered is the question what sorts of if-clauses are in fact allowed to excuse a man from blame. Clearly 'I could not have kept my promise because I was kidnapped' will exculpate me while 'I could not have kept my promise because I am by nature a person who takes promises very lightly' will not. Translated into the hypothetical form, these become respectively 'I would have kept my promise if I had not been kidnapped' and 'I would have kept my promise if I had been a more conscientious person'. Again it is clear that the first exculpates while the second does not. The philosophical difficulties, however, are to decide just why some 'would . . . ifs' excuse while others do not and to provide a criterion for distinguishing the exculpating from the non-exculpating cases. Forcible seizure exculpates; but do threats or psychological compulsion? And if, as some suggest, desires are internal forces which operate on the will, do they exculpate in the way in which external forces do? The problem of freewill is puzzling just because it seems impossible, without indulging in sheer dogmatism, to know just where to stop treating desires as 'compelling forces'.

Now before tackling this difficulty it will be prudent to examine what goes on in a place where questions of responsibility are settled every day and have been settled daily for hundreds of years, namely a court of law. Lawyers have evolved a terminology of remarkable flexibility, refinement, and precision and, although there may be a difference between moral and legal verdicts, it would be strange if the logic of lawyers' talk about responsibility were very different from our ordinary moral talk.

To establish a verdict of 'guilty' in a criminal case it is necessary to establish that the accused did that which is forbidden by the law or, in technical language, committed the *actus reus*, and also that he had what is called *mens rea*. This last phrase is sometimes translated 'guilty mind' and in many modern textbooks of jurisprudence it is supposed to consist of two elements, (a) foresight of the consequences and (b) voluntariness. But, whatever the textbooks may say, in actual practice lawyers never look for a positive ingredient called volition or voluntariness. A man is held to have *mens rea*, and therefore to be guilty, if the *actus reus* is proved, *unless* there are certain specific conditions which preclude a verdict of guilty. "What is meant by the mental element in criminal liability (*mens rea*) is only to be understood by considering certain defences or exceptions, such as Mistake of Fact, Accident, Coercion, Duress, Provocation, Insanity, Infancy."[1] The list of pleas that can be put up to rebut criminal liability is different in different cases; but in the case of any given offence there is a restricted list of definite pleas which will preclude a verdict of guilty.

This is not to say that the burden of proof passes to the defence. In some cases, such as murder, it is necessary for the prosecution to show that certain circumstances were not present which would, if present, defeat the accusation. The essential point is that the concept of a 'voluntary action' is a negative, not a positive one. To say that a man acted voluntarily is in effect to say that he did something when he was not in one of the conditions specified in the list of conditions which preclude responsibility. The list of pleas is not exhaustive; we

1. Professor H. L. A. Hart: *Proceedings of the Aristotelian Society*, 1948–9. Aristotle in effect defines 'the voluntary' in the same negative way as what is done not under compulsion and not through ignorance.

could, if we wished, add to it; and in making moral judgements we do so. For example we sometimes allow the fact that a man acted impulsively to exonerate him morally or at least to mitigate his offence in a case in which the law would not allow this. But it remains true that, in deciding whether an action was voluntary or not, we do not look for a positive ingredient but rather for considerations that would preclude its being voluntary and thereby exonerate the agent. In moral cases the most important types of plea that a man can put forward are (a) that he was the victim of certain sorts of ignorance, and (b) that he was the victim of certain sorts of compulsion.

[2]

Ignorance. A man may be ignorant of many elements in the situation in which he acts. For example he may not know that it was a policeman who told him to stop, that the stuff he put in the soup was arsenic, that the money he took was not his own. In such cases he would be blamed only if it was thought that he ought to have known or taken the trouble to find out. And his vicious trait of character was not contumacy or callousness or greed or disregard for any moral principle, but carelessness; and carelessness can amount to a vice. Fire-arms are so notoriously dangerous that the excuse 'I didn't know it was loaded' will not do. The reason why he is blamed for carelessness and not for the specific vice for which he would have been blamed if he had done any of these things intentionally is that, although he intended to do what he did, he did not intend to break a moral rule. He intended to take the money, but not to steal. His action was not, therefore, a manifestation of the particular vice that the actions of thieves manifest. Ignorance of fact excuses or reduces the seriousness of an offence; but there is one type of ignorance that never excuses; and that is, in legal contexts, ignorance of the law and, in moral contexts, ignorance of right and wrong.

Now why should ignorance of fact excuse while ignorance of rules does not? Why should a man who takes someone else's money, thinking it to be his own, be guiltless of anything (except possibly carelessness), while a man who takes it, knowing it not to be his own but because he sees nothing wrong in taking other people's money, be held guilty and therefore blameworthy? We are not here concerned with the question why some types of action should be stigmatized as 'wrong', but solely with the question why ignorance of what is wrong should not be held to exculpate.

The reason is that while the man who thought the money was his own did not intend to act on the maxim 'It is permitted to take other people's money', the thief does act on this maxim. If a man does something because he does not think it wrong he cannot plead that he did not choose to do it, and it is for choosing to do what is *in fact* wrong, whether he knows it or not, that a man is blamed. The situation is exactly analogous to that in which some non-moral capacity is concerned. 'I would have solved the problem, if I had known all the data' would, if substantiated, allow me to get full marks. But 'I would have solved the problem if I had known more mathematics' would not. Since competence at mathematics is not a moral trait of character, men are not blamed for lack of it; but they are given low marks and denied prizes.

[3]

Compulsion. So long as 'compulsion' is used in the literal sense it is not difficult to see why it should be held to exonerate. If a man is compelled to do something, he does not choose to do it and his action is not a manifestation of his moral character or principles. Now, since the purpose of blame and punishment is to change a man's character and principles, neither blame nor punishment is called for in such a case. It would be unjust to punish him since the rules for punishing lay down that a man who acts under compulsion is not to be punished; and the rules lay this down because, with due allowance for superstition and stupidity, we do not have pointless rules. Once more we must be careful to avoid the mistake of saying that the justice of a sentence turns on the question whether the accused is likely to be reformed by it. What is at issue here is not our reason for exonerating this accused, but our reason for making a *general* exception in the case of men whose actions are not expressions of their moral character. Physical compulsion is an obvious case where this is so.

But what if the source of compulsion is within the man himself? It is not an accident that we use 'compulsion' in a psychological way and exonerate compulsives. There are two questions that are relevant here. In the first place we ask whether the man could have resisted the 'compulsion'; and we decide this in the way that we decide all 'could have' questions. We look for evidence of his past behaviour in this, and also in related matters; for the behaviour of the compulsive is usually odd in matters unconnected with his special compulsion; and we compare his case with other known cases. Once the capacity to resist the compulsion is established beyond reasonable doubt we do not allow unsupported sceptical doubts about his capacity to resist it in a particular case to rebut the conclusion that he could have helped it. And we do not allow this because there is no way of establishing or refuting the existence of a capacity except by appeal to general evidence. If the capacity has been established and all the necessary conditions were present, we would not say that, in this case, he was the victim of a compulsion. Indeed a 'compulsion' is not something that could be said to operate in a particular case only; for to say that a man has a psychological compulsion is to say something about his behaviour over a long period. A compulsion is more like a chronic disorder than like a cold; and it is still less like a sneeze.

It is also relevant to raise the question whether he had any motive for doing what he did. Part of the difference between a kleptomaniac and a thief lies in the fact that the former has no motive for what he does; and he escapes blame because the point of blame is to strengthen some motives and weaken others. We are sometimes inclined to take the psychologists' talk about compulsions too seriously. We think that a man is excused because he has a 'compulsion', as if the compulsion could be pointed to in the way that an external object which pushed him could be pointed to. But compulsions are not objects inside us; and we use the word 'compulsion', not because we have isolated and identified the object which caused him to do what he did, but because we want to excuse him in the same sort of way that we excuse someone who is literally pushed; and we want to excuse him for the same sort of reason. We know that it will do no good to punish him.

Desires. A man might plead that he would have acted otherwise if he had not had a strong desire to do what he did; but the desire was so strong that, as things were, he could not have acted otherwise. Would this plea be allowed to exonerate him? In some cases it would; for there are, as we have seen, cases of addiction in which we allow that a man is not to blame since his craving was too strong for him. But in most cases it would be considered frivolous to say 'I would have done the right thing if I hadn't wanted to do the wrong thing'; for it is just for this that men are blamed.

To distinguish an overwhelming desire from one that the agent could have resisted is not always easy; but the criterion that we in fact use for making the distinction is not difficult to understand. We know from experience that most men can be trained to curb some desires, but not others; and we assume that what is true in most cases is true in a given case unless special reasons are given for doubting this. Now it might seem that, although this evidence enables us to predict that we shall be able to train the man to curb his desire in future, it sheds no light on the question whether he could have curbed it on the occasion in question. I shall say more about this question of moral training later; here I only wish to point out that we have no criterion for deciding whether a man could have resisted a desire on a given occasion other than general evidence of his capacity and the capacity of others like him. We do not, because we cannot, try to answer this question as if it referred solely to the given occasion; we treat it as a question about a capacity.

Character. Finally a man might plead that he could not help doing what he did because that's the sort of man he is. He would not have done it if he had been more honest or less cowardly or less mean and so on. This sort of plea is paradoxical in the same sort of way that the plea of ignorance of moral rules and the plea that he did it because he wanted to are paradoxical. And all three paradoxes stem from the same source, the uncritical extension of 'ought implies can' and of the exculpatory force of 'he could not have acted otherwise' to cases which they will not cover. We know that these pleas are not in fact accepted; the puzzle is to see why.

The plea 'I could not help it because I am that sort of person' might be backed up by an explanation of how I came to be that sort of person. Just as the discovery of a compelling cause exonerates, so, it might be argued, to reveal the causes of my character being what it is is to show that I could not help being what I am and thus to exonerate me. But this argument is fallacious. In the first place to discover the cause of something is not to prove that it is inevitable. On the contrary the discovery of the cause of a disease is often the first step towards preventing it.

Now it is logically impossible to prevent something happening if we know the cause of it, since it could not have a cause unless it occurred and therefore it was not prevented. So when we talk of preventing diseases or accidents we are not talking about preventing cases which have occurred but about ensuring that there are no future cases. Similarly, if I know how Jones came to be a dishonest man I cannot prevent him from being dishonest now; but it may be possible to prevent others from becoming dishonest and to cure Jones of his dishonesty.

Secondly, the discovery of a cause of something has no

necessary bearing on a verdict about that thing. We know that a man has come to be what he is because of three main types of cause, heredity, education, and his own past actions. These three factors are not independent of each other and it is not the business of a philosopher to say exactly what is the effect of each or which is the most important for moral training. The question 'Granted that we want people to be better and that we have fairly clear ideas about what "being better" means, should we try to breed a superior race or pay more attention to education?' is not a philosophical question. But it is the business of a philosopher to show in what ways these 'causes' are related to responsibility.

Now these three factors also play a part in situations in which non-moral verdicts are given. Leopold Mozart was a competent musician; his son Wolfgang was given a good musical education and practised his art assiduously. Each of these facts helps to explain how he was able to compose and play so well. There is plenty of evidence that musical ability runs in families and still more of the effects of teaching and practice. But, having learnt these facts, we do not have the slightest tendency to say that, because Mozart's abilities were 'due' to heredity, teaching, and practice, his compositions were not 'really' his own, or to abate one jot of our admiration. In the same way, however a man came by his moral principles, they are still *his* moral principles and he is praised or blamed for them. The plea that, being what he is he cannot help doing what he does, will no more save the wicked man than it will save the bad pianist or actor who has the rashness to expose his incompetence in public. Nor is he saved by being able to explain how he has come to be what he is.

Hereditary tendencies are not causes and do not compel, although a man may inherit a tendency to some form of psychological compulsion. In general to say that a man has a tendency to do something is to say that he usually does it; and to add that the tendency is hereditary is to say that his father also used to do the same sort of thing; and neither of these facts has any tendency to exculpate.

The belief that heredity or a bad upbringing excuse a man's present character is partly due to the false belief that to explain something is to assign an antecedent cause to it and that, to be voluntary, an action must be uncaused. But there is also a good reason for this belief. In fact we do sometimes allow these factors to exculpate; and if the question of explanation was as irrelevant to the question of responsibility as I have suggested it would be hard to understand why we do this. Why do we tend to deal less harshly with juvenile delinquents who come from bad homes than with those who have had every chance? The question is not one of justice, since it is not a question whether Jones ought to be punished, but whether the law should lay down that people whose bad characters are due to certain causes should be punished. We must therefore ask what is our reason for differentiating between two boys whose characters and actions are the same but who come respectively from bad and good homes. And the reason is that in the first case we have not had a chance to see what kindness and a good education could do, while in the second we know that they have failed. Since punishment involves the infliction of pain and since it is a moral rule that unnecessary pain should not be inflicted, there is a general presumption that people should not be punished if the same end could be achieved without the infliction of pain. This consideration is, of course, irrelevant to the question whether Jones should be punished; but it is highly relevant to the question whether a distinction should be made between those whose characters have come to be what they are because of a bad education and those whose characters are bad in spite of a good one.

But suppose a man should plead that he cannot now help doing what he does because his character was formed by his own earlier actions? This also will not excuse him. The logic of this plea is that he did X because he was, at the time, the sort of man to do X and that he became this sort of man because he did Y and Z in the past. But if he cannot be blamed for doing X now, can he be blamed for having done Y and Z in the past? It would seem that he cannot, for he will exculpate himself in exactly the same way.

Once again the argument presupposes that if his present character can be explained in terms of what happened in the past he necessarily escapes blame. The assumption is that a man's actions form a causal chain in which each necessitates the next. Now, if we suppose that, to be free, an action must be uncaused, either we shall find a genuinely uncaused action at the beginning of the chain or we shall not. If we do not, then no action is culpable; and if we do, then we must suppose that, while most of our actions are caused and therefore blameless, there was in the past some one uncaused action for which alone a man can be held responsible. This theory has in fact been held, although even in the history of philosophy it would be hard to find another so bizarre. The objections to it are clear. In the first place we praise and blame people for what they do now, not for what they might have done as babies; and secondly this hypothetical infantile action could hardly be said to be an action of the agent at all, since it is *ex hypothesi* inexplicable in terms of his character.

The conclusion of the foregoing argument is that 'He could not have acted otherwise' does not always exculpate and, in particular, that it does not exculpate if the reason which is adduced to explain just why he could not have acted otherwise is that he was a man of a certain moral character. We have seen that 'He could have acted otherwise' is to be construed as 'He would have acted otherwise, if . . .' and we have seen which types of 'if' are not allowed to exculpate. We must now see why they are not.

[4]

What is moral character? The key to the logical relationships between the five types of judgement seems to lie in the judgement of moral character (5). For (2) is thought to be a necessary condition of (1), (3), and (4) only because we exclude those cases of incapacity to act otherwise in which the incapacity lies in the moral character. If it is due to an external force or to a 'compulsion' (which we talk of as if it were an external force), or to some non-moral defect, the incapacity to act otherwise is allowed to excuse; but not if it is due to a moral defect. And it is now necessary to provide some criterion for deciding what a moral defect is.

Moral traits of character are tendencies or dispositions to behave in certain ways. How are they to be distinguished from other tendencies? If any tendency were to count as 'moral' we should have to say that conformity to physical laws was a universal trait of human character and that susceptibility to colds was part of the moral character of a particular man.

The first and most obvious limitation lies in the fact that the names of virtues and vices are not purely descriptive words. They are terms of praise and blame used to express approval and disapproval and to influence the conduct of the person whose character is appraised and also of others. These three functions are tied together in a way that should by now be familiar. Appraising, praising, and blaming are things that men *do* and can only be understood on the assumption that they do them for a purpose and use means adapted to their purpose. The logic of virtue- and vice-words is tailor-made to fit the purposes and conditions of their use.

Men would not employ a special form of speech for changing the character and conduct of others unless they had a pro-attitude towards those changes; so that the first limitation that can be put on 'moral character' is that traits of character are tendencies to do things that arouse approval or disapproval. But moral verdicts do not just express the attitudes of the speaker; they are couched in impersonal language and imply accepted standards because the traits of character that a given man wants to strengthen or inhibit in others are usually those that other men also want to strengthen and inhibit. The impersonal language of morals implies a rough community of pro- and con-attitudes. Moreover men would not have adopted the moral language they have unless it was likely to achieve its purpose; and its purpose is achieved because most men dislike disapprobation. The power of moral language is greatly enhanced by the very facts which make impersonal moral language possible. No one likes to be universally condemned and most men are willing to take considerable pains to avoid it.

But this limitation is not enough. There are many things for which men are applauded and condemned which do not count as parts of their moral character. A great musician, mathematician, actor, or athlete is applauded and rewarded for what he does and his ability may be called a 'virtue', but not a moral virtue. Conversely, if a man fails to save a life because he cannot swim, we may regret his incapacity and urge him to learn, but his incapacity is not called a vice.

A man may fail to achieve some worthy object because he is physically or intellectually incompetent, too weak or too stupid. But he may also fail because he is too cowardly or too dishonest or has too little regard for the welfare of others. Why do we call the first set of traits 'non-moral' and never condemn them, while the second are called 'moral' and condemned? It is clear that it will not help to say that we intuit a non-natural relation of fittingness which holds between blameworthiness and dishonesty or meanness but not between blameworthiness and physical weakness or stupidity. For this is only to say that the former traits deserve blame while the latter do not and that we cannot understand why.

To discover why we draw the line in the way that we do we must first ask exactly where we draw it; and all that is necessary for this purpose is to construct two lists, the one of moral traits, the other of non-moral. Cowardice, avarice, cruelty, selfishness, idleness would go into the first list; clumsiness, physical weakness, stupidity, and anaemia into the second. The second list will, of course, contain items of many different sorts, since we are interested, not in the way in which non-moral characteristics differ from each other, but in the distinction between moral and non-moral.

If we construct these lists we shall find that the items in list 1 have two properties in common which the items in list 2 do not have. (a) We believe that if a man's action can be explained by reference to a list 1 characteristic, he could have acted otherwise. And it would appear at first sight that this is the crucial feature which distinguishes moral from non-moral characteristics. Why does a schoolmaster punish a lazy boy but not a stupid one for equally bad work if not because he believes that the lazy boy could have done better while the stupid boy could not? But why does the schoolmaster believe this? In fact he appeals to the evidence of past performance. On the libertarian view this would scarcely be relevant, since the boy might not have been lazy in the past but was lazy at just that moment. And perhaps his momentary laziness was no more under his control than the stupid boy's stupidity? An analysis on these lines could hardly fail to lead to the paradoxical conclusion that no one has any reason whatever for ascribing responsibility. And even if it were possible to answer the question whether he could have acted otherwise, we should be left with the question why this is considered relevant to the propriety of holding him responsible.

Moreover it would be circular to make the phrase 'he could have acted otherwise' the distinguishing criterion of moral characteristics; since, as we have seen, it is necessary to make use of the distinction between actions explained by reference to moral, and actions explained by reference to non-moral characteristics in order to elucidate the phrase 'he could have acted otherwise'.

(b) There is, however, another element which all the characteristics in list 1 have and those in list 2 do not. It is an empirical fact that list 1 characteristics can be strengthened or weakened by the fear of punishment or of an adverse verdict or the hope of a favourable verdict. And when we remember that the purpose of moral verdicts and of punishment is to strengthen or weaken certain traits of character it is not difficult to see that this feature, so far from being synthetically connected with the notion of a 'moral' characteristic, a virtue or a vice, is just what constitutes it. What traits of character can be strengthened or weakened in this way is a matter of empirical fact. Knives can be sharpened, engines decarbonized, fields fertilized, and dogs trained to do tricks. And men also can be trained, within certain limits, to behave in some ways and not in others. Pleasure and pain, reward and punishment are the rudders by which human conduct is steered, the means by which moral character is moulded; and 'moral' character is just that set of dispositions that can be moulded by these means. Moral approval and disapproval play the same role. It is not just an accident that they please and hurt and that they are used only in cases in which something is to be gained by pleasing or hurting.

We might therefore say that moral traits of character are just those traits that are known to be amenable to praise or blame; and this would explain why we punish idle boys but not stupid ones, thieves but not kleptomaniacs, the sane but not the insane. This is not to say that amenability to praise and blame is what justifies either of these in a particular case; that, as we have seen, is a question to be decided by reference to the rules. But a breach of a moral rule is only considered to be culpable when it is attributable to the agent's character, his vice or moral weakness; and our theory is intended to explain just what is included in and what excluded from 'moral character' and to explain why this distinction should be considered relevant to responsibility.

According to this explanation there is no need to postulate any special insight into necessary connexions between the five moral judgements with which we started; for the whole weight of the analysis is now seen to rest on the proposition that people only do those things which are either objects of a direct pro-attitude (i.e. that they want to do or enjoy doing for their own sake) or are believed to produce results towards which they have pro-attitudes. It is absurd to ask why a man who thinks that praise and blame will alter certain dispositions which he wishes to alter should praise and blame them. For this is a special case of the question 'Why do people adopt means that they believe to be the best means of achieving their ends ?'; and this is an absurd question in a way in which 'Why does a man deserve blame only if he acted voluntarily and has broken a moral rule ?' is not.

Nevertheless this way of tracing the connexions between pro-attitudes, moral rules, verdicts on character, and ascriptions of responsibility is obviously too simple and schematic. It is more like an account of the way in which moral language would be used by people who knew all the facts and thoroughly understood what they were doing than like a description of the way in which moral language is actually used. In practice these connexions are much looser than the theory suggests; and there are two reasons for this. In the first place there is the inveterate conservatism of moral language. Even when it is known that a certain type of conduct, for example homosexuality, is not amenable to penal sanctions or moral disapproval, it is difficult to persuade people that it is not morally wrong.

The second reason is more respectable. We are still very ignorant of the empirical facts of human nature, and this ignorance both makes it wise for us to make moral judgements in accordance with a more or less rigid system of rules and also infects the logic of moral language. Our moral verdicts do not, therefore, always imply that the person condemned has in fact done something 'bad' or 'undesirable' in a non-moral sense. An act of cowardice or dishonesty might, by chance, be attended with the happiest consequences; but it would still be blamed. But this fact does not involve any major modification in the theory that bad traits of character are those which (a) tend to bring about undesirable results in most cases and (b) are alterable by praise and blame. For, in deciding whether a trait of character is vicious or not, we consider its effects in the majority of cases. We do not want to reinforce a tendency to behave in a certain way just because it turns out, on rare occasions, to be beneficial. And, in making a moral judgement, we do not consider the actual consequences of the action concerned. Nor do we even need to consider the consequences that such actions usually have. A man has broken faith or been cowardly or mean; we condemn him forthwith without considering why such actions are condemned. The fact that deceitful, cowardly, and mean actions are, by and large, harmful is relevant, not to the questions: 'Has Jones done wrong ? Is he a bad man ? Does he deserve to be blamed ?', but to the question 'Why are deceitfulness, cowardice, and meanness called "vices" and condemned ?'.

This theory enables us to understand why it is not only moral weakness that is blamed, but also wickedness; and it also enables us to distinguish between moral weakness and addiction in a way that the libertarian theory could not. A wicked character can be improved by moral censure and punishment; and if we really thought that a man was so bad as to be irremediable we should, I think, cease to blame him, though we might impose restraints on him as we would on a mad dog. Moral weakness is considered to be a less culpable state, since the morally weak man has moral principles which are good enough, but fails to live up to them. He is therefore more likely to be improved by encouragement than the wicked man is. What he needs is the confidence which comes from knowing that others are on the side of his principles. But both he and the wicked man differ from the addict or compulsive in that the latter will respond neither to threats nor to encouragement.

[5]

Moral Principles. Traits of character, then, are dispositions to do things of which a spectator (including the agent himself) approves or disapproves and which can be, if not implanted or wholly eradicated, at least strengthened or weakened by favourable and adverse verdicts. But they are dispositions to *do* things, in the active sense of 'do', dispositions to choose certain courses of action. It is not, therefore, an accident that the names of virtues and vices, such as 'generosity' and 'avarice', are motive-words which necessarily imply a pro-attitude towards doing the things called 'generous' or 'greedy' for their own sake. And since moral principles are also dispositions to choose, they also must be classed as 'pro-attitudes'. How do they differ from other pro-attitudes?

(a) In the first place a pro-attitude does not count as a moral principle unless it is a relatively dominant one and concerned with an important matter. However regularly I choose to drink coffee for breakfast no one would call this disposition to choose one of my moral principles. To act on principle is consistently to pursue a policy of doing certain sorts of things for their own sake; and for this reason 'acting on principle' must be sharply distinguished from 'acting from a sense of duty', although we shall see later that the two are connected. The reason for distinguishing them is that to act from a sense of duty is consistently to pursue a policy of obeying certain rules for the sake of obeying those rules; it is therefore a special case of acting on principle. 'Acting on principle' cannot, therefore, be identified with either the 'sense of duty' or the 'impulses' which, according to some philosophers, are the only types of motive. It is distinguished from 'acting on impulse' by regularity and consistency and from 'acting from the sense of duty' by the fact that the man who acts on principle does what he does for its own sake.

Now since a moral principle is a disposition to choose, a man cannot be said to have a certain moral principle if he regularly breaks it, and we discover what a man's moral principles are mainly by seeing how he in fact conducts himself. But this is not the only test. A man's moral principles are 'dominant' in the sense that he would not allow them to be over-ridden by any pro-attitude other than another moral principle. Thus a man may belong to many organizations and be allowed by the laws of his country to do something that he is not allowed to do by the rules of his trade union, profession, or church. When a conflict of principles or loyalties arises he may wonder what he ought to do; but it is part of the force of the phrase 'moral principle' that he cannot (logically) wonder what he ought to do if there is a moral principle on one side and not on the other. If I regard something as immoral, then, however trivial it may be and however great may be the non-moral advantages of doing it, I cannot debate with myself whether I ought to do it; and we discover what our own moral principles are very often by putting just this sort of question to ourselves.

A similar limitation in the use of the phrase 'moral principle' comes out in our attitude to compensation. A man will not lightly give up a moral principle; nor will he lightly give up anything else that he regards as valuable. But our attitude towards giving up a moral principle differs from all other cases. If a man has a picture that he values very highly he may reject a low price and be more inclined to part with it if the bid is raised. But if a man refuses a bribe of ten pounds and you offer him a hundred, he might say: "You don't understand; it is not a question of how much; doing that sort of thing is against my moral principles". Indeed he must say this, if it is really a matter of moral principle, unless he can manage to bring the acceptance of the offer under some other moral principle. It is for this reason that Napoleon's dictum that every man has his price sounds so cynical; it implies that no man has any moral principles.

(b) But consistency in action is not the only test of a man's moral principles. Although a man cannot claim that it is against his moral principles to be cowardly or mean if he regularly does cowardly or mean things, he can do such things occasionally and still justify this claim. His claim is justified if he is prepared to condemn his own actions and if he feels remorse. His moral principles are not those on which he always acts, but those which he acknowledges or avows and those about which he feels remorseful when he breaks them. His moral principles are those on which, in his more reflective moments, he honestly says that he would like to act; they are the moral principles of the person he is striving to become.

I shall return to this point in the last section of this chapter.

(c) A principle is not usually called a moral one unless the person who adopts it is prepared to apply it universally. If a man says that he does something as a matter of principle, he cannot (logically) make exceptions unless another moral principle is involved. However narrow in scope it may be, a moral principle must be applied to all cases that are alike in all relevant respects. If there are two people of roughly similar character, tastes, and habits, it may well be that a man likes one of them better than the other. If asked why, he may be unable to give a reason; he just happens to like Jones, although he concedes that Smith is just as virtuous, charming, and amusing. And, although there is an oddity about his taste that might interest a psychologist, there is nothing logically odd about it. But he is abusing language if he says that it is a matter of moral principle with him to pay his debts and he pays Jones, while refusing to pay Smith, without being able to give any reason for the discrepancy.

The logical fact that a pro-attitude is not called a 'moral principle' unless a man is prepared to universalize it has led some philosophers to suppose that it can be proved that we ought to be impartial. But this is to commit the fallacy of deducing a moral injunction from a feature of moral language. A man who has no principles that he is prepared to apply impartially has no moral principles; but we cannot prove that he ought to have any moral principles by pointing out how the phrase 'moral principles' is used.

(d) The fact that a man's moral principles are those which he acknowledges in his more reflective moments throws some light on the connexion between moral principles and rules. A man's moral principles are those on which he thinks he ought to act and the word 'ought', like all deontological words, is only used in connexion with rules and therefore in connexion with relatively long-range principles and policies that we avow and adopt in our more reflective moments.

Moreover these deontological words contextually imply a background of general agreement; so that, in deliberating about what to do, we tend to use the language of 'ought' only in connexion with principles of action that we know to be generally approved. Now, for reasons given in chapter 14, moral codes never contain injunctions to people to pursue their own pleasure; and most moral rules are concerned with the welfare of others. These pervasive features of moral codes infect the logic of deontological words. It is odd to describe a man as a 'conscientious egoist' or to say that pleasure-seeking is his highest moral principle, because people do not in fact use the language of 'ought' when they are being deliberately and consistently selfish. And the reason for this is that it is hard to dissociate this word from its moorings in the language of advice, exhortation, and command. Nevertheless, if a man regularly decides that he ought (in the verdict-giving sense of 'ought') to do whatever brings him pleasure or profit, his dominant pro-attitude is towards his own pleasure or profit. Whether or not we choose to call selfishness a moral principle with him, depends on the criterion we are using for the phrase 'moral principle'. If he behaves selfishly without acknowledging his wickedness and without feeling remorse, we could say that selfishness was one of his moral principles; and we hesitate to say this partly because he almost certainly does not address himself in the language of 'ought' (in the self-hortatory sense) and partly because we are reluctant to believe that he really is what he makes himself out to be.

[6]

Can a man choose to act against his own moral principles or choose to change them? Some moral principles are fundamental in the sense that we can give no reasons for adopting them; they do not follow from any higher principles. And it follows that a man cannot, at the moment of choosing, question the validity of the principle on which he chooses to act. For to do this would be to criticize the principle in the light of a higher principle; and in that case the principle in question is not a fundamental one. A man cannot condemn the principle on which he acts unless he has a con-attitude towards it; and in that case it is not a fundamental pro-attitude.

Now this seems to entail that a man cannot choose to act against his own moral principles, that he cannot choose to do what he knows to be wrong. But this is not so. Self-criticism is possible because, in criticizing my own character or conduct, I apply, not the principles on which I act, but the principles that I acknowledge on those occasions when there is no question of their being manifested or not manifested. I can, for example, think that I ought to be less greedy, vindictive, or sanctimonious than I am, and this implies a con-attitude towards these particular traits in my character. But I cannot (logically) condemn any of these vices in myself while at the same time exercising them. For if I behave vindictively while at the same time condemning myself for doing so, I am a weak-willed but not a vindictive person. If, on the other hand, I deliberately choose to do something vindictive, then I am a vindictive person; and I can still claim that to be vindictive is against my principles only in the sense that, in my more reflective moments, I am prepared to condemn what I did.

The answer to the question whether a man can choose to change his moral principles is partly logical, partly empirical. In the case of principles that are not fundamental there is no logical difficulty, since we adopt these for reasons and both can and should abandon them if we find that the reasons are bad reasons, although it may be in practice difficult to do so. Traditionally a large part of moral philosophy has consisted in the attempt to show that many moral principles are subordinate in this way to one or a few very general principles, such as the Golden Rule or the Greatest Happiness Principle.

But, although there is no logical difficulty in the notion of trying to change a subordinate principle, there must, at any given moment, be some principles that are, here and now, fundamental moral principles for me. If this were not so, we could not talk about *choosing* or *trying* to change a principle, since this implies having a pro-attitude towards making the change. And it is here that the logical difficulty arises.

To try to change a principle implies having a pro-attitude towards making the change, and this implies that the principle is not a fundamental one. But it does not follow from this that there are any moral principles that are unchangeable. The fact that it makes no sense for me to ask whether I ought to act on a certain principle that is for me a fundamental one has often been cited as a proof that there are self-evident principles. For is not to say that it is senseless to question the principle to say that it is self-evident? But this argument confuses the practical impossibility of asking a certain question at a certain time with the logical impossibility of asking it at any time; and it also confuses the role of the advocate with that of the judge.

So long as a man is considering whether or not to act in a certain way, he addresses himself in the split-personality language of 'you ought'. But sooner or later he must make up his mind; he must decide. No doubt perpetual indecision is logically possible; but in many cases not to decide is to take a momentous decision, since the situation alters and the opportunity for choosing has passed. Moreover the logic of practical language is adapted to the practice of ordinary men, not to that of mental paralytics.

Sooner or later, then, he must proceed to a verdict "This is what I ought to do; this is the principle on which I shall act". And it is logically impossible for him to question this decision only in the sense that, if he questioned it, he would be returning to the standpoint of the advocate and it would not be a decision. It does not follow that at some future time he might not reconsider the decision and wonder whether he had been right. But to question the morality of a decision or principle is to criticize or appraise it in the light of a higher principle. Could this principle be questioned in its turn? Unless it were tautologous (in which case it could not serve as a moral principle at all, since it would be compatible with every course of action), it could be. Self-guaranteeing moral principles are impossible; and the demand for them rests on the failure to notice that 'there must always be some moral principle that I cannot now question' does not entail 'There must be some moral principle that I cannot ever question'. Every sentence must (logically) end with a full stop; but there is no point in any sentence at which a full stop must (logically) be put.

A man can, therefore, question the morality of his own principles and try to change them; but he cannot do so while applying them or if he has no pro-attitude towards making the change. Whether or not he can change them if these logical conditions are satisfied is an empirical question, to which the only answer is: "Sometimes. He may not always succeed; but he can always try". And since no one, not even the man himself, knows the limits of what he can do if he tries, it is a question to which no more precise answer can be given. There are moral principles which it is difficult to imagine any man wanting to change, because it is difficult to imagine what it would be like to adopt the contrary principle or to have a pro-attitude towards adopting it. But we must not confuse the difficulty of imagining something with its logical impossibility.

What sort of principles a man adopts will, in the end, depend on his vision of the Good Life, his conception of the sort of world that he desires, so far as it rests with him, to create. Indeed his moral principles just *are* this conception. The conception can be altered; perhaps he meets someone whose character, conduct, or arguments reveal to him new virtues that he has never even contemplated; or he may do something uncharacteristic and against his principles without choosing to do it and, in doing it, discover how good it is. Moral values, like other values, are sometimes discovered accidentally. But the one thing he cannot do is to *try* to alter his conception of the Good Life; for it is ultimately by reference to this conception that all his choices are made. And the fact that he cannot choose to alter this conception neither shields him from blame nor disqualifies him from admiration.

CHAPTER 21

Postscript

[1]

I HAVE tried in the course of this book to elucidate the concepts used in moral discourse and their connexions with each other; and I have referred at several points to very ancient controversies, between objectivists and subjectivists, deontologists and teleologists, libertarians and determinists. These controversies are perennial and it would be absurd to claim to settle them. It would be still more absurd to claim to settle them in favour of one side or the other, since it would be most unlikely for any theory to survive so long if it were wholly mistaken.

Nor could the issues be settled wholly by logical argument; for they are partly matters of individual psychology. We may ask what 'we' mean by a certain word; but we do not all mean the same thing and, if we did, it would be impossible to understand why it is that, in a philosophical dispute, which is concerned with the meanings of words that are the common property of everybody, the points made by the protagonists on each side seem to their opponents so absurd, tenuous, and far-fetched. There may be, and usually is, a large measure of agreement on matters of morality; but the disagreement that persists is not wholly on matters of logic.

Consider, for example, the reactions of two different people who are told that something they have done is wrong or immoral and who accept the criticism as just. For one of them the immediate effect of this criticism may be to make him think about the past. He thinks in terms of having broken a rule and his dominant emotion is shame, a sense of guilt or sin, a sense of his incapacity to live up to his ideals. Moreover it is almost certain that he will tend to think of the ideals he has failed to live up to and the rules he has broken as being not primarily *his* ideals and rules at all, but as being 'objective', as belonging to a special order of reality that he did not create but which is imposed on him. In this way it is easier for him to understand how he came to fail; and because it is easier for him to understand his failure in this way it is more comforting.

Another man will think primarily of the future; his dominant reactions will not be shame but a desire to put right the wrong he has done, if this is possible, and a desire to do better in future. For him morality is more a matter of what he ought to do now and in future than a matter of what he has done in the past. Shame and guilt, since they are concerned with a past that is dead and gone, will seem to him, not to be of the very essence of self-condemnation, but important only as spurs to future effort. And since he thinks more in terms of decisions for the future than of remorse for the past, he will not feel the same need to represent moral rules and ideals as imposed on him from without and will not derive the same comfort from so doing. Indeed it will seem to him to be a slavish attitude. For him rules and moral laws are important enough as guides in cases of doubt and as correctives for tendencies in his own conduct of which he disapproves in his reflective, self-critical moments; but they will not be so important as the policies and principles which he, as a free rational agent, chooses to adopt. Is it likely that two such men will agree about the meaning of the word 'wrong', especially if they make the logical assumption that it must refer to just one thing or have just one primary use?

But although these psychological considerations deserve more recognition than they usually receive, they must not be overestimated. To a very large extent the theories which seem to some philosophers paradoxical and far-fetched really are paradoxical and far-fetched. They misrepresent not only the way in which others use moral language but the way in which the theorist himself uses it. No man, for example, ever really believed that 'good' meant 'what I desire' or that altruism was disguised selfishness or that obligations were denizens of a special, non-natural world. These are absurd, one-sided theories of which the only value lies in the fact that they emphasize elements in moral language that might otherwise be overlooked. And they are arrived at by pursuing, often with great ingenuity and logical rigour, tendencies which are endemic in our actual language to the neglect of other tendencies no less important.

For, whether it be a virtue or a vice, it is a fact that ordinary language is untidy; almost everything that we say would have to be qualified by the phrase 'for the most part' if it were not so obvious that this is the case that we can afford to dispense with the phrase in practice. But if, as philosophers sometimes do, we forget the untidiness of the logic of ordinary language, we shall find ourselves deducing consequences from uses of language that are incompatible with each other. And then we shall feel bound to reject one or other of the implications and, whichever we reject, we shall have a one-sided theory to offer. Philosophy is, for this reason, full of paradoxes; for a philosopher cannot but stress those features of language which seem to him important, and these may not seem to be the important ones to another philosopher. But as long as we see the paradoxes for what they are and know why it is that we reach them they do little harm. Sometimes, however, philosophical theories rest on sheer logical confusions and, at the risk of some repetition, I shall end by summarizing the most important of these.

(1) The most important and pervasive is that of transferring to discussions of moral discourse the logical concepts that have been successfully used to elucidate the discourse of mathematics or science. This has led philosophers to misrepresent knowing how to lead one's life as knowledge of theoretical truths, either about human nature or about a special realm of 'values'. This error, combined with the realization that truths of fact do not entail imperatives and that neither truths of fact nor imperatives entail decisions, has led to the doctrine that moral words must stand for special entities and to the postulation of a special faculty to account for our knowledge of

moral truths. The crucial difference between practical and theoretical discourse has been misrepresented as a difference between sets of objects described instead of represented as a difference in the role performed by different types of expression.

(2) Neglect of the distinction between the meaning of a word and the contextual background of its use and of the fact that an expression may have different implications in different contexts has led to partial analyses being offered as 'the meaning of X' or 'the way in which the word "X" is used', this latter fallacy being only the old fallacy of *unum nomen unum nominatum* in modern dress. The logical liaisons of a given word are many and various and, although a given expression always has some contextual implications, what it implies in one context may be very different from what it implies in another. Once this fact is appreciated it is easier to see why what is a truism to one philosopher can seem to be a plain falsehood to another. The first has treated one set of logical liaisons as valid in all contexts, the second another set.

(3) Teleological writers have often been accused of 'denying morality altogether' or failing to account for moral obligation 'in the strict sense'. In a way this accusation is an impertinence that they rightly ignore; but in another way it is just, since they have attempted to define deontological words in terms of purpose, happiness, desire, pleasure, or good. And in so doing they have confused logical questions about the meaning of the words 'ought', 'right', 'duty', 'just', and 'obligatory' with practical questions about what rules we ought to adopt and psychological questions about what pro-attitudes men in fact have. This procedure is rightly denounced as involving a failure to understand the peculiar part which deontological concepts actually play in choosing, advising, commanding, and exhorting.

But the deontologist, while rightly emphasizing the connexion between 'ought' and rules, has been led to treat desires and purposes as 'merely empirical' concepts, the proper concern of the psychologist, not of the moral philosopher. And this has led him into the wildly extravagant assertion that all traditional moral philosophy rests on a mistake. By distinguishing between the standpoint of the legislator and that of the judge we can do justice to the deontologist's insight that the question whether a verdict is just and the question whether the judge ought to pronounce it are questions of fact which have nothing to do with purposes, and also to the teleologist's insight into the fact that rules are made to serve the purposes of men.

(4) The oversimplification involved in treating all pro-attitudes, that is to say all logically complete answers to the question 'What shall I do?', as 'desires' or 'inclinations' has resulted, not only in over-simple psychology, but also in the fatal tendency to represent all voluntary action as selfish; and this in turn is so flagrant a paradox that it has led to the treatment of the sense of duty as a non-natural force which must be a force, since it opposes the desires, and yet cannot be just another natural force, since it pronounces a verdict. But to suppose that, the sense of duty apart, all men would act selfishly is to suppose something for which we can have no evidence, since we know of no societies in which there is no concept of obligation; and it is something which is quite certainly untrue of men as we know them.

[2]

Moral philosophy is a practical science; its aim is to answer questions in the form 'What shall I do?'. But no general answer can be given to this type of question. The most a moral philosopher can do is to paint a picture of various types of life in the manner of Plato and ask which type of life you really want to lead. But this is a dangerous task to undertake. For the type of life you most want to lead will depend on the sort of man you are. Decisions and imperatives do not follow logically from psychological or biological descriptions; but the sort of life that will in fact be satisfactory to a man will depend on the sort of man that he is. Generalization is possible only in so far as men are psychologically and biologically similar. There are some types of life that we can say outright that no man would find satisfactory; but practical advice is not necessary when it is obvious. In cases which are difficult to decide it is vain, presumptuous, and dangerous to try to answer these questions without a knowledge both of psychology and of the individual case.

My purpose has been the less ambitious one of showing how the concepts that we use in practical discourse, in deciding, choosing, advising, appraising, praising and blaming, and selecting and rejecting moral rules are related to each other. The questions 'What shall I do?' and 'What moral principles should I adopt?' must be answered by each man for himself; that at least is part of the connotation of the word 'moral'.

Index

The principal references are indicated by heavy type.

321